An Introduction to AutoCAD
Release 14

An Introduction to AutoCAD Release 14

A. Yarwood

Registered Developer

LONGMAN

Addison Wesley Longman Limited
Edinburgh Gate, Harlow
Essex CM20 2JE, England
and Associated Companies throughout the world

First published 1998

British Library Cataloguing in Publication Data
A catalogue entry for this title is available from the British Library

ISBN 0-582-32656-7

Set by 24 in 10/13pt Melior
Produced by Longman Singapore Publishers (Pte) Ltd
Printed in Singapore

Contents

List of plates

Colour plates are between pages 146 and 147.

Preface

AutoCAD Release 14, which was published in July 1997, is designed to work only in Windows 95 or Windows NT. Other platforms are no longer supported. The contents of this book describe the use of the software package operating in Windows 95. Its contents, apart from some of the methods of working in NT, will be as suitable for NT users as for Windows 95 users.

The package will function in a PC fitted with at least an 80846 CPU, but preferably with a Pentium 90 or faster. It will operate with 16 Mbytes RAM, but will work better with a minimum of 32 Mbytes. If working with NT 32 Mbytes Ram is the minimum requirement.

There are many enhancements over Release 13 introduced with Release 14. Among these are:

Faster operation.

Faster plotting. Plot previews without having to go through Plot.

Startup and Setup Wizard, with a range of drawing templates if required.

Improved polylines. Improved hatching with solid fill hatching.

Improved layer control. Ability to easily rename or erase layers.

An AutoSnap system, which operates apart from or together with Osnap.

XREF system allowing dynamic links between drawings.

Internet Browser.

Raster images can be inserted into drawings and printed with drawings.

A Learning Assistance CD-ROM available with animated help screens.

Ability to save to Release 12, Release 13 or AutoCAD LT formats.

The book is designed to be suitable as a text for students in Further and Higher Education or for beginners new to Release 14. There is no possibility of a book the size of this one able to fully describe using such a complex package as AutoCAD Release 14. The manuals associated with the software run into many thousands of pages, necessary to fully describe all aspects of working in Release 14. The purpose of this book is to encourage beginners to commence learning how to use the software to construct both 2D and 3D drawings. Once reasonably proficient with the use of the software, it is hoped readers will then be encouraged to go on to learn more about how to use the software for more advanced work.

The book contains what is basically a course of work. Starting from first principles; going on to set examples and exercises in the construction of 2D drawing; proceeding on to examples and exercises in constructing 3D solid model drawings; then to examples and exercises in the rendering of 3D models. A set of four appendices, which include plotting, a glossary of tools, a short list of set variables, a glossary of computer terms and completes the contents of the book.

An eight-page insertion contains colour plates of AutoCAD screens showing 2D drawings, 3D models and renderings of 3D models. Many of the colour plates show renderings of 3D solid models which have been included as examples and exercises throughout the book.

Aims of the book
To provide a text covering sufficient details of the use of AutoCAD Release 14 for Windows 95 to make it suitable for students in Further or Higher Education or beginners to Computer Aided Design (CAD) wishing to learn how to use AutoCAD Release 14.

A. Yarwood
Salisbury 1997

Acknowledgements

The author wishes to acknowledge with grateful thanks the help given to him by members of the staff at Autodesk Ltd.

Trademarks

The following are registered trademarks of Autodesk Inc.:

Autodesk®, AutoCAD®.

The following are trademarks of Autodesk Inc.:

ACAD™, DXF™.

IBM® is a registered trademark of the International Business Machines Corporation.

MS-DOS® is a registered trademark, and Windows™ a trademark of the Microsoft Corporation.

A. Yarwood is a Master Developer with Autodesk Ltd.

Registered Developer

CHAPTER 1

Release 14 for Windows 95

Introduction

This chapter is an outline of the method of starting AutoCAD Release 14 for Windows 95, together with the terms used throughout the book when describing how to construct drawings with the aid of the software. Also included in this chapter are details of the configuration of AutoCAD Release 14 and some details of the R14 window.

Although many different types of digitiser can be used when working with R14, in this book only methods of working with a two-button mouse as the digitiser are given. In general when working with a two-button mouse, the left-hand button is the **Pick** button and the right-hand button the **Return** button (Fig. 1.1).

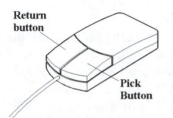

Fig. 1.1 The buttons of a two-button mouse

Terms

R14: An abbreviated form of AutoCAD Release 14.

Cursor: Several types of cursor will be seen when using R14. Some of these are shown in Fig. 1.2. Cursors can be moved under mouse control. Move the mouse and the cursor currently in action moves as the mouse is moved.

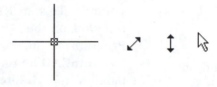

Fig. 1.2 Some of the types of cursor seen in R14

Left-click: Place the cursor under mouse control onto a feature and press the **Pick** button of the mouse.

Right-click: Place the cursor under mouse control onto a feature and press the **Return** button of the mouse.

Double-click: Place the cursor under mouse control onto a feature and press the **Pick** button of the mouse twice in rapid succession.

Fig. 1.3 The pick box associated with Osnaps and AutoSnap

Fig. 1.4 The symbol on the **Return** or **Enter** key of the keyboard

Fig. 1.5 The tool tip for the **Polyline** icon

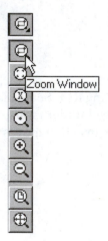

Fig. 1.6 The **Zoom** flyout

Drag: Move the cursor under mouse control, hold down the **Pick** button and move the mouse. The feature moves with the mouse movement.

Select: Move the cursor onto a feature and press the **Pick** button of the mouse.

Pick: The same action as select. The two terms are used throughout this book and can be regarded as having the same meaning.

Pick button: the left-hand button of the mouse.

Pick box: An adjustable square associated with picking features of a construction (Fig. 1.3).

Enter: Type the given word or letters at the keyboard.

Return: Press the **Return** or **Enter** key of the keyboard (Fig. 1.4). Usually, but not always, has the same result as a *right-click* – i.e. pressing the **Return** button of the mouse.

Esc: The **Esc** key of the keyboard. In R14 pressing the **Esc** key has the effect of cancelling the current action taking place.

Tool: The name given to a command in recent releases of AutoCAD.

Icons: A common graphic feature in all Windows applications – a small item of graphics representing a tool or a function of the software in use.

Tool tip: The name of the tool represented by an icon, which appears when the cursor under mouse control is placed onto a tool icon (Fig. 1.5).

Flyout: A number of tool icons have a small arrow in the bottom right-hand corner of the icon. Such icons will produce a flyout (Fig. 1.6) when the cursor is placed onto the icon and the **Pick** button of the mouse is held down.

Starting R14

When the files for R14 are first loaded into a computer, an AutoCAD R14 shortcut start-up icon is loaded into the Windows 95 start-up window. To start R14, either *double-click* on this shortcut icon or *left-click* on the Windows 95 **Start** button, followed by another on **Programs** in the popup list which appears, followed by another on the **AutoCAD R14** name in the program list and yet another on the name **AutoCAD R14** in the list of R14 specific files which appears. Figure 1.7 shows this sequence as well as the shortcut icon.

When R14 starts, the **Start Up** dialogue box appears in an R14 window, usually with the **Use a Template** part of the dialogue box showing (Fig. 1.8). Either select one of the templates from the **Select a Template** list box, or if wishing to make up one's own template, *left-click* on the **Use a Wizard** button, followed by yet another on **Advanced Setup** in the **Select a Wizard** list box (Fig. 1.9). Pressing

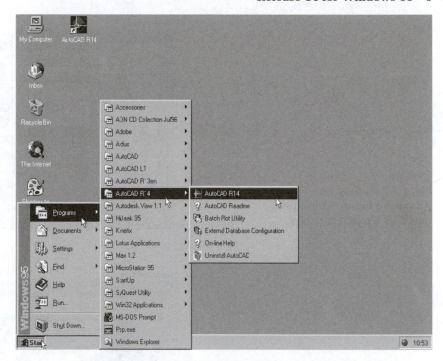

Fig. 1.7 The start-up window
of Windows 95

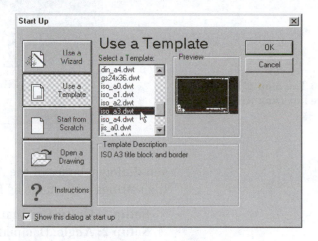

Fig. 1.8 The R14 **Start Up**
dialogue box

the **OK** button brings up the **Advanced Setup** dialogue box, which
contains six sub-dialogue boxes, the first of which is shown in Fig.
1.10.

My template

For the purpose of this book, all drawings were constructed on a
drawing template which I saved to the name **ay.dwt** (my own initials
ay, followed by the R14 template file extension ***.dwt**). In the six

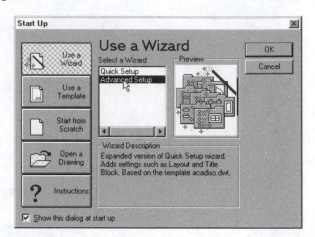

Fig. 1.9 Selecting the **Advanced Setup** option from the **Start Up** dialogue box

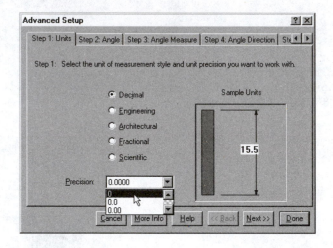

Fig. 1.10 The **Step 1: Units** dialogue box from **Advanced Setup**

sub-dialogue boxes of the **Advanced Setup** dialogue, this template file settings were made as follows:

Setup 1: Units: Decimal with Precision 0.
Setup 2: Angle: Decimal Degrees with Precision 0.
Setup 3: Angle Measure: East.
Setup 4: Angle Direction: Counter-clockwise.
Setup 5: Area: Width 420. Length 297.
Setup 6: Title Block: None.
Setup 7: Layout: No to **Do you want to use advanced Paper Space layout capabilities?**

Then *left-click* on the **Done** button, followed by calling **Save As** from the **File** pull-down menu. In the **Save Drawing As** dialogue box, save the template to the name **ay.dwt** as indicated in Fig. 1.11.

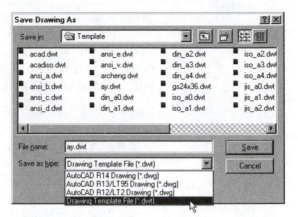

Fig. 1.11 The **Save Drawing As** dialogue box

Notes

1. The drawing template **ay.dwt** is the one in which the majority of the drawing appearing in the pages of this book will be constructed.
2. If you wish to have your own drawing template, it can be constructed from the **Advanced Setup** dialogue boxes as shown. The file name you will use may well be your initials followed by the template extension **.dwt**.
3. AutoCAD R14 drawings are usually saved to a format with a file extension of **.dwg**. Templates in which drawings are constructed are saved in a file format with an extension of **.dwt**.

The Preferences dialogue boxes

A *left-click* on **Tools** in the menu bar brings a pull-down menu to screen. In that menu *left-click* on **Preferences...** (Fig. 1.12). The

Fig. 1.12 Selecting **Preferences...** from the **Tools** pull-down menu

Fig. 1.13 Setting for no scroll bars in the R14 window

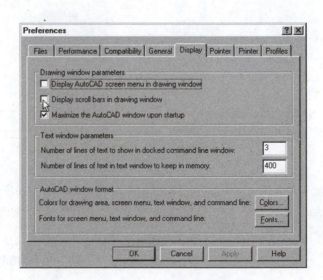

Preferences dialogue box appears. This dialogue box, like the **Advanced Setup** dialogue box, has a number of sub-dialogue boxes, seven in all. For our purposes, with illustrations throughout the book, apart from two of the sub-dialogue boxes, the default settings will be accepted. The two different settings will be made in:

Display: Fig. 1.13. *Left-click* in the **Display scroll bars in the drawing window** check box to turn it off (no tick in the check box). Personally, I find this allows me a little more area in which to construct. However, remember, if you are dealing with very large drawings, it will usually be an advantage to have the scroll bars in the drawing window. This enables all parts of the drawings to be scrolled, yet allows the operator to work in an area in which details are not too small to see clearly.

Pointer: Figure 1.14. In the **Cursor size** area of the dialogue box *enter* 100 in the **Percentage of screen size** box. This displays the cursor cross hairs right across the drawing area in the R14 window. I personally find this an advantage when constructing drawings in R14.

Now save the template again to the chosen file name – in this case **ay.dwt**.

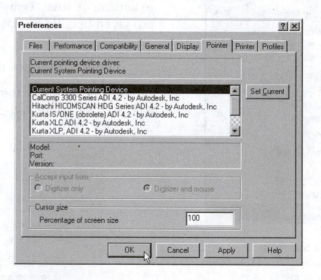

Fig. 1.14 Setting the cursor cross hairs at 100 per cent

Notes

1. The colours of the various parts of the R14 window can be changed from the **Display** sub-dialogue. *Left-click* on the **Colors...** button of the dialogue box and the **AutoCAD Window Colors** dialogue box appears (Fig. 1.15). Either select the colour of the part of the R14 window which you wish to change from the **Window Element** list

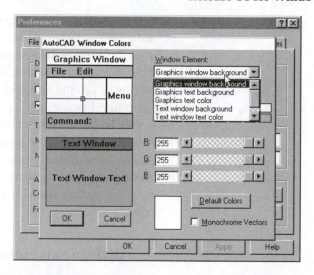

Fig. 1.15 The **AutoCAD Window Colors** dialogue box

or *left-click* in that part of the window showing to the left of the dialogue box. Then another *left-click* in the colour box below the **Window Element** list box. The colour of the window element changes.

2. Colours of the R14 screen will also be changed if changes are made from the Windows 95 **Control Panel** in the **Appearance** dialogue box of **Display settings** (Fig. 1.16).

3. Another setting you may wish to save is in the **General** sub-dialogue box. This is the **Automatic Save every ---- minutes**. But be

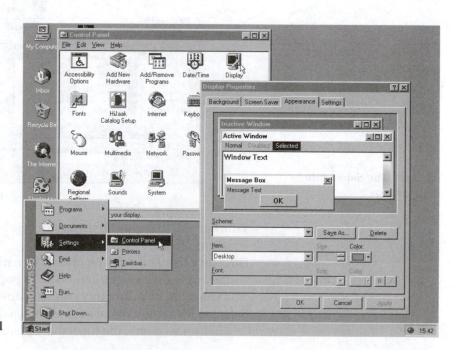

Fig. 1.16 The **Display Properties** dialogue box from the Windows 95 **Control Panel**

careful setting this figure, because there are occasions when an automatic save time can cause problems. It is far better to accustom your working methods to saving your work every 10 or 15 minutes. This is a good working habit to get accustomed to. The default setting of 120 minutes is probably a good timing for automatic save for general working.

4. It may be necessary to change or add to the printers in the **Printers** sub-dialogue box, but usually this only requires setting once to the printer or plotter in uses with your computer.

5. Take care when changing settings in **Preferences** if you are not the only one using the computer. Changes may cause problems for other users.

Dialogue and other boxes

Dialogue boxes

Several types of boxes will be seen when using R14. A dialogue box showing some of the features common to many dialogue boxes is the **Select File** dialogue appearing when **Open...** is selected from the **File** pull-down menu. Figure 1.17 shows this dialogue box with details of its various parts. Note the following:

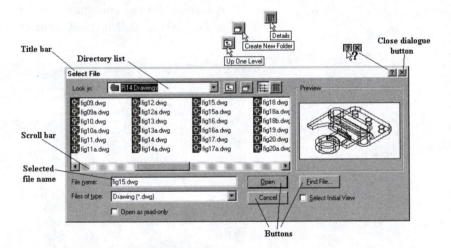

Fig. 1.17 The **Select File** dialogue box.

Title bar: All dialogue boxes have a title bar, in which the name of the box is given.

Directory list: *Left-click* on either the name in the directory list or on the arrow on its right-hand end. A popup list appears from which a selection of a directory can be made (Fig. 1.18).

Selected file name: When a file is selected from the file list with a *left-click* on its name, the file name appears in this box. A *left-click* on

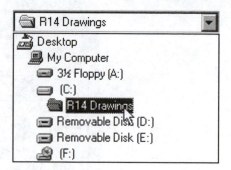

Fig. 1.18 The file popup list from the **Select File** dialogue box

the **Open** button of the dialogue box and the drawing from the file will appear on screen. A *double-click* on the file name in the file list will have the same result.

Scroll bar: If too many file names appear in the file name list, a scroll bar below the list allows the list to be scrolled sideways.

Icons: Three of the four icons to the right of the directory list box are given above the dialogue box in Fig. 1.17 with their tool tips showing.

Close dialogue box button: Common to all dialogue boxes. A *left-click* on the button and the dialogue box disappears from screen.

The Help ? button: *Left-click* on this button and a large **?** appears hanging onto the cursor. Move the cursor to any area of the dialogue box and *left-click* and a **Help** box appears describing the use for that area of the dialogue box. Figure 1.19 shows the help box which appears with a *left-click* in the directory list box.

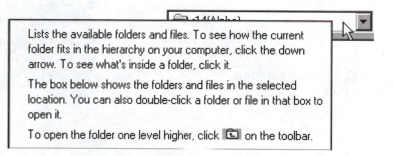

Fig. 1.19 The **Help** box for the directory list box

Buttons: buttons of this type are a common feature in dialogue boxes. Figure 1.20 shows the result of a *left-click* on the **Find File...** button. Figure 1.20 also shows the popup list appearing with a *left-click* on the **Size:** name, showing that the icons representing the drawings in the selected directory can be increased in size if required.

Preview area: When a file name is selected, an icon which is a small copy of the drawing represented by the file appears in the **Preview** box.

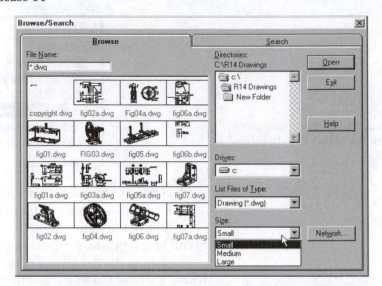

Fig. 1.20 The **Browse/Search** dialogue box

Note: Other dialogue boxes may have other features. The features shown above show a reasonable representation of a general dialogue box.

Message boxes

Figure 1.21 shows a typical **AutoCAD Message** box. Its meaning is quite clear.

Fig. 1.21 A typical **AutoCAD Message** box

Other forms of boxes

Some have been shown in previous pages of this chapter – Figs 1.8 to 1.15.

Dd calls to bring dialogue boxes to screen

Some dialogue boxes are called to screen from command names in pull-down menus. An example is shown in the **File** menu – Fig. 1.12. Where dialogue boxes are so called, their names are followed by three full stops (**...**) signifying that the name is associated with a dialogue box.

Fig. 1.22 The toolbars in the
R14 start-up window

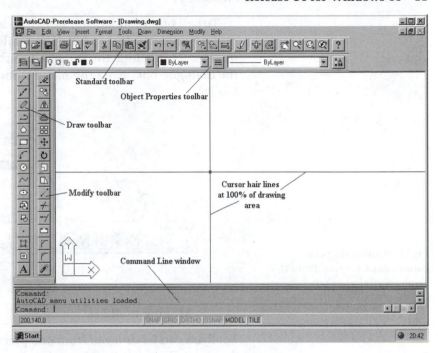

Some of the dialogue boxes can be called by *entering* **dd** calls at
the Command window. Examples are:

ddgrips:	Grips.
ddim:	Dimension Styles.
ddinsert:	Insert.
ddlmodes:	Layer & Linetype (layers showing).
ddltype:	Layer & Linetype (linetypes showing).
ddosnap:	Osnap.
ddptype:	Point Style.
ddstyle:	Test Style.
dducs:	UCS Control.
ddunits:	Units Control.
ddvpoint:	Viewing Presets.

Fig. 1.23 Selecting **Toolbars...**
from the **View** pull-down
menu

Tools, toolbars and tool tips

All operations in R14 when constructing drawings can be carried
out with selection of tools, which are all represented by tool icons
in **toolbars**. At start-up, R14 usually shows a window with four
toolbars showing. These four hold the tools most likely to be used
when using R14 to construct a drawing. Figure 1.22 shows the start-
up R14 window with its four toolbars.

To call other toolbars on screen, select **Toolbars...** from the **View** pull-down menu (Fig. 1.23). The **Toolbars** dialogue box appears as in Fig. 2.24 in which the **Dimensions** toolbar has been selected from the dialogue box. Note the name **Dimensions** in the title bar of the toolbar.

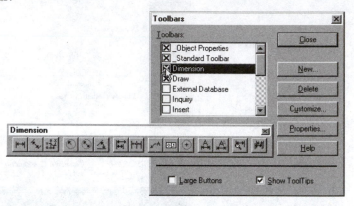

Fig. 1.24 Selecting the
Dimensions toolbar from the
Toobars dialogue box

Moving toolbars

Toolbars can be *dragged* from one place on screen to another. Move the cursor hairs under mouse control until they point into the title bar of the toolbar. The cursor changes to an arrow type. *Drag* the toolbar to a new position, the toolbar ghosts. Release the mouse button and the toolbar reappears in its new position. Figure 1.25 shows the **Solids** toolbar being so moved.

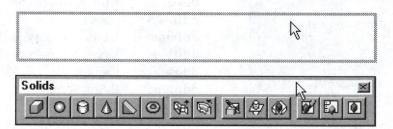

Fig. 1.25 Moving a toolbar

Changing the shape of a toolbar

Figure 1.26 shows the **Surface** toolbar being twice changed in shape. The cursor is moved under mouse control onto an edge of the toolbar. The cursor changes shape as shown and by moving the mouse the toolbar is changed in shape.

Calling commands (tools)

There are four ways in which a tool (command) can be called into action. To call the **Line** tool, either:

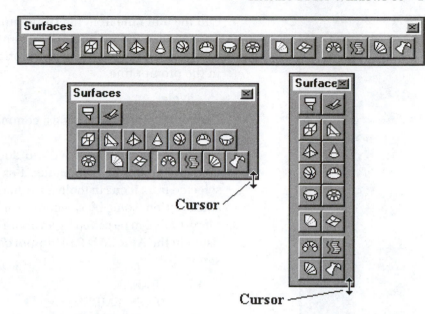

Fig. 1.26 Changing the shape
of a toolbar

Fig. 1.27 Selecting **Line** from
the **Draw** toolbar

1. *Left-click* on the **Line** tool icon from the **Draw** toolbar (Fig. 1.27).
   The Command window shows **_line from point:** and the prompt
   line below the Command window shows the prompt **Creates
   straight line segments line** describing the action of the **Line** tool
   (Fig. 1.28).

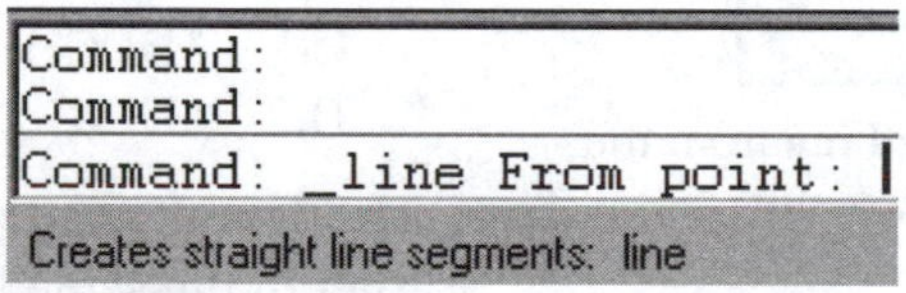

Fig. 1.28 The Command Line
and prompt line when the
Line tool icon is selected

```
Command:
Command:
Command: _line From point: |
Creates straight line segments: line
```

2. *Enter* **line** at the Command window. Figure 1.29 shows the resulting
   prompt in the Command window. Note that nothing appears in the
   prompt line.

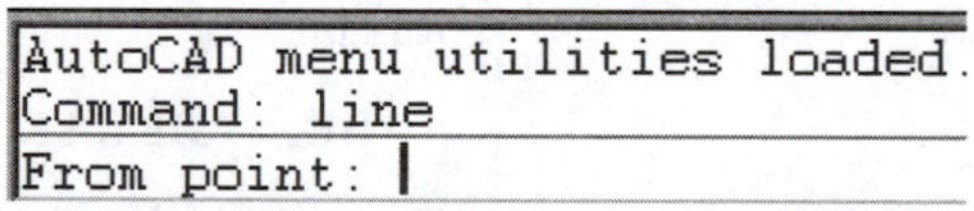

Fig. 1.29 The Command
window when **line** is *entered*

```
AutoCAD menu utilities loaded.
Command: line
From point: |
```

3. *Enter* the abbreviation **l** for Line in the Command window. Figure
   1.30 shows the resulting prompt in the window. Note that nothing
   appears in the prompt line.

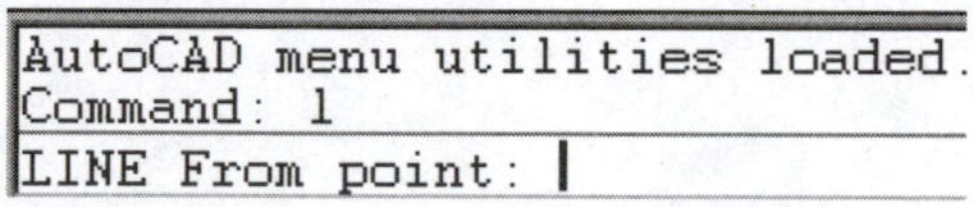

Fig. 1.30 The Command
window when **l** is *entered*

```
AutoCAD menu utilities loaded.
Command: l
LINE From point: |
```

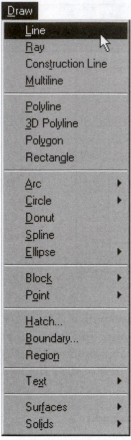

Draw

Line
Ray
Construction Line
Multiline

Polyline
3D Polyline
Polygon
Rectangle

Arc ▶
Circle ▶
Donut
Spline
Ellipse ▶

Block ▶
Point ▶

Hatch...
Boundary...
Region

Text ▶

Surfaces ▶
Solids ▶

Fig. 1.31 Calling **Line** from the **Draw** pull-down menu

4. Call the tool **Line** from the **Draw** pull-down menu (Fig. 1.31). The Command window shows the same as when the **Line** tool is selected from its icon. The description of the tool's action appears in the prompt line.

Notes

1. The four methods of calling a command (tool) are common to the use of all tools.
2. In practise, the operator will no doubt decide upon his/her own methods of calling commands. For example some tools may be selected from icons in toolbars, others may be called by *entering* an abbreviation, some by selection from a pull-down menu.
3. Many tools can be called by an abbreviation. The abbreviations are listed in the **AutoCAD R14/support/acad.pgp** file, part of which is shown below:

     BR, *BREAK
     CE, *COPYEMBED
     CF, *CHAMFER
     CH, *CHANGE
     CL, *COPYLINK
     C,   *CIRCLE
     CC, *COPYCLIP
     CO, *DDCOLOR
     CP, *COPY
     CR, *DDCHPROP
     D,   *DIM

4. The default **acad.pgp** file in R14 contains many more abbreviations than in the same file of previous releases, resulting in an operator being able to use many abbreviations without having to add them to the file.
5. If you do wish to add abbreviations to the file, use an editing programme such as the MS-DOS Edit to make changes using the format:

     BR, *BREAK

6. Once again however, if you are not the sole user of the computer being operated it is advisable to leave the acad.pgp file alone, in case your changes confuse other operators using the machine.

Questions

1. What does the term *left-click* mean?
2. How can the cross hairs cursor of R14 be changed to cover the full length and width of the R14 window?
3. How is R14 started?
4. What is a *tool tip*?
5. What is the difference between a file with the extension **.dwt** to one with the extension **.dwg**?
6. How are the R14 window colours changed?
7. What is the purpose of the **?** button seen at the top right hand of many dialogue boxes?
8. What is a message box?
9. There are four methods of calling commands (tools) in R14. Can you name them?
10. In which file are R14 command abbreviations held?

CHAPTER 2

Introduction

The advantages of using CAD software

There are many advantages in using a Computer Aided Design (CAD) software package for constructing technical drawings. Among these advantages are:

1. Any technical drawing which can be produced 'by hand' can be created in a CAD package.
2. Drawing with the aid of CAD is much quicker than working 'by hand'. A skilled operator can produce drawings as much as 10 times as fast, or more, than when working 'by hand'.
3. There is less tedium when working with CAD. Features such as text which can be very tedious when entered freehand can be added to a drawing with the minimum of effort.
4. Drawings can be inserted into other drawings, without having to redraw them.
5. Parts of drawings can be copied, moved, mirrored, arrayed etc. without the need to redraw. In fact a basic rule when drawing with CAD is:

   Never draw the same detail twice

6. Adding dimensions to a drawing is very fast and, when using associative dimensioning, reduces the possibility of dimensioning error.
7. Drawings created in CAD can be saved as files on a disk system, considerably reducing the amount of space required for the storage of drawings.
8. Drawings can be printed or plotted to any scale from the same drawing, reducing the need to make a separate drawing for each scale.

There are some disadvantages when comparing hand drawing with CAD drawing, the most serious being the initial expense in the setting up of the necessary equipment, particularly in a large design office. There is also the disadvantage that CAD is sometimes unsuitable for the making of some design sketches, some of which may need to be drawn freehand. A further disadvantage lies in the need to fully train an operator new to CAD draughting.

System requirements to run R14

Software

1. AutoCAD Release 14. As regards this book's contents – the Windows 95 version of R14.
2. Windows 95 or Windows NT.

Hardware

1. PC fitted with an Intel 80486 or Pentium CPU.
2. A minimum of 16 Mbytes memory (RAM), preferably more.
3. Hard disk, with at least 70 Mbytes of free space to allow AutoCAD R14 files to load.
4. Up to 100 Mbytes free disk space to allow disk swapping.
5. VGA or preferably, higher display monitor and video card. The larger the display monitor the better. A 17 inch (or larger) monitor is preferable to the more normal 14 inch.

Figure 2.1 shows a typical hardware set-up for working with AutoCAD Release 14.

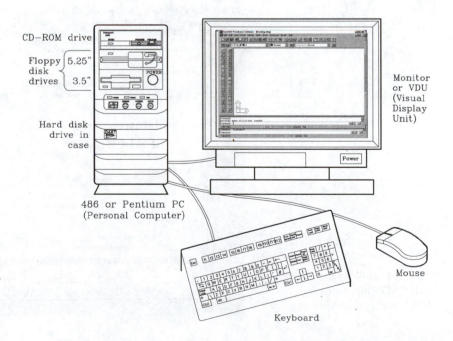

Fig. 2.1 A typical hardware set-up for running AutoCAD Release 14

The AutoCAD R14 window

Upon start-up, the R14 window appears as shown in Fig. 2.2. The features of the start-up window are:

Title bar: Shows the R14 icon, the name **AutoCAD**. When a drawing is opened the title bar includes the name of the drawing. In the title bar there are the three buttons:

Minimise – a *left-click* on the button and the R14 window closes, but is held as an icon in the Windows 95 task bar.

Maximise – a *left-click* on the button and the R14 window expands to fill the screen.

Close – a *left-click* on the button and R14 is closed and the window disappears.

Menu bar: Includes the names of the menus of R14. A *left-click* on any of the menu names brings the named pull-down menu on screen.

Standard toolbar: Usually included just under the menu bar. Includes the tool icons of those tools, in frequent use, but not used for drawing construction.

Object Properties toolbar: Just under the **Standard** toolbar. Includes tools associated with layers.

Draw toolbar: Usually *docked* against the left-hand side of the R14 window. Contains most of the drawing tools.

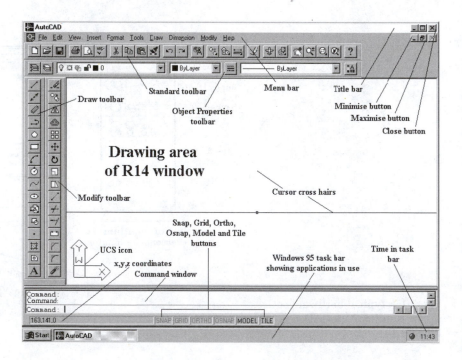

Fig. 2.2 Details of the AutoCAD Release 14 for Windows 95 window

Modify toolbar: Usually docked against the **Draw** toolbar. Contains tools such as **Erase**, **Mirror** etc. – tools for modifying parts of drawings.

Cursor cross hairs: Those shown in Fig. 2.2 have been set for 100 per cent – right across the window in both directions.

Command window: This is a window – can be enlarged or decreased in size vertically. Contains a history of actions taken from the start of a construction. The default for the number of lines held in the text window is 400 – set in the **Preferences/Display** dialogue box.

Prompt bar: Shows the *x,y,z* coordinates of the position of the intersection of the cursor cross hairs and 6 buttons – **SNAP**, **GRID**, **ORTHO**, **OSNAP**, **MODEL** and **TILE**. A *double-click* on any of the first three toggles SNAP, GRID or ORTHO. A *double-click* on OSNAP brings the **Osnap Settings** dialogue box to screen; a *double click* on MODEL switches the screen to Paper Space, when the TILE button greys out. A *double-click* on the greyed out TILE button brings back Model Space. More about these features in later chapters.

   When the cursor is placed over a tool icon or when a tool is selected from a menu bar, the prompt bar shows a description of the action of the chosen tool and the other features disappear.

Windows 95 Task bar: shows details of the applications in action concurrently with R14 and includes the Windows 95 **Start** button from which other programmes can be called. The time is always running at the right-hand end of the task bar.

Changing the R14 window

Figure 2.3 shows another R14 window, in which the four default toolbars have been removed and the **Osnaps** toolbar placed against the right-hand side of the window. This window allows more space in the drawing area and also gives instant access to the osnaps, which are in very frequent use when constructing drawings. Some operators may prefer this window, but toolbars in use at the moment must be floating somewhere on screen, or all tool commands *entered* in the Command window.

   Note that if R14 is shut down (*left-click* on the **Close** button), on the next start up, the same window will appear – i.e. without the four toolbars.

Help

An extensive help system is available in R14. Help can be called in several ways:

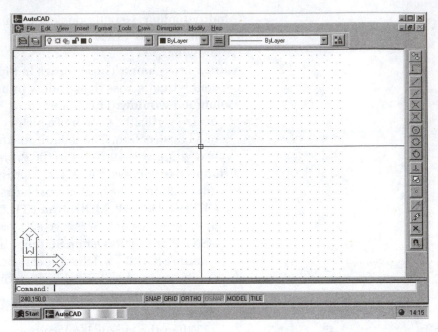

Fig. 2.3 Another R14 window

Fig. 2.4 Selecting **AutoCAD Help Topics** from the **Help** pull-down menu

1. *Left-click* on **Help** in the menu bar, followed by another on **AutoCAD Help Topics** in the pull-down menu which appears (Fig. 2.4). The **Help Topics: AutoCAD Help** window appears. *Enter* the name of the topic which is required in the box numbered **1** (Fig. 2.5). The list of help topics changes to show the *entered* name highlighted. *Left-click* on the **Display** button and help topic window for the topic name appears (Fig. 2.6). In the example shown here, the name

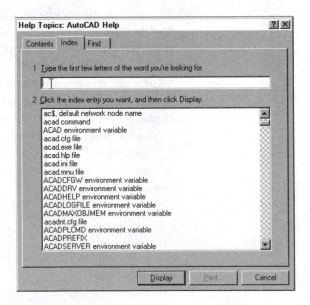

Fig. 2.5 The **Help Topics: AutoCAD Help** window

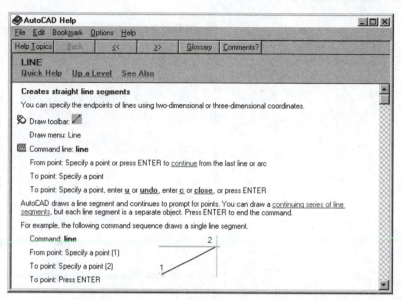

Fig. 2.6 The **LINE** help window

entered was line. In the **LINE** help window, note that some words are in green. A *left-click* on any of the green words brings up another help window with details of help for the named topic.

2. *Enter* help in the Command Window. The **AutoCAD: Help Topics** window appears.
3. When a tool is in action, pressing the **F1** key brings up the help window for that tool.
4. At any time, either *enter* help or a **?** in the Command window and the **Help Topics: AutoCAD Help** window appears.

Floating and docked toolbars

A toolbar such as the **Draw** toolbar, can be placed anywhere on screen in a re-sized shape, by placing the cursor in its title bar and *dragging* the toolbar to a suitable position on screen. Figure 2.7 shows the **Draw** toolbar in a 'floating' position in the R14 window.

A toolbar can also be moved from its floating position by placing the cursor within its title bar and *dragging* it to either side, to the top, or to the bottom of the R14 window. The toolbar assumes the shape of the side in which it is placed and becomes *docked* tight against that side. Figure 2.8 shows the **Draw** toolbar being *dragged* to the left-hand side of the R14 window. When in position the mouse button is released and the details in the toolbar reappear.

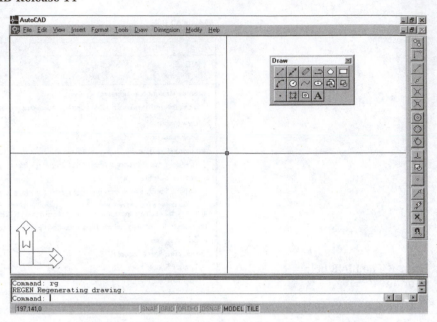

Fig. 2.7 A floating toolbar

The AutoCAD coordinate system

Drawings are constructed in AutoCAD in either a 2D (two-dimensional) system or a 3D (three-dimensional) system. When working in 2D the coordinates are expressed in terms of X and Y. X units are measured horizontally and Y units vertically. With this system, any point in the R14 window can be referred to in terms of *x,y*. Thus the point *x,y* = 70,40 is 70 units horizontally to the right of an origin where

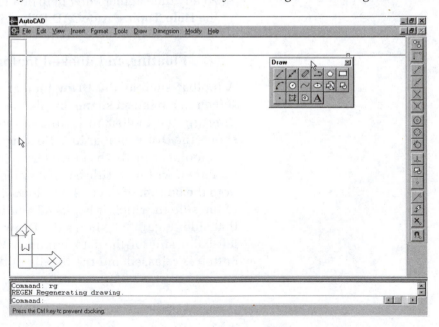

Fig. 2.8 *Docking* a toolbar against the side of the R14 window

$x,y = 0,0$ and 40 units vertically above the $x,y = 0,0$ origin. Figure 2.9 shows a number of 2D coordinate points in an R14 window.

Coordinates points can be measured in negative figures. Thus the point $x,y = -100,-50$ is a point 100 units to the left of an origin $x,y = 0,0$ and 50 units below the origin 0,0.

3D coordinates include a third direction measured in terms of Z. In R14, +ve Z is as if coming towards the operator from the R14 window perpendicular to the screen. This means that −ve Z is perpendicularly from the screen away from the operator.

Note that the coordinate reading in the prompt line of R14 shows a three number coordinate e.g. $x,y,z = 70,40,0$. This is because when taking 2D coordinates Z units are at 0 – lying on the surface of the screen.

More about 3D coordinates in a later chapter (Chapter 13).

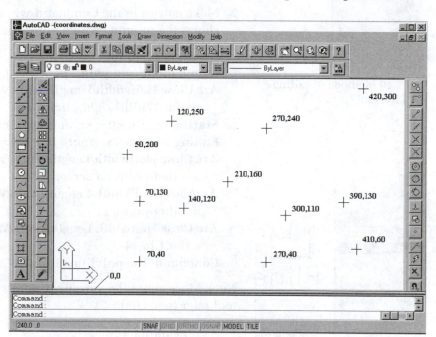

Fig. 2.9 2D coordinate points in an R14 window

Examples of drawing with tools (Fig. 2.14)

Example 1

1. Either (Fig. 2.10):
    (a) *Left-click* on the **Line** tool from the **Draw** toolbar, or:
    (b) *Enter* l in the Command window, or:
    (c) *Enter* line in the Command window, or:
    (d) Select **Line** from the **Draw** pull-down menu.

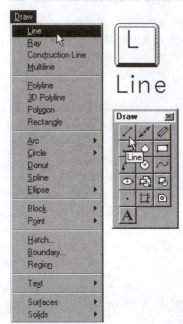

Fig. 2.10 Methods of calling the **Line** tool

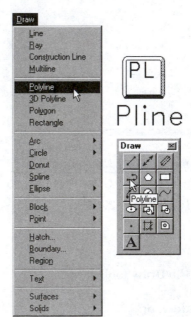

Fig. 2.11 Methods of calling the **Polyline** tool

2. Note the prompts in the Command window for each of the methods used. In all of them the prompt **Line from point:** will appear. *Left-click* at any point in the R14 window. The prompt changes to **To point:**. *Left-click* at another point. The prompt repeats to **To point:**. Continue *left-clicks* anywhere on screen.

3. When satisfied that lines can be easily drawn *enter* c (for Close). The line closes to the first *picked* point and a polygon is formed.

Example 2

1. Either (Fig. 2.11):
   (a) *Left-click* on the **Polyline** tool from the **Draw** toolbar, or:
   (b) *Enter* pl in the Command window, or:
   (c) *Enter* pline in the Command window, or:
   (d) Select **Polyline** from the **Draw** pull-down menu.

2. Make entries in the Command window as follows. The bold type shows the prompts which appear in the Command window:

Command: _pline
Command: From point: *pick* any point on screen
Arc/Close/Halfwidth/Length/Undo/Width/<Endpoint of line>: *enter* w (for Width) *right-click*
Starting width <0>: *enter* 2 *right-click*
Ending width <2>: *right-click* (to accept the 2)
Arc/Close/Halfwidth/Length/Undo/Width/<Endpoint of line>: *pick* another point on screen
Arc/Close/Halfwidth/Length/Undo/Width/<Endpoint of line>: *pick* another point
Arc/Close/Halfwidth/Length/Undo/Width/<Endpoint of line>: *enter* c (for Close)
Command: the polyline closes

Note: More about the various prompts associated with the polyline tool later (page 68).

Example 3

1. Either (Fig. 2.12):
   (a) *Left-click* on the **Circle** tool from the **Draw** toolbar, or:
   (b) *Enter* c in the Command window, or:
   (c) *Enter* circle in the Command window, or:
   (d) Select **Circle** from the **Draw** pull-down menu.

2. Make entries in the Command window as follows:

Command: _circle 3P/2P/TTR/<Center point>: *pick* a point
Diameter/<radius>: *pick* another point
Command: the circle forms

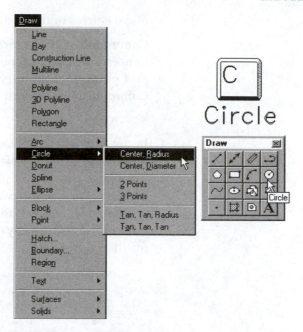

Fig. 2.12 Methods of calling
the **Circle** tool

Example 4

1. Either (Fig. 2.11):
    (a) *Left-click* on the **Arc** tool from the **Draw** toolbar, or:
    (b) *Enter* a in the Command window, or:
    (c) *Enter* arc in the Command window, or:
    (d) Select **Arc** from the **Draw** pull-down menu.

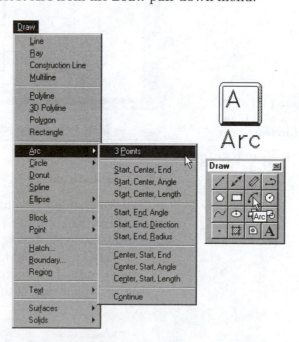

Fig. 2.13 Methods of calling
the **Arc** tool

2. Make entries in the Command window as follow:

Command: _arc Center/<Start point>: *pick* a point
Center/End/<Second point: *pick* another point
End point: *pick* another point
Command: the arc forms

Notes

1. In the prompts in the Command window, names enclosed in the brackets **< >** are the default prompts.
2. To change the default prompt *enter* the initial letter of the other prompts. An example was given in the second example when the w entered stood for **Width** of the polyline.
3. Pressing the **Return** key of the keyboard will usually have the same result as a *right-click*.

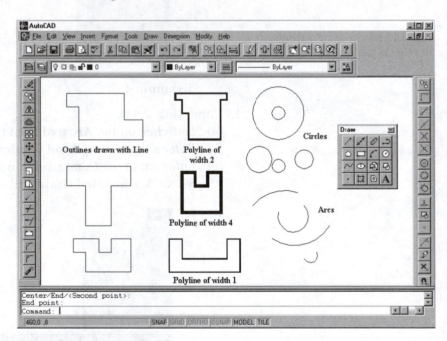

Fig. 2.14 Examples of constructions with **Line**, **Polylines**, **Circle** and **Arc**

Questions

1. Can you list five advantages of using a CAD software programme such as R14 for the production of technical drawings when compared to producing the same drawings using 'hand methods'.
2. Can R14 be run in a Macintosh computer?
3. How can the cursor cross hairs be changed so as to only stretch across 25 per cent of the screen?

4. Can you name the several methods by which **Help** can be obtained in R14?
5. What is meant by 'docking' a toolbar?
6. What is meant by 'floating' a toolbar?
7. What is the difference between the coordinate points $x,y = 20,100$ and $x,y = -20,-100$?
8. How many coordinate units are there between $x,y = 100,230$ and $x,y = 100,415$?
9. How many coordinate units are there between $x,y = 10,65$ and $x,y = -120,65$?
10. Can you name the four methods by which commands (tools) can be called in R14?

Exercises

1. *Left-click* on each of the names in the menu bar and examine the commands (tools) in each pull-down menu which appears on screen.
2. *Left-click* on each of the tool icons in the **Draw** toolbar in turn to check which tools each of the icons represent.
3. *Left-click* on each of the tool icons in the **Modify** toolbar to check the names of the tools each of the icons represents.
4. Move the mouse so that the cursor is at one of the corners of the R14 window. What happens to the cursor?
5. *Left-click* in the popup list box or on the arrow to the right of the box named **By Layer** in the **Object Properties** bar. Examine the list which appears. What do you think the icons in the list represent and why are they there?
6. Move the cursor cross hairs onto the top edge of the Command window. The cursor changes. *Drag* this new cursor upwards to enlarge the window. Then *drag* it back.
7. *Left-click* on the **Minimise** button at the right corner of the title bar. The name bar of R14 in the Windows 95 task bar should lose its highlighting. Then *left-click* on the R14 name bar in the task bar. The R14 window should again fill the screen.
8. *Left-click* on the **Maximise** button to the right-hand of the **Minimise** button. Check what happens to the R14 window.
9. *Drag* the **Draw** toolbar away from the edge of the R14 window and change its size. Then *drag* the toolbar back to one side of the window and *dock* it against the side. Try the same at the top, bottom and both sides of the R14 window.

10. *Enter* setvar in the Command window. The Command line changes to:

Command: *enter* setvar *right-click*
Variable name or ?: *enter ? right-click*
Variable(s) to list <*>: *right-click*

and an **AutoCAD Text Window** appears showing the AutoCAD set variables. It is too early for the beginner to think about set variables, but it is worth while examining the list in the window. Methods of working AutoCAD often depends upon the settings of the variables.

CHAPTER 3

Accurate construction of drawings

Introduction

There are several methods by which drawings can be accurately constructed in R14 to given dimensions. They are based upon the AutoCAD coordinate system. The coordinate system of AutoCAD is in *x,y,z* coordinate units, thus the operator must decide on the units of measurement determined by the coordinate unit. For example, opening my **ay.dwt** template produces an R14 window 420 units wide (X units) and 297 units high (Y units). An A3 drawing sheet in landscape format is 420 mm wide by 297 mm high. Thus when working in a template such as **ay.dwt** it can be assumed that each coordinate unit is equivalent to 1 millimetre. If such a drawing is printed or plotted full size, then the measurements on the printed/ plotted drawing will be in millimetres.

Most of the drawing shown as examples and/or exercises in this book have been constructed on **ay.dwt**. Their dimensions are therefore assumed to be in millimetres. There are some exceptions, particularly when the drawings are of buildings, building plots etc.

For the time being we are only concerned with two-dimensional drawings. This means that only X and Y coordinates will be given in the drawings in this chapter.

Method 1 – absolute units

The absolute coordinates method requires the entry at the keyboard of the position of each and every point in a construction.

Each of the following examples were constructed by first selecting the required tool from the **Draw** toolbar. Selection from the **Draw** pull-down menu, *entry* of tool names or their abbreviations in the Command window could equally as well be the chosen method.

Figure 3.1 shows the tool icons and their tool tips used for the examples as they would be selected from the **Draw** toolbar.

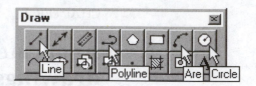

Fig. 3.1 The **Draw** toolbar
showing tools selected for the
examples

Example 1 (Fig. 3.2)

Select the **Line** tool from the **Draw** toolbar. The prompt in the
Command window becomes:

Command:_line from point: *enter* 20,250 *right-click*
To point: *enter* 130,250 *right-click*
To point: *enter* 130,180 *right-click*
To point: *enter* 20,180 *right-click*
To point: *enter* c (for Close) *right-click*
Command:

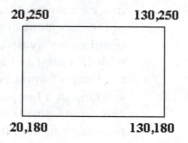

Fig. 3.2 Example 1

Example 2 (Fig. 3.3)

Select the **Line** tool from the **Draw** toolbar. The prompt in the
Command window becomes:

Command:_line from point: *enter* 20,150 *right-click*
To point: *enter* 50,150 *right-click*
To point: *enter* 50,110 *right-click*
To point: *enter* 80,110 *right-click*
To point: *enter* 80,150 *right-click*
To point: *enter* 110,150 *right-click*
To point: *enter* 110,70 *right-click*
To point: *enter* 80,70 *right-click*
To point: *enter* 80,90 *right-click*
To point: *enter* 50,90 *right-click*
To point: *enter* 50,70 *right-click*
To point: *enter* 20,70 *right-click*
To point: *enter* c (for Close) *right-click*
Command:

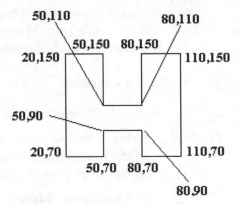

50,110   80,110
50,150 80,150
20,150   110,150
50,90
20,70   110,70
50,70 80,70
80,90

Fig. 3.3 Example 2

Example 3 (Fig. 3.4)

Select the **Polyline** tool from the **Draw** toolbar. The prompt in the Command window becomes:

> **Command: _pline**
> **From point:** *enter* 180,250 *right-click*
> **Current line width is 0**
> **Arc/Close/Halfwidth/Length/Undo/Width/<Endpoint of line>:** *enter* w (for Width) *right-click*
> **Starting width <0>:** *enter* 1 *right-click*
> **Ending width <1>:** *right-click* (to accept)
> **Arc/Close/Halfwidth/Length/Undo/Width/<Endpoint of line>:** *enter* 270,250 *right-click*
> **Arc/Close/Halfwidth/Length/Undo/Width/<Endpoint of line>:** *enter* 270,220 *right-click*
> **Arc/Close/Halfwidth/Length/Undo/Width/<Endpoint of line>:** *enter* 250,220 *right-click*
> **Arc/Close/Halfwidth/Length/Undo/Width/<Endpoint of line>:** *enter* 250,180 *right-click*
> **Arc/Close/Halfwidth/Length/Undo/Width/<Endpoint of line>:** *enter* 200,180 *right-click*
> **Arc/Close/Halfwidth/Length/Undo/Width/<Endpoint of line>:** *enter* 200,220 *right-click*

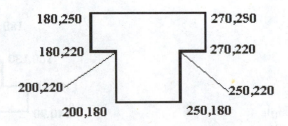

180,250   270,250
180,220   270,220
200,220   250,220
200,180   250,180

Fig. 3.4 Example 3

Arc/Close/Halfwidth/Length/Undo/Width/<Endpoint of line>:
  enter 180,220 *right-click*
Arc/Close/Halfwidth/Length/Undo/Width/<Endpoint of line>:
  enter c (for Close) *right-click*
Command:

Example 4 (Fig. 3.5)

In Fig. 3.5 some of the coordinate numbers have not been included in the illustration. Select the **Polyline** tool from the **Draw** toolbar. The prompt in the Command window becomes:

Command: _pline
From point: *enter* 180,150 *right-click*
Current line width is 1
Arc/Close/Halfwidth/Length/Undo/Width/<Endpoint of line>:
  enter 200,150 *right-click*
Arc/Close/Halfwidth/Length/Undo/Width/<Endpoint of line>:
  enter 200,130 *right-click*
Arc/Close/Halfwidth/Length/Undo/Width/<Endpoint of line>:
  enter 220,130 *right-click*
Arc/Close/Halfwidth/Length/Undo/Width/<Endpoint of line>:
  enter 220,110 *right-click*
Arc/Close/Halfwidth/Length/Undo/Width/<Endpoint of line>:
  enter 240,110 *right-click*
Arc/Close/Halfwidth/Length/Undo/Width/<Endpoint of line>:
  enter 240,90 *right-click*
Arc/Close/Halfwidth/Length/Undo/Width/<Endpoint of line>:
  enter 140,90 *right-click*
Arc/Close/Halfwidth/Length/Undo/Width/<Endpoint of line>:
  enter 140,110 *right-click*
Arc/Close/Halfwidth/Length/Undo/Width/<Endpoint of line>:
  enter 160,110 *right-click*
Arc/Close/Halfwidth/Length/Undo/Width/<Endpoint of line>:
  enter 160,130 *right-click*
Arc/Close/Halfwidth/Length/Undo/Width/<Endpoint of line>:
  enter 180,130 *right-click*

Fig. 3.5 Example 4

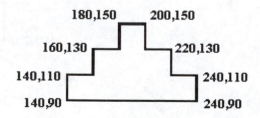

Arc/Close/Halfwidth/Length/Undo/Width/<Endpoint of line>:
enter c (for Close) *right-click*
Command:

Example 5 (Fig. 3.6)

Select the **Circle** tool from the **Draw** toolbar. The prompt in the Command window becomes:

Command: _circle 3P/2P/TTR/<Centre point>: *enter* 340,220
right-click
Diameter/<Radius>: *enter* 50 *right-click*
Command: *right-click* (back to Circle command sequence)
CIRCLE 3P/2P/TTR/<Centre point>: *enter* 340,220 *right-click*
Diameter/<Radius> <50>: *enter* 30 *right-click*
Command:

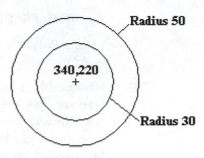

Fig. 3.6 Example 5

Example 6 (Fig. 3.7)

Select the **Arc** tool from the **Draw** toolbar. The prompt in the Command window becomes:

Command: _arc Center/<Start point>: *enter* 280,100 *right-click*
Center/End/<Second point>: *enter* 330,140 *right-click*

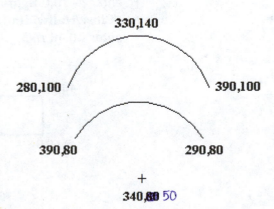

Fig. 3.7 Example 6

End point: *enter* 390,100 *right-click*
Command: *right-click* (back to Arc prompts)
Center/<Start point>: *enter* c (for Center) *right-click*
Center: *enter* 340,50 *right-click*
Start point: *enter* 390,80 *right-click*
Angle/Length of chord<End point>: *enter* 290,80 *right-click*
Command:

Method 2 – relative units

In the relative method of construction each of the coordinates are *entered* relative to the last set – i.e. including the distance from the last set. To differentiate between absolute and relative entry, @ is *entered* before the figures of the coordinate point relative to the last point.

Example 1 (Fig. 3.8)

Select the **Polyline** tool from the **Draw** toolbar. The Command line changes to:

Command: _pline
Current line width is 0
Arc/Close/Halfwidth/Length/Undo/Width/<Endpoint of line>:
   enter w (for Width) *right-click*
Starting width <0>: *enter* 0.7 *right-click*
Ending width <1>: *right-click* Note 1 because only 1 decimal
   point
Arc/Close/Halfwidth/Length/Undo/Width/<Endpoint of line>:
   enter @130,0 *right-click*
Arc/Close/Halfwidth/Length/Undo/Width/<Endpoint of line>:
   enter @0,–70 *right-click*
Arc/Close/Halfwidth/Length/Undo/Width/<Endpoint of line>:
   enter @–70,0 *right-click*
Arc/Close/Halfwidth/Length/Undo/Width/<Endpoint of line>:
   enter @0,40 *right-click*

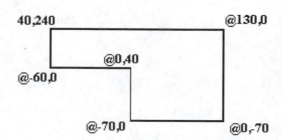

Fig. 3.8 Example 1

Arc/Close/Halfwidth/Length/Undo/Width/<Endpoint of line>:
enter @–60,0 *right-click*
Arc/Close/Halfwidth/Length/Undo/Width/<Endpoint of line>:
enter c (for Close) *right-click*
Command:

Note: Some of the *x* and *y* coordinate units in this example were given as negative. The following rules apply:

+ve x   horizontally to the right
–ve x   horizontally to the left
+ve y   vertically upwards
–ve y   vertically downwards

Thus @130,0 is 130 units horizontally relative to the last constructed point; @0,–70 is 70 units vertically downwards relative to the last constructed point.

Example 2 (Fig. 3.9)

When constructing with the aid of the relative coordinates method, lines at an angle relative to the horizontal are constructed by keying the < symbol from the keyboard. Thus, a line drawn with the *entry* **@100<45** is 100 units distance from and at an angle of 45° to the horizontal.

This example shows the use of angles constructed using the relative coordinates method. Call the **Polyline** tool. The Command line shows:

Command: _pline
From point: *enter* 55,165 *right-click*
Current line width is 0
Arc/Close/Halfwidth/Length/Undo/Width/<Endpoint of line>: *enter*
    w (for Width) *right-click*
Starting width <0>: *enter* 1 *right-click*

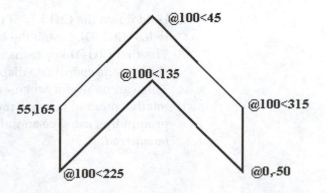

Fig. 3.9 Example 2

Ending width <1>: *right-click* (to accept)
Arc/Close/Halfwidth/Length/Undo/Width/<Endpoint of line>:
 enter @100<45 *right-click*
Arc/Close/Halfwidth/Length/Undo/Width/<Endpoint of line>:
 enter @100<315 *right-click*
Arc/Close/Halfwidth/Length/Undo/Width/<Endpoint of line>:
 enter @0,–50 *right-click*
Arc/Close/Halfwidth/Length/Undo/Width/<Endpoint of line>:
 enter @100<135 *right-click*
Arc/Close/Halfwidth/Length/Undo/Width/<Endpoint of line>:
 enter @100<225 *right-click*
Arc/Close/Halfwidth/Length/Undo/Width/<Endpoint of line>:
 enter c (for Close) *right-click*
Command:

Notes

1. The default method of measuring angles in AutoCAD is starting with 0° to the right (eastwards) angles are measured in an anticlockwise (counter clockwise or ccw) direction back to 360° eastwards. Figure 3.10 shows the angles at 45° intervals as measured in this way.

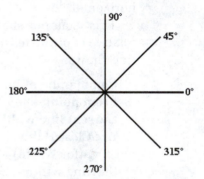

Fig. 3.10 The default ccw
measurement of angles

2. Hold down the **Ctrl** key of the keyboard and then press the **D** key twice (**Ctrl+D**). Watch the coordinate display in the prompt line. The first **Ctrl+D** key turns off the coordinate display, the second changes the coordinate display from absolute to relative numbers. This can be useful when *entering* angular coordinates using the relative method because the coordinate numbers showing in the prompt line can give an indication of the direction of the angle to be *entered*.

Method 3 – directional drawing

When drawing lines or polylines, once the first point has been *entered*, subsequent points (in answer to the **To point:** prompts can be determined by moving the cursor in the direction in which the line or pline should be drawn and *entering* the distance at the Command line prompt. If all lines of the construction are to be vertical and horizontal, turning **ORTHO** on (*double-click* on the **ORTHO** button in the prompt line) will ensure accurate positioning of the line (pline) direction.

Example 1 (Fig. 3.11)

1. Turn on **ORTHO**.
2. Call the line tool and *left-click* anywhere in the drawing window.
3. *Drag* the rubber band of the line to the right and *enter* 100 at the Command line, followed by a *right-click*. A line 100 units long will be drawn.

Command: _line
From point: *left-click* anywhere on screen.
To point: *drag* the rubber band to the right and *enter* 100 *right-click*
To point: *drag* the rubber band downwards and *enter* 60 *right-click*
To point: *drag* the rubber band to the left and *enter* 40 *right-click*
To point: *drag* the rubber band downwards and *enter* 60 *right-click*
To point: *drag* the rubber band to the left and *enter* 20 *right-click*
To point: *drag* the rubber band upwards and *enter* 60 *right-click*
To point: *drag* the rubber band to the left and *enter* 40 *right-click*
To point: *enter* c (for Close) *right-click*
Command:

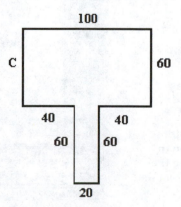

Fig. 3.11 Example 1

Example 2 (Fig. 3.12)

Turn **ORTHO** off. Set the coordinate display in the prompt line to show relative coordinates. By moving the cursor to positions on screen so as to show the required angle in the coordinate display and *entering* the required numbers, construct the figure shown in Fig. 3.12.

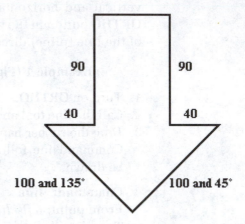

Fig. 3.12 Example 2

The term entity

A single feature in AutoCAD such as a line, an arc, a circle is referred to as an **entity**. The term **object** has the same meaning.

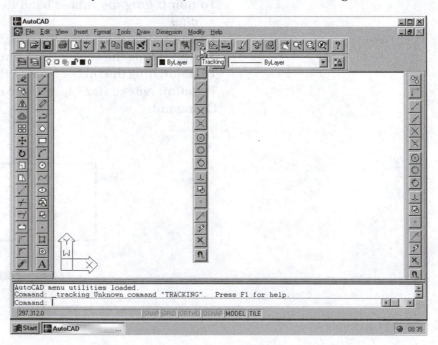

Fig. 3.13 The R14 window showing the **Object Snap** toolbar both *docked* to the right and appearing from the **Tracking** icon

Object snaps (osnaps)

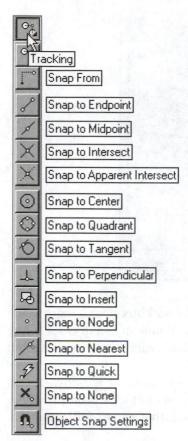

When an object snap is in operation, the positioning of points in the construction of drawings can be made with precision. Their use allows the operator to construct drawings by accurately *snapping* entities to various parts of other entities – to ends, to midpoints, to the intersections of entities etc. Object snaps have to be set, the setting being achieved in a variety of ways:

1. By selection from the **Object Snap** toolbar. The toolbar may be *docked* against the right-hand side of the R14 window, so that it is always handy when required. Even if the toolbar is not so *docked*, it can always be brought on screen by holding a *left-click* on the **Tracking** icon in the **Standard** toolbar at the top of the R14 window. The **Object Snap** toolbar then appears as a flyout as shown in Fig. 3.13.
   Figure 3.14 shows the names (by tool tips) of the object snaps of the icons in the toolbar.

2. Press the **Shift** key and *right-click* and a menu appears with the names of the **Object Snaps** (Fig. 3.15). Any of the object snaps can then be selected by name from the menu.

3. *Enter* ddosnap in the Command window and the **Object Settings** dialogue box appears (Fig. 3.16). An **Object Snap** (osnap), or several snaps can be set by setting the check squares on (*left-click* in the check box against a snap name). In the dialogue box, the size of the snaps *pick* box can be set by movement of the **Aperture size** slider.

Fig. 3.14 The names of the snaps in the **Object Snaps** toolbar

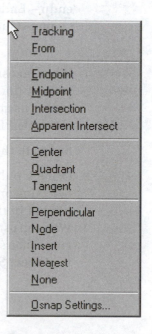

Fig. 3.15 **Shift**/*right-click* brings the **Object Snaps** menu on screen

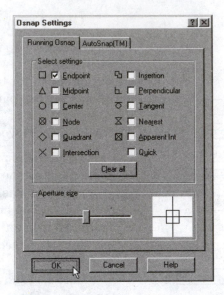

Fig. 3.16 The **Osnap Settings** dialogue box

As the slider is moved so the size of the *pick* box size changes in the viewing box to the right of the slider. When an osnap is set in the dialogue box, it is automatically available each time a drawing tool is called.

4. An osnap can be set by *entry* in the Command window. As an example, if a tool is in action, at any of the tool's prompts, if the abbreviation for the osnap is *entered*, that osnap will function. Examples of the abbreviations are:

   endp – Endpoint; **mid** – Midpoint; **int** – Intersect; **cen** – Center; **qua** – Quadrant; **tan** – Tangent; **nod** – Node; **per** – Perpendicular.

   Notes

1. When an osnap is called from the toolbar, a prompt appears in the prompt line of R14 describing the action of the osnap and also stating its abbreviation. As an example, when the **Endpoint** osnap is selected from the toolbar, the prompt line shows:

   Snaps to the closest endpoint of a line or arc: endp

2. Osnaps only come into action when a drawing tool is in use. Selecting one at any other time brings up an Unknown Command prompt in the Command window.

3. When an osnap is called a *pick* box appears at the intersection of the cursor hairs. The size of the *pick* box is governed by its settings in the **Object Snaps** dialogue box.

Examples of the use of osnaps

1. Figure 3.17 shows the use of the osnaps Endpoint, Midpoint, Intersection, Center and Quadrant. The relative osnap icons with their tool tips from the toolbar are included in the illustration.
2. Figure 3.18 shows the use of the osnaps Tangent, Node, Nearest and Settings. The relative osnap icons with their tool tips from the toolbar are included in the illustration.

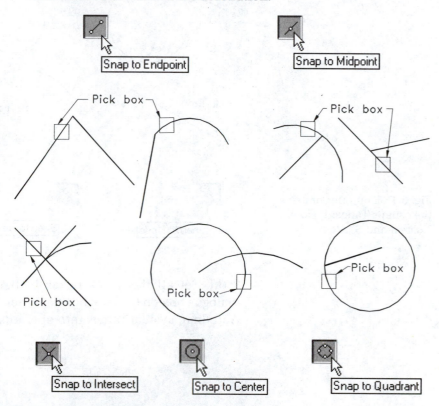

Fig. 3.17 Examples of using the osnaps Endpoint, Midpoint, Intersection, Center and Quadrant

Notes

1. If the osnap **Snap to None** is selected, all osnaps are turned off for that one selection.
2. If the osnap **Snap to Quick** is selected the snap point is the nearest to the selected point within the *pick* box. This is of particular value when several snap points have been turned on in the **Osnaps Settings** dialogue box.

AutoSnap

With the **Osnap Settings** dialogue box on screen, *left-click* on the **AutoSnap(TM)** label. The **AutoSnap** dialogue box appears (Fig.

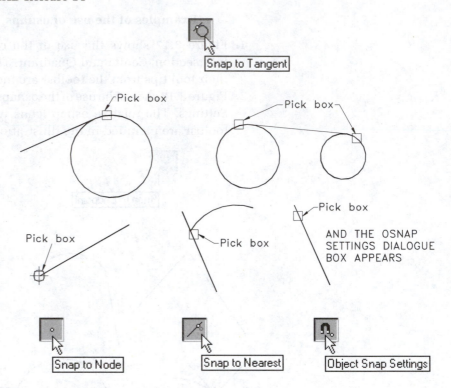

Fig. 3.18 Examples of using the osnaps Tangent, Node, Nearest and Settings

3.19). Set all the check boxes in the **Select settings** area of the dialogue box on (ticks in boxes). When the osnaps are now used, the AutoSnap system comes into operation.

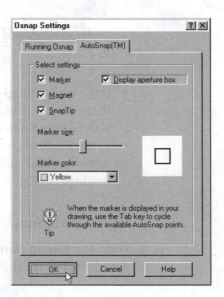

Fig. 3.19 The **AutoSnap(TM)** dialogue box

There are three parts of AutoSnap when it is set to be in action –
a **Marker**, a **Magnet** and a **Snap Tip**. If wished any one of these can
be turned off if required:

1. If the marker is turned off no pick box appears with the AutoSnap.
2. If the magnet is turned off, AutoSnap does not lock to the nearest
   snap point.
3. If the snap tip is turned off it doesn't show when osnaps are
   selected.

Notes

1. If, when the **Magnet** of AutoSnap is on, the osnap *pick* box is
   dragged by the AutoSnap marker box to the nearest snap point,
   depending upon which snaps have been set in the **Osnaps Settings**
   dialogue box.
2. If several osnaps are set on in the **Osnaps Settings** dialogue box,
   when AutoSnap is active, pressing the **Tab** key of the keyboard will
   toggle through all the possible snap points one after the other. As
   an example, Fig. 3.20 shows three plines. With all osnaps set on in
   Osnap Settings and with AutoSnap active, if another pline is
   drawn, pressing the **Tab** key will toggle between endpoint, midpoint
   and intersection osnaps. The Snap tip will show which of the snap
   points will be snapped onto.
3. It will be seen from Fig. 3.20 that a different shape marker will show
   for each of the AutoSnap markers, depending upon which osnap is
   in use.
4. AutoSnap only functions for osnaps already selected or set.

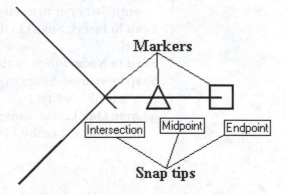

Fig. 3.20 AutoSnap markers
and Snap tips

The osnaps

The osnap *pick* box appears only when an osnap is in operation,
either selected from the **Object Snap** toolbar, set in the **Osnap**

Settings dialogue box or *entered* in the Command window. If an osnap is in operation the *pick* box appears at the intersection of the cursor cross hairs, whenever a drawing tool is in use. When the osnap *pick* box is present, the next *picked* point will snap onto the part of the *picked* entity to which the osnap refers. Osnaps are available for the following points on any entity:

Snap From: Fig. 3.21. Draw a circle. Select the **Line** tool. The Command window shows:

> **Command:** _line From point *left-click* on the **Snap From** icon.
> _from Base point: *enter* qua (for quadrant)
> of *pick* the circle **<Offset>:** *enter* 180,150. The start point for a line jumps to the coordinate point 180,150
> **To point:** *enter* 280,150 *right-click*
> **To point:** *right-click*
> **Command:**

Snap to Endpoint: Snaps to the nearest endpoint of the selected entity.
Snap to Midpoint: Snaps to the middle point of the selected entity.
Snap to Intersect: Snaps to an intersection of entities covered by the *pick* box.
Snap to Apparent Intersect: Available for use when working in 3D.
Snap to Center: Snaps to the centre of a selected circle or arc.
Snap to Quadrant: Snaps to the nearest quadrant point of a selected circle.
Snap to Tangent: Snaps to a tangent point on a selected arc or circle from another entity.
Snap to Perpendicular: Snaps on an entity to form a perpendicular entity from or to a selected point.
Snap to Insert: Snaps to the insertion point of an insert (see Chapter 11).
Snap to Node: Snaps to the centre of a **Point**.
Snap to Nearest: Snaps to the nearest point covered by the *pick* box on a selected entity.
Snap to Quick: If an osnap is in operation, snaps to that osnap point on a selected entity.

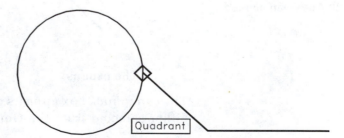

Fig. 3.21 An example of the use of **Snap From**

Snap to None: Turns off any osnaps in operation.

Object Snap Settings: Brings the **Osnap Settings** dialogue box on screen.

Grid and Snap

Grid points at any chosen intervals can be set in the drawing area either from the **Drawing Aids** dialogue box (called from the **Tools** pull-down menu – Fig. 3.22), or by *entry* in the Command window. Once set, grid can be toggled on/off by pressing the function key **F7** of the keyboard.

Snaps can be set at any chosen intervals, either from the **Drawings Aids** dialogue box or by *entry* in the Command window. Once set snaps can be toggled on/off by pressing the function key **F9**.

Figure 3.23 shows **Snap** set to 5 and **Grid** set to 10 in the **Drawing Aids** dialogue box. Note in the dialogue box, **Blips** are turned off, but this choice is the operator's.

Setting Snap and Grid from the Command line

To set **Snap**:

> **Command:** *enter* snap *right-click*
> **Snap spacing or On/Off/Aspect/Rotate/Style <10>:** *enter* 5 *right-click*
> **Command:**

To set **Grid**:

> **Command:** *enter* grid *right-click*
> **Grid spacing (X) or ON/OFF/Snap/Aspect <0>:** *enter* 10 *right-click*
> **Command:**

With **Snap** set to 5 and on, the cursor under mouse control can only be moved either horizontally or vertically in steps of 5. As the cursor is moved it snaps at 5 unit intervals. The snap setting does not,

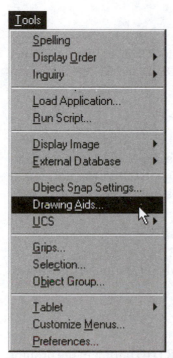

Fig. 3.22 Selecting **Drawing Aids...** from the **Tools** pull-down menu

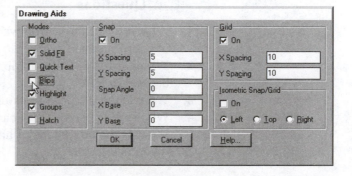

Fig. 3.23 The **Drawing Aids** dialogue box

however, affect the positioning of points *entered* in coordinates at the Command line.

With **Grid** set to 10 and on, dots appear in the R14 drawing area at 10 unit intervals horizontally and vertically.

Snap and Grid can be used as useful adjuncts to accurate drawing.

Notes

Both grid and snap can be set:

1. From the **Drawing Aids** dialogue box.
2. From the Command line.
3. By toggling from the function keys **F7** for **Grid** and **F9** for **Snap**.
4. By toggling with *double-clicks* on the **GRID** and **SNAP** buttons in the prompt line of the R14 window.

Ortho

When **Ortho** is set on, the drawing of features such as lines and polylines under mouse control is restricted to either the horizontal or vertical directions (the X axis or Y axis directions). This facility is of value particularly when setting out views in orthographic projections (Chapter 7). Ortho can be set on/of:

1. In the **Drawing Aids** dialogue box (Fig. 3.23).
2. From the Command line. *Enter* ortho and the Command line shows:

   Command: *enter* ortho *right-click*
   ON/OFF <Off>:

3. By toggling from the function key **F8**.
4. By toggling with *double-clicks* on the **ORTHO** button in the prompt line of the R14 window (Fig. 3.24).

Fig. 3.24 The buttons in the R14 prompt line

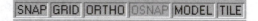

Questions

1. What is the difference between drawing using the absolute method of coordinate entry and the relative method?
2. Which is the default rotational direction for the sizes of angles to be read in R14?
3. What is the purpose of using **ORTHO**?
4. When using osnaps how can the size of the *pick* box be altered?
5. What is the advantage of having a *pick* box of a fairly large size when using osnaps?

6.   Can you describe the use of the osnap **Snap From**?
7.   What happens with a *left-click* on the osnap icon **Object Snap Settings**?
8.   What is **AutoSnap**?
9.   What is the purpose of setting the **Magnet** action of AutoSnap?
10. Which function keys can be used to toggle **Grid?**; **Ortho?**, **Snap?**

Exercises

1.   Practise toggling on/off the controls **Grid**, **Snap** and **Ortho** using the various methods described on page 45.
2.   Practise using the shortcut **Ctrl+D** watching the coordinates showing in the prompt line and noting the changes which occur.
3.   Select tool icons one after the other from the **Draw** toolbar and note the descriptions of the tools' actions showing in the prompt line.
4.   Call **Help** for each of the controls given in the exercises. The exercises below have been worked in an R14 window set-up as in my template **ay.dwt**. See page 3.
5.   Using the absolute coordinates method of construction and with either the **Line** or the **Polyline** tool copy the drawing given in Fig. 3.25. Do not attempt to include the coordinate figures.

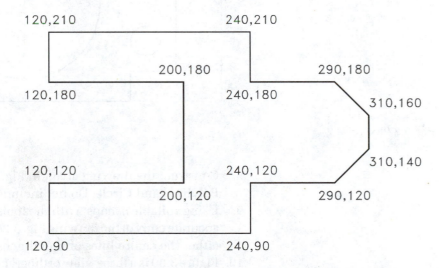

Fig. 3.25 Exercise 5

6.   Using the relative coordinates method of construction and with the **Line**, **Circle** and **Arc** tools construct the drawing shown in Fig. 3.26. Do not attempt including the dimensions.
7.   With the aid of the tools **Line** (or **Polyline**) and **Circle** construct the drawing given in Fig. 3.27. Do not include either the centre lines or the dimensions.

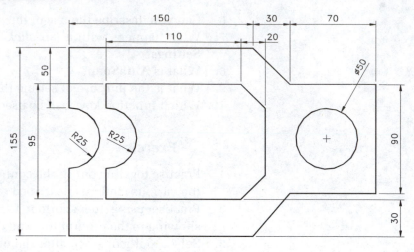

Fig. 3.26 Exercise 6

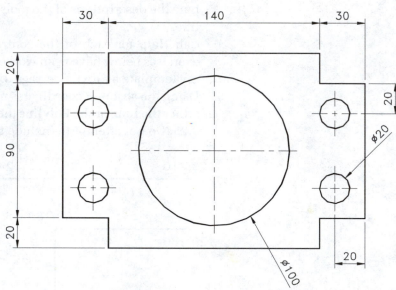

Fig. 3.27 Exercise 7

8. Construct the drawing given in Fig. 3.28 with the aid of **Line** (or **Polyline**) and **Circle**. Do not include the dimensions.
9. Using suitable osnaps, with the tools **Circle** and **Arc** construct an accurate copy of the drawing Fig. 3.29. Make no attempt to include either the centre lines or the dimensions in your drawing.
10. Figure 3.30 is a three-view orthographic projection (see Chapter 7) of a simple engineering component. Construct an accurate copy of the given drawing. It is advisable to set **ORTHO** on for this type of drawing. Do not attempt including either the centre lines or the dimensions.

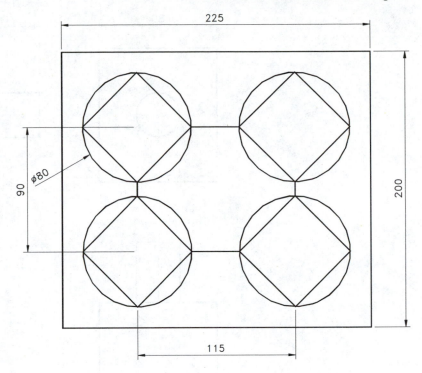

Fig. 3.28 Exercise 8

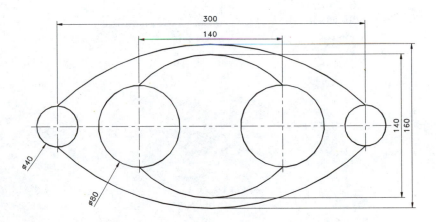

Fig. 3.29 Exercise 9

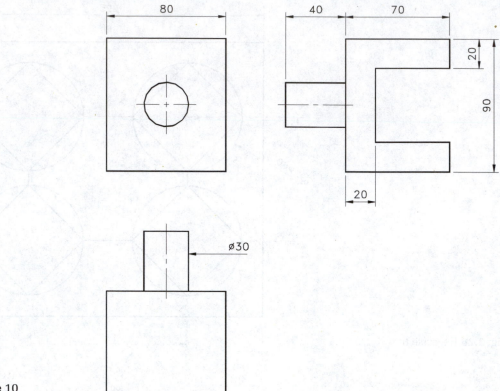

Fig. 3.30 Exercise 10

CHAPTER 4

Settings from dialogue boxes

Introduction

Some references have already been made to settings in dialogue boxes in previous chapters. Some of the dialogue boxes mentioned in previous chapters will be described in this chapter in fuller detail. Dialogue boxes can be called to screen in a variety of ways:

From pull-down menus: Whenever a name appears in a pull-down menu followed by three fullstops (**...**) selecting that name brings a dialogue box to screen. Figure 4.1 shows the pull-down menu from **Format**, which includes several names followed by ....

From tool icons: Selection from some tool icons will cause the appropriate dialogue box to appear. As an example, Fig. 4.2 shows the **Boundary Hatch** dialogue box resulting from a *left-click* on the **Hatch** tool from the **Modify** toolbox.

By dd calls: Many dialogue boxes can be called to screen by the *entry* of a dd call. See page 10.

Fig. 4.1 Selecting a dialogue box name from the **Format** pull-down menu

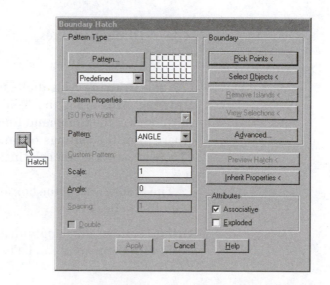

Fig. 4.2 The **Boundary Hatch** dialogue box called from the **Hatch** tool icon

From within other dialogue boxes: Some dialogue boxes can be brought to screen by *left-clicks* on dialogue box buttons within dialogue boxes on screen. When the name of a button in a dialogue box includes three full stops (**...**) a *left-click* on that button brings up a dialogue box. A *left-click* on the **Pattern...** button of the **Boundary Hatch** box (Fig. 4.2) brings up the **Hatch pattern palette** dialogue box (Fig. 4.3).

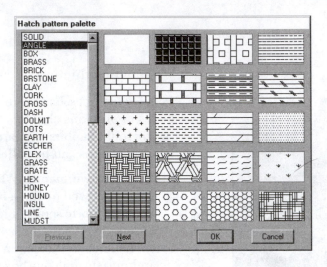

Fig. 4.3 The **Hatch pattern palette** dialogue box

Note: In many dialogue boxes, check boxes or check circles against a name can be used to set the named feature on or off. A tick in a check box means the item is on, if empty it is off. A dot in a check circle signifies the feature is on; empty check circles show the feature is off.

Dialogue boxes

Drawing Aids

Call the **Drawing Aids** dialogue box to screen with a *left-click* on **Drawing Aids** from the **Tools** pull-down menu or by *entering* ddrmodes at the Command line, followed by a *right-click* (Fig. 4.4). Apart from the settings of **Snap** and **Grid**, already mentioned in Chapter 3, several other settings can also be made from this dialogue box.

The **Modes** area of the box allows the following to be set on or off from their check boxes:

Ortho: Confines *dragging* with the mouse along only the X and Y axes.
Solid Fill: If on, areas can be hatched with solid fill (see Chapter 5).

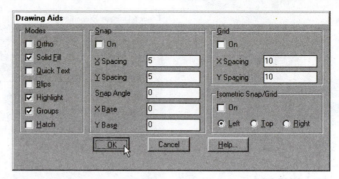

Fig. 4.4 The **Drawing Aids** dialogue box

Quick Text: If on, text is seen after being placed, by only an outlined box. If **Quick Text** is in action, this saves times regenerating and zooming drawings containing text.

Blips: If on, tiny crosses appear at all *picked* and *entered* coordinate points. These disappear on a redraw or regeneration of the screen. Some operators prefer blips to be off.

Groups: If on, groups can be formed from a number of entities. If off, such groups cannot be formed.

Hatch: If on, associative hatching includes the hatch area boundaries. See Chapter 8.

The Isometric Snap/Grid area

Snap and grid and the Isometric planes for isometric drawing can be set within this area of the dialogue box. See Chapter 7.

Layer & Linetype Properties

Left-click on the **Layers** icon in the **Object Properties** toolbar (Fig. 4.5). The **Layer & Linetype Properties** dialogue box appears (Fig. 4.6). This dialogue box is in two parts. *Left-click* on the **Linetype** label at the top of the dialogue box and the linetype part of the dialogue box appears (Fig. 4.7).

In the **Layer** part of the dialogue box, a *left-click* on the **New** button brings up a new line in the dialogue box – **Layer1**, **Layer2** etc., each with its own group of icons for controlling the named layer.

In the linetype part of the dialogue box *left-click* on the **Load...** button and the **Load or Reload Linetypes** dialogue box appears from

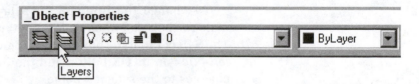

Fig. 4.5 The **Layers** icon in the **Object Properties** toolbar

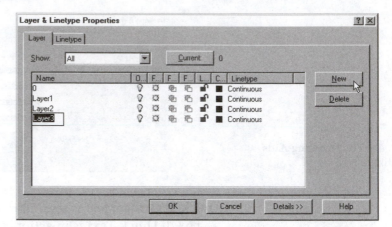

Fig. 4.6 The **Layer and Linetype Properties** dialogue box

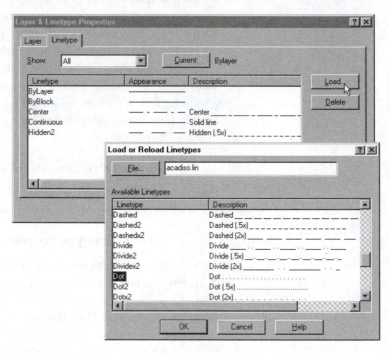

Fig. 4.7 The **Linetype** part of the dialogue box

which a selection can be made from the large range of linetypes clearly displayed. Those linetypes not seen in the **Linetype** box can be scrolled for viewing. Selecting one of the displayed linetypes, followed by a *left-click* on the **OK** button and the selected linetype loads in the **Linetype** dialogue box, from which it can be selected for adding to a layer.

To change the linetype for a layer, in the **Layer** part of the dialogue box, *left-click* on the linetype name (usually **Continuous**). The **Select Linetype** box appears. Select a linetype from the box and *left-click* on its **OK** button and the linetype name in the **Layer** box changes to the selected name.

The layer icons

Layers can be turned on or off, frozen, thawed, locked or have their colours changed. *Left-click* on the icons have the actions as shown in Fig. 4.8, in which the icon tool tips are included.

The actions from using the layer tools are:

On/Off: When a layer is turned off – *left-click* on the icon, its colour greys and any constructions on the layer disappear.

Freeze/Thaw in all viewports: A *left-click* on the icon freezes all constructions in all viewports – the constructions disappear, but are not held in memory, making redraws and regenerations speedier than when a layer is turned off.

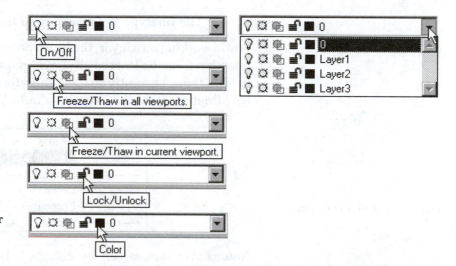

Fig. 4.8 The icons in the **Layer** box of the **Object Properties** toolbar

Fig. 4.9 The colour **ByLayer** popup list

Freeze/Thaw in current viewport: The same action as the previous icon, except that the action takes place only in the viewport currently being used. More about viewports in Chapter 14.

Lock/Unlock: If a layer is locked, further constructions can be added to that layer, but no modifications can take place on the constructions already on the layer.

Color: Shows the colour for any entities constructed when that layer is currently in operation. To change a colour *left-click* on the required colour in the popup list shown in Fig. 4.9. To change the colour attributed to a layer, *left-click* on the **Color** icon in the **Layer and Linetype** dialogue box. This will bring up a **Select Color** dialogue box (Fig. 4.10), from which the required colour can be selected.

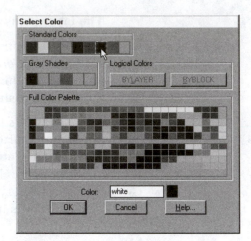

Fig. 4.10 The **Select Color**
dialogue box

The linetype ByLayer popup list

While working on a layer, the linetype being used can be changed by
selection from the linetype **ByLayer** popup list (Fig. 4.11). This lists
the linetypes currently loaded and allows the operator to select a
new linetype from the list with a *left-click* on its name.

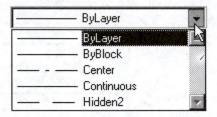

Fig. 4.11 The **ByLayer** popup
list

Note: Layer names can be changed. In the **Layer and Linetype
Properties** dialogue box, *left-click* on the name of a layer. A **Details**
box appears at the bottom of the dialogue box. In the **Name:** part of
the **Details** box, erase the name (e.g. **Layer2**) and *enter* the required
name.

Grips

Select **Grips...** from the **Tools** pull-down menu. The **Grips** dialogue
box appears (Fig. 4.12). If the **Enable Grips** check box is set on (tick
in the check box), when an entity is selected, without a tool being in
action, a small coloured *pick* box appears at each vertex of the
selected entity. Then if one of the grips (the *pick* boxes) is selected,
that grip changes colour and the Command line shows:

Command: ** STRETCH **
<Stretch to point>/Base point/Copy/Undo/eXit:

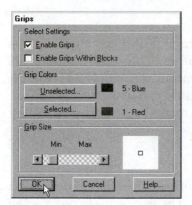

Fig. 4.12 The **Grips** dialogue box

Pressing the **Return** key or the Space bar of the keyboard cycles through five modify tools (commands), any one of which can be used to **Stretch**, **Move**, **Rotate**, **Mirror** or **Scale** the entity. More about these **Modify** tools in Chapter 6.

Figure 4.13 shows the result of using the three options **Stretch**, **Rotate** and **Scale** with grips in action.

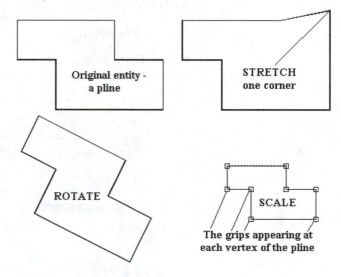

Fig. 4.13 The action of **Grips**

Units

Select **Units...** from the **Format** pull-down menu and the **Units Control** dialogue box comes on screen (Fig. 4.14). From the popup lists under **Precision:** the decimal places to which all figures can be set is selected both for units and angles. Throughout this book, both **Units** and **Angle** are set to show no decimal figures after the decimal point.

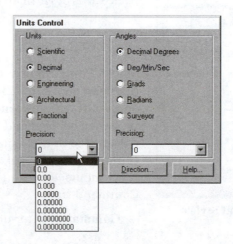

Fig., 4.14 The **Units Control** dialogue box

Dimensions Styles

Select **Dimension Style...** from the **Format** pull-down menu and the **Dimensions Styles** dialogue box appears. Three further dialogue boxes – **Geometry**, **Format** and **Annotation** are associated with this dialogue box. Because the whole of Chapter 9 is devoted to dimensions, a fuller explanation of settings in the four dialogue boxes will be left until then.

Text Style

Select **Text Style...** from the **Format** pull-down menu and the **Text Style** dialogue box appears (Fig. 4.15). The text font can be selected

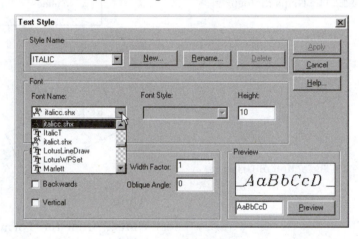

Fig. 4.15 The **Text Style** dialogue box

from a range of different fonts from the **Font name:** popup list or, if a number of fonts have already been loaded, from the **Style name:** popup list. The parameters for text can be set in the dialogue box – height, width, the angle at which it slopes, whether upside down, backwards or vertically placed on screen. More about text in Chapter 7.

Point Style

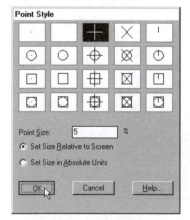

Fig. 4.16 The **Point Style** dialogue box

Select **Point Style...** from the **Format** pull-down menu and the dialogue box, Fig. 4.16 appears, from which a point style can be chosen. It will be seen from the dialogue box that a variety of point types can be used and their size can be varied as a percentage of the screen size or as so many units in size. To see the action of setting different point styles, *left-click* in any of the boxes in the dialogue box, set its size and *left-click* on the **OK** button. Then at the Command line:

Command: *enter* pt (for Point) *right-click*

POINT Point: *left-click* at required position on screen, or *enter* coordinates

And the selected form of point appears at the selected position. Some examples of different sizes are given in Fig. 4.17.

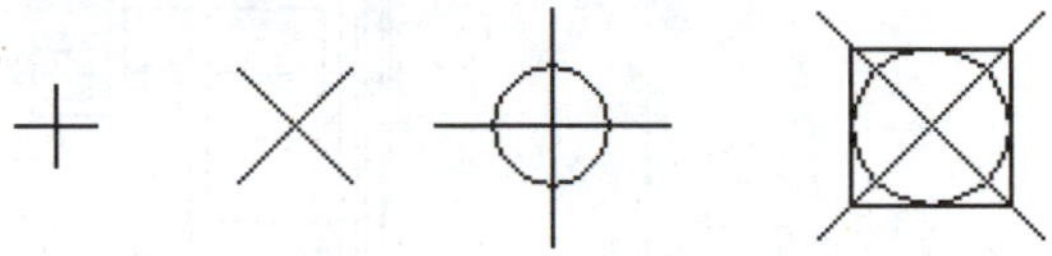

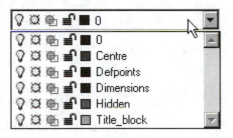

Fig. 4.17 Different styles of points

Layers

The use of layers is an important concept when using any CAD (computer aided design) software package. As an example, the three-view third angle orthographic projection of Fig. 4.19 has been constructed on the layers shown in Fig. 4.18.

Fig. 4.18 The layers on which the drawing Fig. 4.19 was constructed

Layers can be imagined as being similar to tracings in drawings which have been drawn 'by hand' methods. Tracings are constructed so as to lie one on top of the other throughout a drawing. Tracings can be removed in the same manner that layers can be frozen or turned off. Tracings can be replaced in a sequence in the same way that layers can be turned back on or thawed. When a tracing is on top of the others, it can be drawn on in a similar manner to which constructions can be added to the current layer in an R14 drawing.

Colours and linetypes in layers

When working on layers it is advisable to draw the constructions on each layer in a different colour. This makes for easier working because the operator can determine by colour alone which layer is being worked on. Many layers may have different line types as indicated in the pictorial drawing Fig. 4.20 in which the layers on which Fig. 4.19 were drawn have been treated as if they were tracings which are shown separated from each other. Figure 4.20

includes the layer names, the colours and line types used for the constructions on the layers.

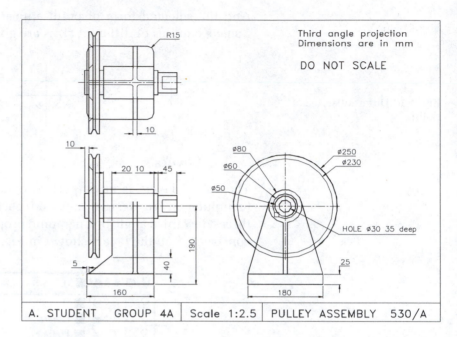

Fig. 4.19 Example of a drawing constructed on layers

Additions to the ay.dwt template

At this stage it might be advisable to add a number of layers to the template file which is to be used when working drawings in this

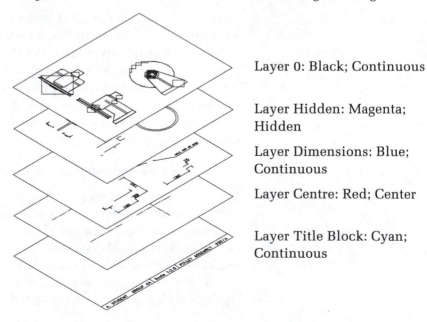

Layer 0: Black; Continuous

Layer Hidden: Magenta; Hidden

Layer Dimensions: Blue; Continuous

Layer Centre: Red; Center

Layer Title Block: Cyan; Continuous

Fig. 4.20 The layer names, colours and line types on which Fig. 4.19 was drawn

book. The layer table and the suggested colours and linetypes shown in Figs 4.18 and 4.20 show a very appropriate set of layer, colours and line types for general mechanical engineering drawings. If the layers are included in the template used for working the drawings in this book, there will be no need to set up a group of layers each time a drawing is attempted. So, set up layers as shown in Fig. 4.18 on your **initials.dwt** template and save the file to your chosen template name.

The settings of layers

As has been shown in earlier pages of this chapter, the colours and linetypes applied to layers can be set from dialogue boxes. To choose the layer on which to work, either:

1. *Left-click* on the layers box in the **Objects Properties** toolbar. The layer popup list appears. A *left-click* on the name of the layer to be worked on makes that layer the current layer, ready for constructions to be placed on it, using the linetype and colour associated with that layer.
2. *Left-click* on the **Layers** icon in the **Object Properties** toolbar and in the **Layer & Linetype Properties** dialogue box which appears, *left-click* on the layer name in the dialogue box, followed by another *left-click* on the **Current** button at the top of the dialogue box. The selected layer name appears to the right of the button. Note that a layer which has been frozen or turned off cannot be selected as the current layer.
3. *Entering* layer, or la at the Command line brings up the **Layer & Linetype Properties** dialogue box.

Questions

1. What is the meaning of three fullstops (...) after a name in a pull-down menu?
2. Can you name half a dozen dialogue boxes which can be called to screen from the Command line using 'dd' calls?
3. In which dialogue box is **Snap** set?
4. What is the purpose of setting **Ortho**?
5. What happens when the following functions keys are pressed: **F7**, **F8**, **F9**?
6. What happens with a *left-click* on the **Layers** icon in the **Object Properties** toolbar?
7. Why are layers so important when working with a CAD software package?

8.   What is the difference between freezing a layer and turning it off?
9.   What is the purpose of **Grips**?
10. How is the point style set?

Exercises

In order to construct the drawings in answer to the exercises which
follow, it is best to set up a template file which includes layers as
suggested in Fig. 4.18.

1.   Figure 4.21 is a two-view orthographic projection of a cylinder with
     a second cylinder inserted into a hole in the first. Construct the
     drawing to the given dimensions, including the centre and hidden
     lines.
       Do not attempt to include any of the dimensions.

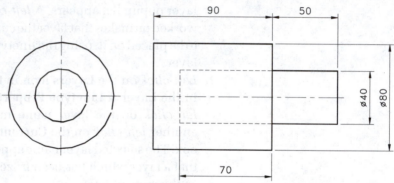

Fig. 4.21 Exercise 1

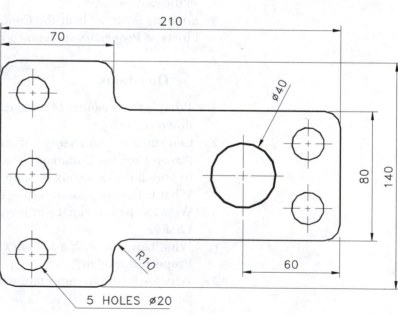

Fig. 4.22 Exercise 2

2. Figure 4.22 is a view of a plate in which several holes have been bored. Make an accurate drawing of the plate, including all the centre lines.

   Do not include any of the dimensions.

3. Figure 4.23 shows a two-view orthographic drawing of a coupling. Working to the given sizes, construct the two views to include all centre and hidden detail lines.

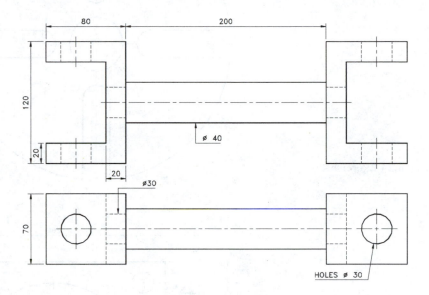

Fig. 4.23 Exercise 3

4. A plate in which with four slots have been cut and a hole has been bored is shown in a two-view orthographic projection in Fig. 4.24. Working to the given dimensions construct the two views, to include all hidden lines and centre lines.

5. A facing from a machine is shown in the drawing of Fig. 4.25. Construct the given drawing to the sizes given to include all the centre lines. Do not include the dimensions

6. Figure 4.26 is a two-view orthographic projection of a pointing device. Construct the two views to the given dimensions and include all hidden detail and centre lines, but not the dimensions.

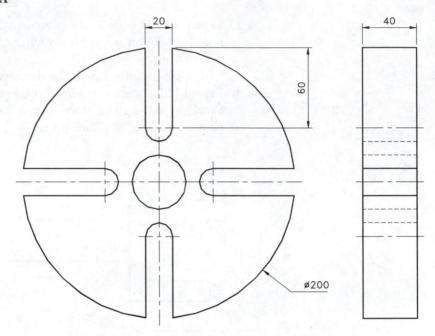

Fig. 4.24 Exercise 4

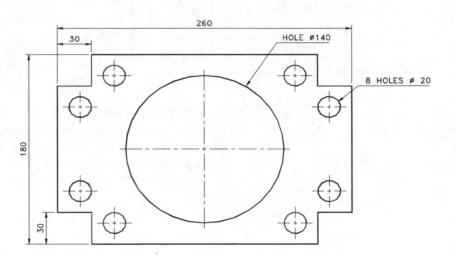

Fig. 4.25 Exercise 5

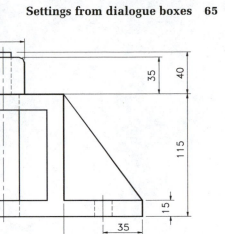

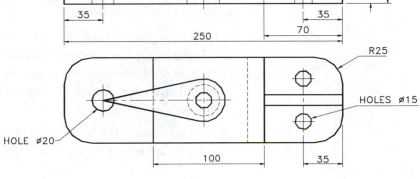

Fig. 4.26 Exercise 6

CHAPTER 5

2D drawing tools

The Draw toolbar

At start-up, the R14 window usually opens with the **Draw** toolbar *docked* against the left-hand side of the window. Figure 5.1 shows a typical R14 start-up window, with the tool **Line** having been selected and a line drawn. Figure 5.2 shows all the tool tips from the **Draw** toolbar.

Note: Only one of the tool icons (**Insert Block**) has a flyout. The tool tips from the **Insert Block** flyout are included in Fig. 5.2.

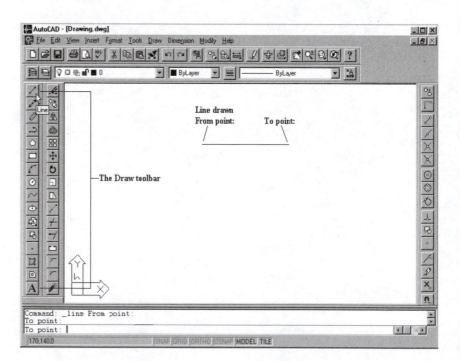

Fig. 5.1 A typical R14 start-up window with a line drawn

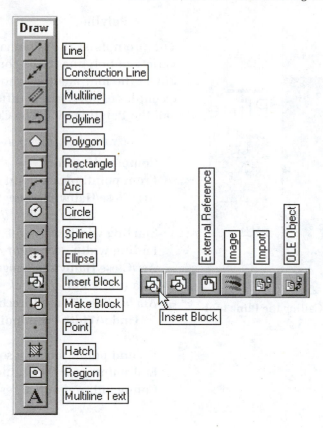

Fig. 5.2 The **Draw** toolbar
showing the tool tips of all its
tools

Calling the Draw tools

Referring back to Chapter 3, it will be remembered that the **Draw** tools (commands) can be called for use in several ways:

From the **Draw** toolbar.
From the **Draw** pull-down menu.
By *entering* a tool name at the Command line.
By *entering* a tool name abbreviation at the Command line.

The results of employing any of these methods will be much the same except for slightly different prompts at the Command line.

Examples of using the Draw tools

Examples of drawing with **Pline** and **Arc** were given in Chapters 2 and 3. Because there are several methods of drawing plines and arcs the use of these two tools is repeated here.

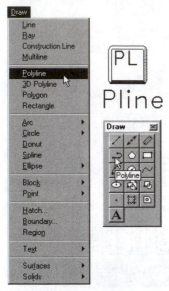

Fig. 5.3 Calling the **Pline** tool

Polyline

The prompts at the Command line for the **Polyline** tool allow a variety of polylines to be constructed. **Polyline** can be called using any of the four methods shown in Fig. 5.3. Figure 5.4 shows three examples of polylines of different widths. To draw the three plines, call the **Polyline** tool. The Command line shows:

Example 1 (Fig. 5.4 – 1)

Command: _pline
From point: *pick* a point on screen
Arc/Close/Halfwidth/Length/Undo/Width/<Endpoint of line>: *enter* w (for Width) *right-click*
Starting width <0>: *enter* 1 right-click
Ending width <1>: *right-click*
Arc/Close/Halfwidth/Length/Undo/Width/<Endpoint of line>: *enter* a (for Arc) *right-click*
Angle/CEnter/CLose/Direction/Halfwidth/Line/Radius/Second point/ Undo/Width/.<Endpoint of arc>: *enter* s (for Second) *right-click*
Second point: *pick* the second point
End point: *pick* the endpoint
Command: *right-click* resumes the pline prompts

Fig. 5.4 Three examples of polylines (plines)

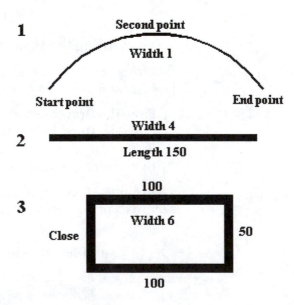

Example 2 (Fig 5.4 – 2)

Arc/Close/Halfwidth/Length/Undo/Width/<Endpoint of line>: *enter* w (for Width) *right-click*

Starting width <1>: *enter* 4 right-click

Ending width <4>: *right-click*

Arc/Close/Halfwidth/Length/Undo/Width/<Endpoint of line>: *enter* l (for Length) *right-click*

Length of line: *enter* 150 *right-click*

Arc/Close/Halfwidth/Length/Undo/Width/<Endpoint of line>: *right-click*

Command: *right-click* resumes up the pline prompts

Example 3 (Fig. 5.4 – 3)

Arc/Close/Halfwidth/Length/Undo/Width/<Endpoint of line>: *drag* the cursor cross hairs to the right and *enter* 100 *right-click*

Arc/Close/Halfwidth/Length/Undo/Width/<Endpoint of line>: *drag* the cursor cross hairs downwards and *enter* 50 *right-click*

Arc/Close/Halfwidth/Length/Undo/Width/<Endpoint of line>: *drag* the cursor cross hairs to the left and *enter* 100 *right-click*

Arc/Close/Halfwidth/Length/Undo/Width/<Endpoint of line>: *enter* c (for Close) *right-click*

Further examples

Figure 5.5 shows four examples of polylines drawn as follows:

Drawing 1: The width of the pline changed with each pline drawn. Despite the changes in width the whole outline is a single entity.

Drawing 2: If the **Starting width** and **Ending width** are different features such as arrows can be drawn. Drawing 2 is, again, a single entity.

Drawing 3: An example with different start and end width, using the **Arc** prompt.

Drawing 4: Two sets of start and end prompts plus use of **Arc**.

Command:

Note: When the **Undo** prompt, not shown in the above sequences, is used, the last part of the pline constructed is undone. Repeated **Undo**'s can be used back to the start point.

The set variable Fill

Many features of R14 are controlled by settings made to set variables. One of the set variables is **Fill**. When **Fill** is set on plines are filled

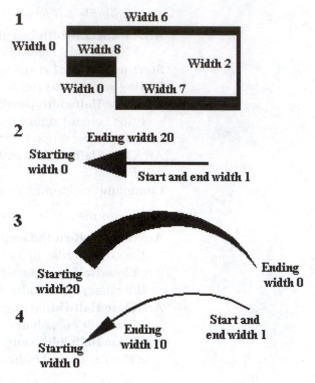

Fig. 5.5 Four further examples
of polylines

(black). When **Fill** is turned off plines are not filled. To set **Fill** on/off:

Command: *enter* **Fill** *right-click*
ON/OFF/<On>: *enter* off *right-click*
Command:

Figure 5.6 shows the examples 2, 3 and 4 given in Fig. 5.5 with **Fill** turned off.

The Polyline Arc prompts

The Arc prompts allow an arc to be drawn to a large number of options. Similar options are available when using the **Arc** tool, shown later.

**Angle/CEnter/CLose/Direction/Halfwidth/Line/Radius/Second point/
Undo/Width/.<Endpoint of arc>:**

It is good practise to experiment with the arc prompts apart from using the polyline tool. Not only can the arc angle, direction, radius, second point and endpoint of the arc be selected, but the arc can also have width.

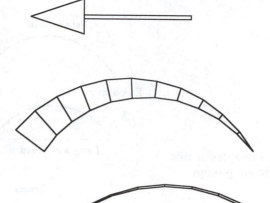

Fig. 5.6 Polylines with **Fill**
turned off

Arc

The **Arc** tool can be called using any one of the four methods shown
in Fig. 5.7. Figure 5.8 shows four examples of arcs drawn with the
aid of the **Arc** tool. When called by any of the methods shown in Fig.
5.7, the Command line shows:

Example 1 (Fig. 5.8 – 1)

Command _arc Center/<Start point>: *pick* the start point
Center/End/<Second point>: *pick*
End point: *pick*
Command: *right-click* (starts arc prompt sequence again)

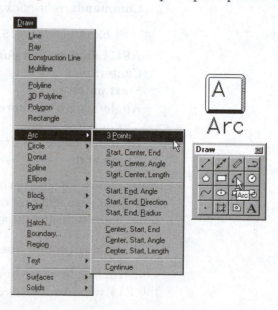

Fig. 5.7 Calling the **Arc** tool

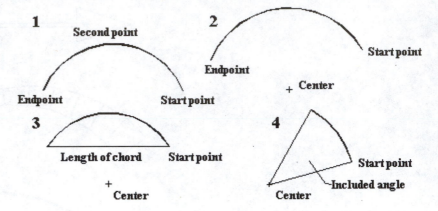

Fig. 5.8 Four examples of arcs drawn to different prompt responses

Example 2 (Fig. 5.78 – 2)

ARC Center/<Start point>: *enter* C (for Center) *right-click*
Center: *pick*
Start point: *pick*
Angle/Length of chord/<End point>: *pick*
Command: *right-click* (starts arc prompt sequence again)

Example 3 (Fig. 5.8 – 3)

ARC Center/<Start point>: *enter* C (for Center) *right-click*
Center: *pick*
Start point: *pick*
Angle/Length of chord/<End point>: *enter* l (for Length) *right-click*
Length of chord: *enter* 100 *right-click*
Command: *right-click* (starts arc prompt sequence again)

Example 4 (Fig. 5.8 – 4)

ARC Center/<Start point>: *enter* C (for Center) *right-click*
Center: *pick*
Start point: *pick*
Angle/Length of chord/<End point>: *enter* a (for Angle) *right-click*
Included angle: *enter* 45 *right-click*
Command:

Note: Figure 5.8 clearly shows that arcs are constructed in R14 in an anti-clockwise (counter clockwise or ccw) direction, with the start point to the right and the arc forming in the anti-clockwise direction.

Construction line

Construction lines are lines of infinite length stretching right across the R14 window and beyond to infinity. They are of value when

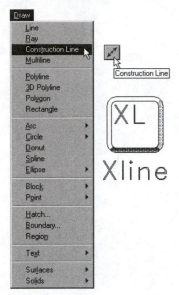

Fig. 5.9 Calling **Construction Line**

laying out a construction to provide guide lines on which a final drawing is to be created. The tool can be called by the use of any of the four methods shown in Fig. 5.9. An example of a set of construction lines is given in Fig. 5.10 and the drawing based on them is given in Fig. 5.11. To draw the construction lines of Fig. 5.10, call the tool and the Command line shows:

Command: _xline Hor/Ver/Ang/Bisect/Offset/<From point>: *enter* h (for Horizontal) *right-click*
Through point: *enter* 50,250 *right-click*
Through point: *enter* 50,160 *right-click*
Through point: *enter* 50,140 *right-click*
Through point: *enter* 50,100 *right-click*
Through point: *enter* 50,80 *right-click*
Through point: *enter* 50,20 *right-click*
Through point: *right-click*
Command: *right-click*
Command: _xline Hor/Ver/Ang/Bisect/Offset/<From point>: *enter* v (for Vertical) *right-click*
Through point: *enter* 50,160 *right-click*
Through point: *enter* 95,160 *right-click*
Through point: *enter* 105,160 *right-click*
Through point: *enter* 150,160 *right-click*
Through point: *enter* 190,160 *right-click*

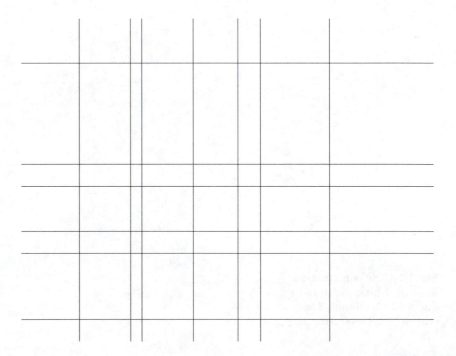

Fig. 5.10 The set of construction lines on which the drawing Fig. 5.11 was based

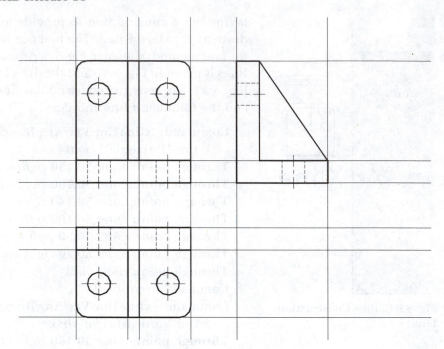

Fig. 5.11 The drawing based
on the construction lines of
Fig. 5.10

Through point: *enter* 205,160 *right-click*
Through point: *enter* 270,160 *right-click*
Through point: *right-click*
Command:

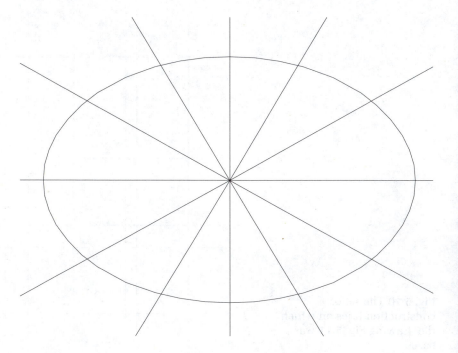

Fig. 5.12 The construction
lines on which the drawing
Fig. 5.13 was based. The
ellipse is not a construction
line

To draw the construction lines at angles, shown in Fig. 5.12 and on which the drawing Fig. 5.13 was based:

Command: _xline Hor/Ver/Ang/Bisect/Offset/<From point>: *enter* a (for Angle) *right-click*
Reference/<Enter angle> <0>: *enter* 30 *right-click*
Through point: *enter* 140,150 *right-click*
Command: _xline Hor/Ver/Ang/Bisect/Offset/<From point>: *enter* a (for Angle) *right-click*
Reference/<Enter angle> <30>: *enter* 60 *right-click*
Through point: *right-click*
Command:

And so on at 30° angles up to 180°.

Construction lines can be drawn to bisect each other or to be offset from each other. It is advisable to experiment with these two options.

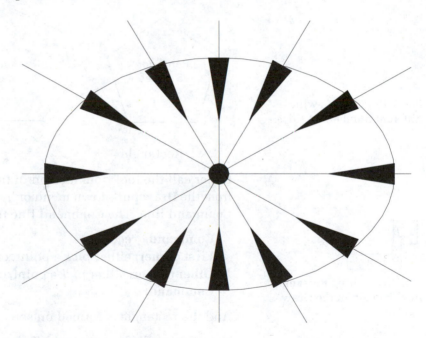

Fig. 5.13 The drawing based on the construction lines of Fig. 5.12

Polygon

The tool can be called by any of the four methods detailed for the tools outlined above. Figure 5.14 shows the tool icon from the **Draw** toolbar. The tool abbreviation is **PG**. Call the tool and the Command line shows:

Command: _polygon Number of sides <4>: *enter* 6 *right-click*
Edge/<Center of polygon>: *enter* 150,200 *right-click*

Fig. 5.14 Calling **Polygon** from its icon in the **Draw** toolbar

Inscribed in circle/Circumscribed about circle (I/C) <I>: *right-click*
Radius of circle: *enter* 60 *right-click*
Command:

Figure 5.15 shows a number of polygons with different numbers of sides constructed with the aid of the tool.

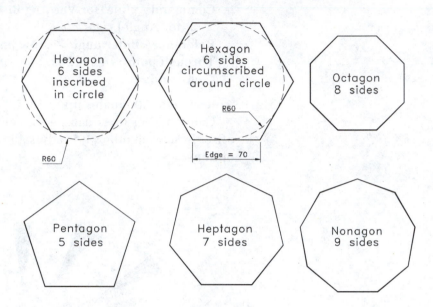

Fig. 5.15 Polygons with different numbers of sides

Rectangle

Either call the tool from its icon in the **Draw** toolbar (Fig. 5.16), or from the **Draw** pull-down menu or by *entering* **RC** or **Rectang** at the Command line. The Command line then shows:

Command _rectang
First corner: either *pick* a point, or *enter* coordinates *right-click*
Other corner: either *pick* a point, or *enter* coordinates *right-click*
Command:

And the rectangle is formed on screen.

Note: The outline created with **Polygon** or **Rectangle** are polylines.

Fig. 5.16 Calling **Rectangle** from its icon in the **Draw** toolbar

Spline

Only one example will be shown for the use of this tool. That is given in Fig. 5.18.

Either select the tool from its icon in the **Draw** toolbar (Fig. 5.17) or from the **Draw** pull-down menu, or *enter* spline at the Command line. To construct the spline of Fig. 5.18:

Fig. 5.17 Calling **Spline** from its icon in the **Draw** toolbar

Command: _spline
Object/<Enter first point>: *enter* 60,190 *right-click*
Close/Fit Tolerance/<Enter point>: *enter* 100,240 *right-click*
Close/Fit Tolerance/<Enter point>: *enter* 140,190 *right-click*
Close/Fit Tolerance/<Enter point>: *enter* 180,240 *right-click*
Close/Fit Tolerance/<Enter point>: *enter* 220,190 *right-click*
Close/Fit Tolerance/<Enter point>: *enter* 260,240 *right-click*
Close/Fit Tolerance/<Enter point>: *enter* 300,190 *right-click*
Close/Fit Tolerance/<Enter point>: *right-click*
Enter start tangent: *enter* 160,190 *right-click*
Enter end tangent: *enter* 300,190 *right-click*
Command:

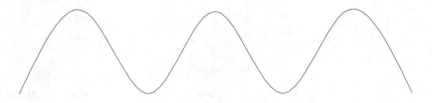

Fig. 5.18 Example of spline

Fig. 5.19 Calling **Ellipse** from its icon in the **Draw** toolbar

Ellipse

Either select the tool from the **Draw** toolbar (Fig. 5.19) or from the **Draw** pull-down menu, or *enter* ellipse or el at the Command line. The Command line then shows:

Command _ellipse
<Axis endpoint 1>/Center: *enter* c (Center) *right-click*
Center of ellipse: *pick* or *enter* coordinates *right-click*
Axis endpoint: *pick* or *enter* coordinates *right-click*
<Other axis distance>/Rotation: *pick* or *enter* coordinates *right-click*
Command:

Notes

1. The longest axis of an ellipse is its **major axis**. The smaller axis is its **minor axis** (Fig. 5.20).
2. Ellipses in R14 can either be constructed as true ellipses or as polylines. The set variable **Pellipse** controls which is to be constructed. When **Pellipse** is set to 0 the resulting ellipse will be true. If set to 1, the ellipse will be a polyline. To set **Pellipse**;

Command: *enter* pellipse *right-click*
New value for PELLIPSE <0>: *enter* 1 *right-click*
Command:

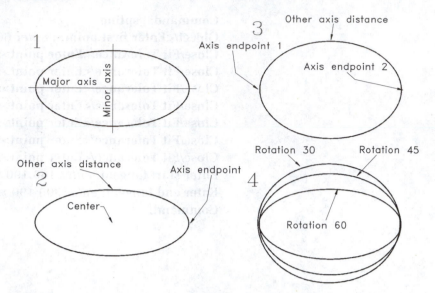

Fig. 5.20 Methods of
constructing ellipses

3. Ellipses can be regarded as the result of looking at circles so as to see their full shape, then rotating them around their horizontal diameter. As the rotation increases, so the vertical axis of the circle becomes smaller and what appears to be an ellipse is seen. The **Rotation** prompt asks for the angle through which the rotation takes place to be *entered*.

4. In R14 ellipses can be drawn by *picking* or *entering* the ends of both axes.

Figure 5.20 shows a number of ellipses constructed in R14. The four drawings show:

1. Major and minor axes of an ellipse.
2. An ellipse constructed from the prompts **Center**, **Axis endpoint** and **Other axis distance**.
3. An ellipse constructed from the prompts **Axis endpoint 1**, **Axis endpoint 2** and **Other axis distance**.
4. Three ellipses constructed to the same major axis lengths with **Rotation** *entered* as 30, 45 and 60.

Insert block and its flyout and Make Block

These tools will be described in Chapter 11.

Point

Point

Fig. 5.21 Calling **Point** from
its icon in the **Draw** toolbar

Point can be called from the **Draw** toolbar (Fig. 5.21) or from the **Draw** pull-down menu or by *entering* point or its abbreviation pt. The type of point is selected from the **Point Style** dialogue box (page 58). When called the Command line shows:

Command _point Point: either *pick* or *enter* coordinates

and continue placing points until all that are required are placed, then *right-click* and the tool actions ends.

Hatch

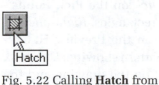

Fig. 5.22 Calling **Hatch** from its icon in the **Draw** toolbar

Hatch can be called from the **Draw** toolbar (Fig. 5.22) or from the **Draw** pull-down menu (as **Hatch...**), or by h or bhatch *entered* at the Command line. Note that *entering hatch* at the Command line does not have the same result.

When the tool is called, the **Boundary Hatch** dialogue box comes on screen. A *left-click* on the **Pattern...** button of the dialogue box brings a second dialogue box on screen – **Hatch pattern palette**. More about hatch and hatching in Chapter 8. One example of hatching is given in Fig. 5.24. This example was constructed as follows:

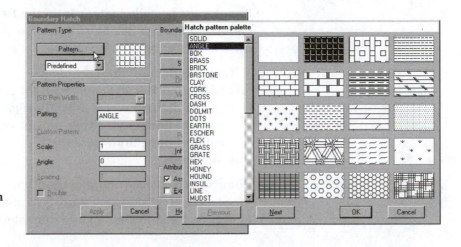

Fig. 5.23 The **Boundary Hatch** and **Hatch pattern palette** dialogue boxes

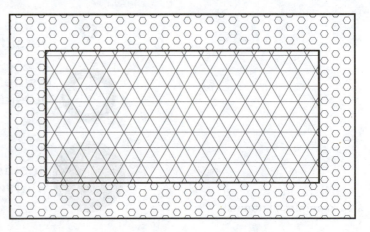

Fig. 5.24 An example of hatching

1. With the **Polyline** tool construct two rectangles of line width 1, the outer 200 × 150, the inner 160 × 90.
2. Call **Hatch**. The **Boundary Hatch** dialogue box appears. *Left-click* on the **Pattern...** button and from the **Hatch pattern palette** dialogue, select the pattern **HEX**.
3. In the **Boundary Hatch** dialogue, *left-click* on the **Pick Points>** button and *pick* a spot between the two rectangles. *Right-click*.
4. The dialogue box reappears. *Left-click* on the **Preview Hatch>** button. The drawing reappears with the pattern showing. *Left-click* on the **Continue** message box appearing on the drawing and the dialogue box reappears.
5. *Left-click* on the **Apply** button. The hatch pattern is applied.
6. Repeat with the inner rectangle with pattern **NET3** set to a **Scale** of 3.

Donut

Donut must be called either from the **Draw** pull-down menu or by *entering* donut, or its abbreviation do at the Command line. When called, the Command line shows:

Command: *enter* do *right-click*
Inside diameter <1>: *enter* 5 *right-click*
Outside diameter <1>: *enter* 10 *right-click*
Center of doughnut: either *pick* or *enter* coordinates *right-click*
Center of doughnut: *right-click*
Command:

Donuts can be placed one after the other until a *right-click* terminates the placing of the donuts. Figure 5.25 gives examples of three donuts of different inside and outside diameters.

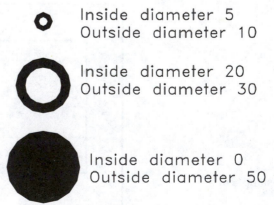

Inside diameter 5
Outside diameter 10

Inside diameter 20
Outside diameter 30

Inside diameter 0
Outside diameter 50

Fig. 5.25 Examples of donuts

Saving a drawing to file

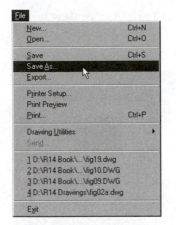

When a drawing is saved in R14 it is usually saved to a filename of the operator's choice with the file name extensions **.dwg**. To save a drawing, select **Save As...** from the **File** pull-down menu (Fig. 5.26). The **Save Drawing As** dialogue box appears (Fig. 5.27). From the **Save in:** list box select the appropriate directory in which to save the drawing file, then *enter* the file name in the **File name:** box, followed by a *left-click* on the **Save** button. The file-name extension ***.dwg** will be automatically added to the file name, if it has not been entered with the file name.

Fig. 5.26 Selecting **Save As...** from the **File** pull-down menu

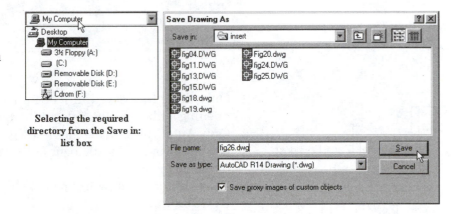

Selecting the required directory from the Save in: list box

Fig. 5.27 The **Save Drawing As** dialogue box

Notes

1. In the **File** pull-down menu note the **Save** command. This is a **Quick Save** tool which saves the drawing to the name already assigned to it. Care must be taken when using the **Save** command because the operator may not wish to use the same file name as a drawing develops in complexity.
2. In R14 drawings can be saved in formats suitable for opening in Release 12 or 13 or in AutoCAD LT or as template (*.dwt) files. See Fig. 5.28 which shows the **Save as type:** popup list.

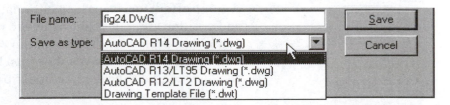

Fig. 5.28 The **Save as type:** popup list from the **Save Drawing As** dialogue box

Opening a drawing file

To open a drawing file to the R14 window, select **Open...** from the **File** pull-down menu. The **Select File** dialogue box appears (Fig.

5.29). Note the icon of the drawing appearing in the **Preview** box of the dialogue.

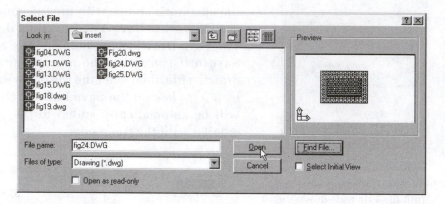

Fig. 5.29 The **Select File** dialogue box

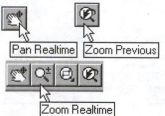

Fig. 5.30 The **Zoom** and **Pan** icons in the **Standard Toolbar**

Notes

1. Only those files saved in R14 format will show previews when opening a file from the **Select File** dialogue box.
2. Only AutoCAD drawing files (*.dwg) or R14 template files (*.dwt) can be opened for the dialogue box. See the **Files of type:** popup list of the dialogue box.
3. The name of the drawing opened will appear in the title bar of the R14 window.

Redraw and Regen

Either select these two controls from the **Edit** pull-down menu or *enter* r (for **Redraw**) or rg (for **Regen**). Both commands refresh the contents of the drawing area. In particular blips (if Blipmode is on) will disappear when either command is called.

Zooms and Pan

A group of four tool icons for manipulating the R14 drawing area size and position are at the right-hand end of the **Standard Toolbar** (Fig. 5.30). These four icons represent the **Zoom** and **Pan** tools. Holding a *left-click* on the **Zoom Window** icon brings down a flyout. This is shown in Fig. 5.31 in which the tool tip of each of the icons is shown.

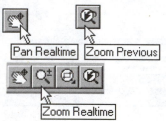

Fig. 5.31 The tool icons in the **Zoom Window** flyout

Zooms

Zooming the R14 drawing area and its contents to different sizes is a very important part of the construction of drawings. Zooming allows even the most minute part of a drawing to be examined, checked or modified.

When any of the zooms – e.g. **Window** – are called from their tool icons, the Command line shows:

Command: '_zoom
All/Center/Dynamic/Extents/Previous/Scale(X/XP)/Window/
<Realtime>: w

with the prompt being the initial letter of the type of zoom chosen.

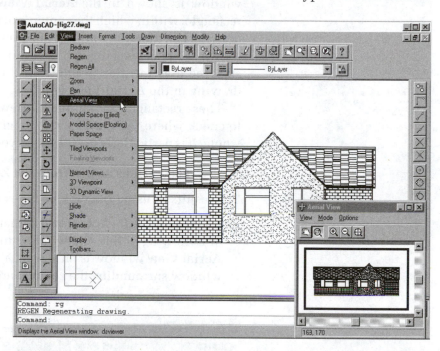

Fig. 5.32 **Zoom** can be called from the **View** pull-down menu

Zoom can be equally as well be called by *entering* z at the Command line, which then shows:

Command: *enter z right-click*
All/Center/Dynamic/Extents/Previous/Scale(X/XP)/Window/
<Realtime>:

And *entering* the required initial letter of the type of zoom required starts of the prompts for that type of zoom.

Zoom can also be called from the **View** pull-down menu as shown in Fig. 5.32, in which a front view of a bungalow is shown in the R14 window.

When zooms are in action, the following message will appear in the Command window:

Press Esc or Enter to exit, or right-click to activate popup menu.

A *right-click* brings up the menu shown in Fig. 5.33.

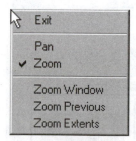

Fig. 5 33 The popup menu which appears with a *right-click* when zooms are active

Aerial View

Select **Aerial View** from the **View** pull-down menu and the **Aerial View** window appears, usually at the bottom right-hand corner as shown in Fig. 5.32. The **Aerial View** window is a true window – it can be enlarged or reduced in size, can be moved around the R14 window and carries its own tool icons. The drawing area of the R14 window is shown in the **Aerial View** as a thick black or white rectangle, within which the contents of the window are shown. If the drawing is within the limits of the drawing area, the drawing area is shown as a black rectangle. If the limits are greater than the drawing size, the drawing area is shown as a thick white rectangle on the drawing in the **Aerial View** window.

These rectangles in the **Aerial View** window allow the operator to check where the drawing on screen relates to the drawing as a whole. It is particularly useful when working on very large drawings.

The various zooms from the Zoom Window flyout

The results of using the various types of **Zoom** are:

Zoom Window: *Left-clicks* at two corners of a window, zoom the part of a drawing within the window to fill the drawing area. If the **Aerial View** window is on screen, a thick white line shows in the window surrounding the zoomed area (Fig. 5.34).

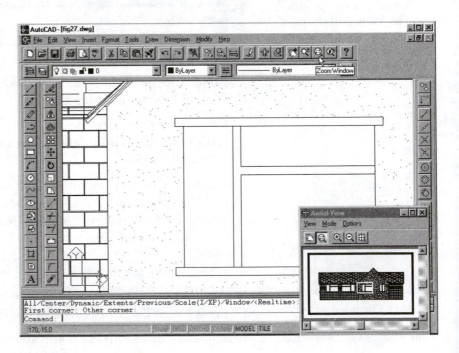

Fig. 5.34 A zoom window

Zoom Dynamic: When called, a thin line window appears with a cross showing at its centre. *Left-click* and the cross changes to an arrow pressing against the right-hand side of the line window. Movement of the mouse horizontally causes the size of the window to change. Movement up and down causes the resized window to move up and down. **Zoom Dynamic** allows an area of a drawing to be dynamically selected and zoomed (*right-click*).

Zoom Scale: Requests a scale factor to be *entered*. *Enter* a figure and the drawing zooms to a scale given by the figure.

Zoom Center: A *left-click* at a point on screen, or *entering* coordinates of a point, followed by a *right-click* and the drawing centres at the point.

Zoom In: Enlarges the drawing by a default scale of 2X.

Zoom Out: Reduces the drawing by a default scale of 5X.

Zoom All: Zooms the drawing so that it is at its full extent, with its edges touching the edges of the R14 drawing area.

Zoom Extents: Similar to **Zoom All**.

Other zooms

Realtime Zoom: If zoom is called by *entering* z at the Command line, the default zoom will be **Realtime**. If this zoom is called, an icon appears in the R14 window. Dragging this icon up scales the drawing larger in size. Dragging it down decreases the scale (Fig. 5.35).

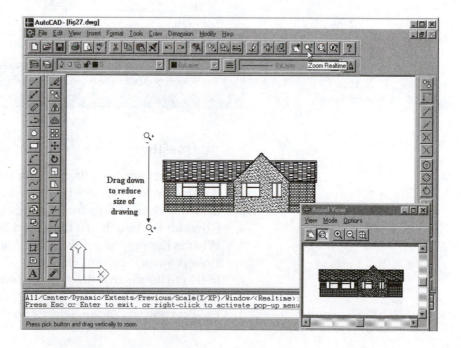

Fig. 5.35 Using **Realtime Zoom**

Zoom Previous: Causes the drawing to revert to the last zoom in operation. Repeated use of **Zoom Previous** and the drawing will eventually zoom back to its scale when first drawn or loaded. Further use of **Zoom Previous** will then have no effect.

Pan

When called the **Pan** icon (a hand) appears on screen and the drawing can be moved in any direction by holding a *left-click* and moving the mouse. In the **Aerial View** window the position of the drawing within the R14 drawing area can be followed by a black line appearing showing the extents of the R14 drawing area (Fig. 5.36).

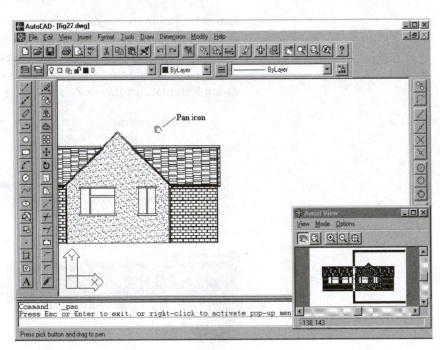

Fig. 5.36 **Pan** in action

Questions

1. How can an arrow be drawn with the tool **Polyline**?
2. If u (for **Undo**) is used when drawing a pline, what is the result?
3. In which default direction are arcs constructed in R14?
4. How can the length of a **Construction Line** be set?
5. What is the purpose of the set variable **Pellipse**?
6. How is a hatch pattern changed?
7. In R14 to how many different file formats can a drawing be saved?
8. When opening a file, when will a preview drawing not appear in the **Preview** box of the **Select File** dialogue box?

9. What is the difference between a **Zoom Dynamic** and a **Zoom Window**?
10. How can the **Aerial View** window be re-sized?

Exercises

1. Figure 5.37 shows a tabbed washer. Using the Polyline, **Circle** and **Arc** tools construct a drawing of the washer. Do not include any of the dimensions.

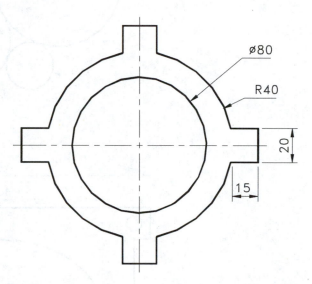

Fig. 5.37 Exercise 1

2. Using the **TTR** prompt of the **Circle** prompts sequence draw the circles of Fig. 5.38 to the dimensions shown. The circles are all touching (tangential) to each other.
3. Figure 5.39 is a view of a cover to be made from a plastic material. Make a full size copy of the drawing without including the dimensions.
4. Construct the four polygons shown in Fig. 5.40. Do not include the dimensions.
5. Figure 5.41 has been constructed with the aid of the tools **Rectangle**, **Arc**, **Polygon** and **Hatch**. Copy the given drawing to the sizes given, but do not add the dimensions.
6. A metal tab is shown in the front view Fig. 5.42. Working with appropriate tools make a full size copy of the tab. Do not include the dimensions.
7. Construct the outlines Fig. 5.43 using **Polyline** and **Arc** tools. Do not add any of the dimensions.
8. With the aid of **Polyline**, **Arc** and **Circle** construct the outlines Fig. 5.44. **Hatch** the areas as shown using any suitable hatch pattern.

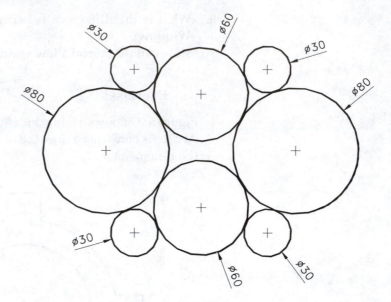

Fig. 5.38 Exercise 2

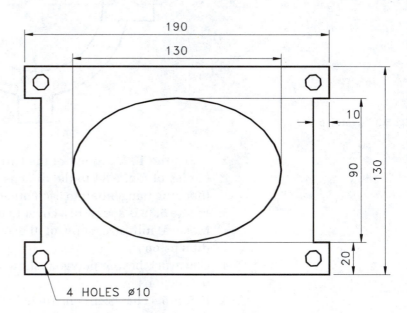

Fig. 5.39 Exercise 3

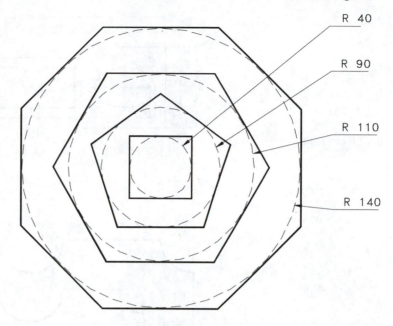

R 40

R 90

R 110

R 140

Fig. 5.40 Exercise 4

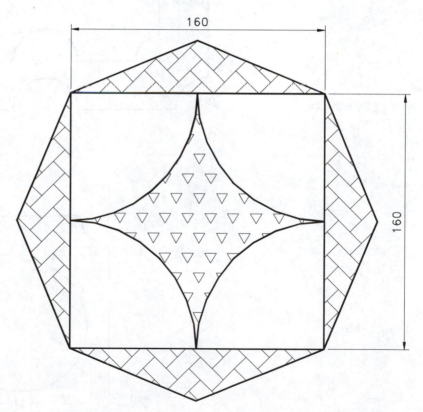

160

160

Fig. 5.41 Exercise 5

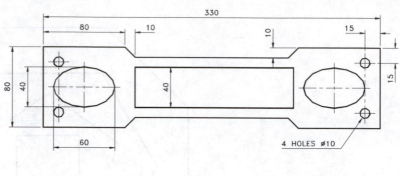

Fig. 5.42 Exercise 6

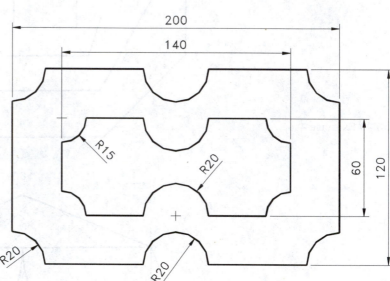

Fig. 5.43 Exercise 7

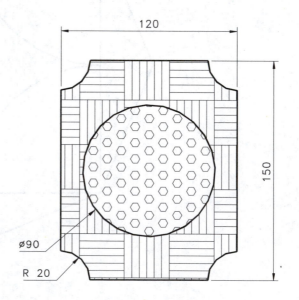

Fig. 5.44 Exercise 8

CHAPTER 6

Modify tools

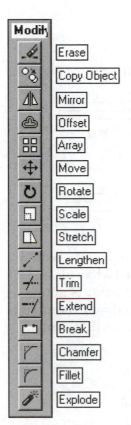

Fig. 6.1 The tools in the
Modify toolbar

Fig. 6.2 The **Modify** toolbar
docked against the **Draw**
toolbar

Introduction

The tools from the **Modify** toolbar (Fig. 6.1) are for modifying or editing entities or groups of entities. Upon start-up of R14 the **Modify** toolbar is usually found *docked* against the **Draw** toolbar at the left-hand edge of the R14 window (Fig. 6.2). The tools can either be selected from the **Modify** toolbar or from the **Modify** pull-down menu (Fig. 6.3), or by *entry* of the tool name or its abbreviation in the Command line. The tools can be used to modify 3D models, but in this chapter we are only concerned with using the tools on 2D drawings.

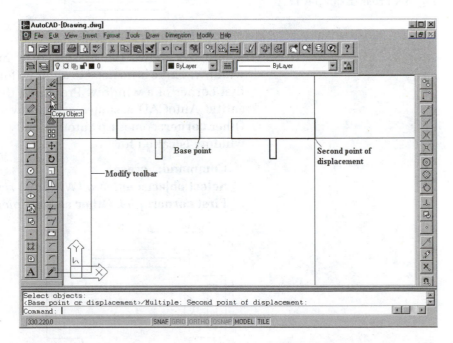

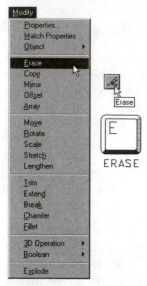

Fig. 6.3 Calling the **Erase** tool

The Modify tools

Erase

The **Erase** tool can be called from the **Modify** toolbar or **Modify** pull-down menu, or by *entering* e or erase at the Command line (Fig. 6.3).

Example 1 – Fig. 6.4

Figure 6.4 shows the erasure of a single entity from a drawing. When called the Command line shows:

> **Command: _erase**
> **Select objects:** *pick* the entity **1 found**
> **Select objects:** *right-click*
> **Command:**

And the entity (object) is erased – right-hand drawing of Fig. 6.4.

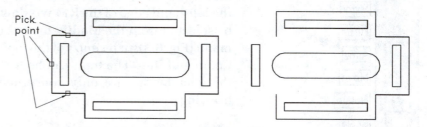

Fig. 6.4 **Erase**. Example 1

Example 2 – Fig. 6.5

Figure 6.5 shows the erasure of a number of objects within a window. There is no need to *enter* w (for Window) when *picking* the first corner of a window. Providing the *picked* point is not on an entity, AutoCAD assumes a window is required and the prompt **Other corner:** comes up automatically. However, in this example, a window is called for.

> **Command: _erase**
> **Select objects:** *enter* w (Window) *right-click*
> **First corner:** *pick* **Other corner:** *pick* **3 found**

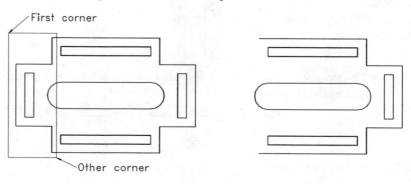

Fig. 6.5 **Erase**. Example 2

Select objects: *right-click*
Command:

And the three objects (entities) within the window are erased – right-hand drawing of Fig. 6.5.

Example 3 – Fig. 6.6

When using the **Erase** tool, if the first point selected is to the right of a drawing and the **Other corner:** to the left, all entities crossed by the resulting window are erased. A crossing window can also be called by *entering* the response c (for Crossing) to erase several entities crossed by the lines of the window. In Fig. 6.6 a crossing window is used. Note that when a crossing window can be used from either side of the drawing from which the erasures are required.

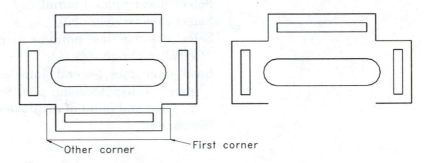

Fig. 6.6 **Erase.** Example 3

Command: _erase
Select objects: *enter* c (for Crossing window) *right-click*
First corner: *pick* **Other corner:** *pick* **3 found**
Select objects: *right-click*
Command:

Copy

The **Copy** tool can be called from the **Modify** toolbar or **Modify** pull-down menu, or by *entering* copy or its abbreviation co at the Command line (Fig. 6.7).

Example 1 – Fig. 6.8

Either a single entity can be copied or entities can be copied several times (**Multiple** option) Fig. 6.8 shows the copying of a single entity, – in this example a pline. Call **Copy**. The Command line shows:

Command: _copy
Select objects: *pick* **1 found**
Select objects: *right-click*
Select objects:<Base point or displacement>/Multiple: *pick*
Command:

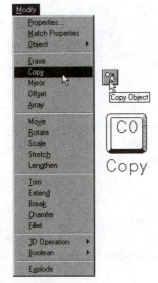

Fig. 6.7 Calling the **Copy** tool

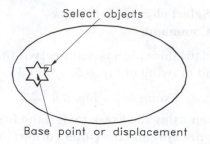
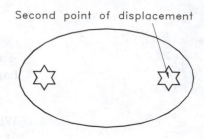

Fig. 6.8 **Copy**. Example 1

Example 2 – Fig. 6.9

Figure 6.9 shows the multiple copying of a single entity. Call **Copy** and the Command line shows:

> **Command: _copy**
> **Select objects:** *pick* **1 found**
> **Select objects:** *right-click*
> **Select objects:<Base point or displacement>/Multiple:** *enter* m (Multiple) *right-click*
> **Base point:** *pick* **Second point of displacement:** *pick* **Second point of displacement:** *pick* **Second point of displacement:** *pick* **Second point of displacement:** *right-click*
> **Command:**

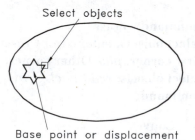
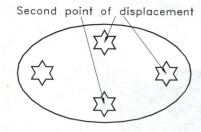

Fig. 6.9 **Copy**. Example 2

Example 3 – Fig. 6.10

Figure 6.10 shows the copying of a group of entities selected within a window. A similar group could be selected from a crossing window if required. Call **Copy** and the Command line shows:

> **Command: _copy**
> **Select objects:** *enter* w (Window) *right-click*
> **First corner:** *pick* **Other corner:** *pick* **5 found**
> **Select objects:** *right-click*
> **Select objects:<Base point or displacement>/Multiple:** *enter* m (Multiple) *right-click*

Base point: *pick* **Second point of displacement:** *pick* **Second point of displacement:** *pick* **Second point of displacement:** *pick* **Second point of displacement:** *right-click*
Command:

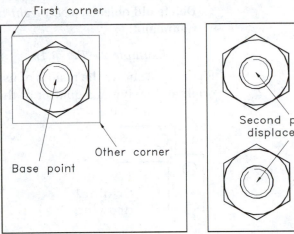

Fig. 6.10 **Copy**. Example 3

Mirror

Fig. 6.11 Selecting **Mirror** from the **Modify** toolbar

Mirror can be called from the **Modify** toolbar (Fig. 6.11), by *entering* mirror, or its abbreviation mi at the Command line.

Example 1 – Fig. 6.12

Figure 6.12 shows the mirroring of a windowed group of entities. The left-hand drawing of Fig. 6.12 shows the *pick* points for the various options, the left-hand drawing shows the resulting mirror effect. Call **Mirror** and the Command line shows:

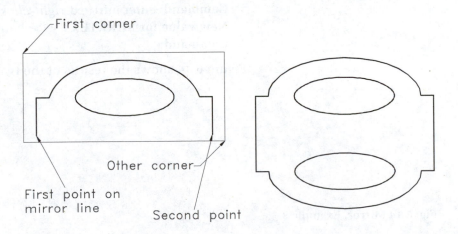

Fig. 6.12 **Mirror**. Example 1

Command: _mirror
Select objects: *enter* w (Window) *right-click*
First corner: *pick* **Other corner:** *pick* **7 found**
Select objects: *right-click*
First point on mirror line: *pick* **Second point:** *pick*
Delete old objects? <N>: *right-click*
Command:

Example 2 – Fig. 6.13

Figure 6.13 shows the results of using **Mirror** twice on what was an original drawing of a quarter of the final drawing.

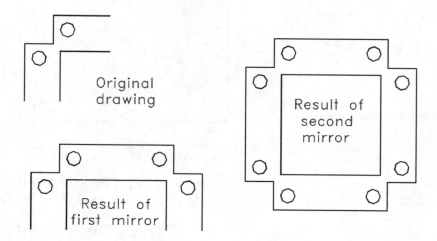

Fig. 6.13 **Mirror**. Example 2

Example 3 – Fig. 6.14

When text is acted upon by **Mirror**, the results depend upon the setting of the set variable **mirrtext**. The variable is set by:

Command: *enter* mirrtext *right-click*
New value for MIRRTEXT <1>: *enter* 0 *right-click*
Command:

Figure 6.14 shows the results of the two settings.

Mirrtext = 1   Mirrtext = 1

Mirrtext = 1

Mirrtext = 0   Mirrtext = 0

Mirrtext = 0

Fig. 6.14 **Mirror**. Example 3

Fig. 6.15 Calling **Offset** from the **Modify** toolbar

Offset

Offset can be called from the **Modify** toolbar (Fig. 6.11), from the **Modify** pull-down menu or, by *entering* offset or its abbreviations of at the Command line.

Examples – Fig. 6.16

Figure 6.16 gives several examples of the results of using the **Offset** tool. When called the Command line shows:

> **Command:** _offset
> **Offset distance or Through <0>:** *enter* 20 *right-click*
> **Select object to offset:** *pick*
> **Side to offset?** *pick*
> **Select object to offset:** *right-click*
> **Command:**

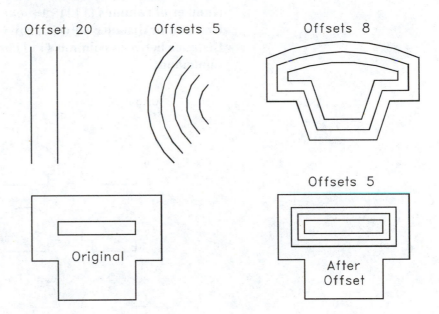

Fig. 6.16 **Offset**. Examples

Notes

1. Instead of *entering* a number in response to the **Offset distance or Through <0>:** prompt, *picking* two points on the screen will determine the distance.
2. The **Side to offset?** prompt can be answered time after time if a number of offsets from the first offset are required before having to resume the command sequence.

Fig. 6.17 Calling **Array** from the **Modify** toolbar

Array

Array can be called from the **Modify** toolbar (Fig. 6.17), from the **Modify** pull-down menu, by *entering* array or its abbreviations ar at the Command line.

There are two types of array – **Rectangular** and **Polar**. Figure 6.18 gives an example of a **Rectangular** array and Figs 6.19 and 6.20 examples of **Polar** arrays.

Example 1 – Fig. 6.18

Call **Array** and the Command line shows:

Command: _array
Select objects: *enter* w (Window) *right-click*
First corner: *pick* **Other corner:** *pick* **5 found**
Rectangular or Polar array (R/P) <R>: *right-click* (accepts R)
Number of rows (---) <1>: *enter* 4 *right-click*
Number of columns (| | |) <1>: *enter* 4 *right-click*
Unit cell or distance between rows (---): *enter* -60 *right-click*
Distance between columns (| | |): *enter* 80 *right-click*
Command:

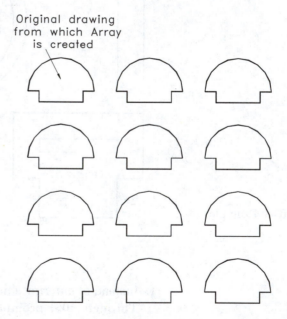

Original drawing from which Array is created

Fig. 6.18 **Array**. Example 1

Notes

1. Rows are the copies made to produce horizontally placed lines of copies. Columns are the copies made to produced vertically placed lines.

2. The row or column distances can be taken from any point on the original from which the array has been developed – vertical distance for rows, horizontal distance for columns.
3. The distance of rows copied downwards in the Y axis direction must be preceded with a **–ve** (minus) sign.
4. The distance of columns copied vertically to the left in the X axis direction must be preceded with a **–ve** (minus) sign.

Example 2 – Fig. 6.19

Command: _array
Select objects: *enter* w (Window) *right-click*
First corner: *pick* **Other corner:** *pick* **4 found**
Rectangular or Polar array (R/P) <R>:
Rectangular or Polar array (R/P) <R>: *enter* p (Polar) *right-click*
Center point of array: either *pick* a point or *enter* coordinates *right-click*
Number of items: *enter* 6 *right-click*
Angle to fill (+=ccw, -=cw) <360>: *right-click*
Rotate objects as they are copied? <Y>: *right-click* (accepts rotate as copied)
Command:

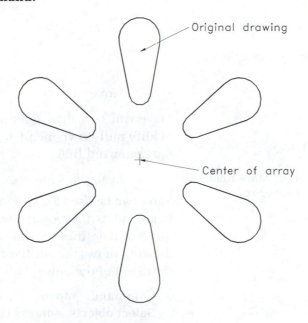

Original drawing

Center of array

Fig. 6.19 **Array**. Example 2

Example 3 – Fig. 6.20

Command: _array
Select objects: *enter* w (Window) *right-click*

First corner: *pick* **Other corner:** *pick* **8 found**
Rectangular or Polar array (R/P) <R>:
Rectangular or Polar array (R/P) <R>: *enter* p (Polar) *right-click*
Center point of array: either *pick* a point or *enter* coordinates
  right-click
Number of items: *enter* 68 *right-click*
Angle to fill (+=ccw, -=cw) <360>: *enter* 180 *right-click*
Rotate objects as they are copied? <Y>: *enter* N (No) *right-click*
Command:

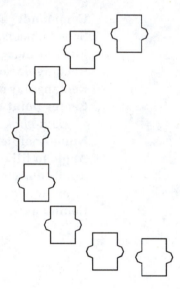

Fig. 6.20 **Array**. Example 3

Fig. 6.21 Calling **Move** from
the **Modify** toolbar

Move

Move can be called for the **Modify** toolbar (Fig. 6.21), from the
Modify pull-down menu, by *entering* move or its abbreviation m at
the Command line.

Example – Fig. 6.22

Move can be used for moving single entities of a number of entities
in a window (or crossing window). Figure 6.22 is an example of a
number of entities moved with the aid of a window. The left-hand
drawing shows the entities to be moved and the right-hand window
the result of the move. Call the tool and the Command line shows:

Command: _move
Select objects: *enter* w (Window) *right-click*
First corner: *pick* **Other corner:** *pick*
Base point or displacement: *pick* **Second point of displacement:**
  pick
Command:

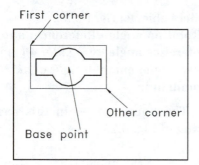

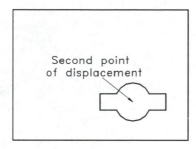

Fig. 6.22 **Move**. Example

Rotate

Fig. 6.23 Calling **Rotate** from the **Modify** toolbar

Rotate can be called for the **Modify** toolbar (Fig. 6.23), from the **Modify** pull-down menu, by *entering* rotate or its abbreviation ro at the Command line.

Two methods of rotation are available, the first by the *entering* of a figure for the rotation (anti-clockwise by default) from the current position of the item being rotated, the second by reference from one angle to a second.

Example 1 – Fig. 6.24

Call **Rotate**. The Command line shows:

Command: _rotate
Select objects: *enter* w (Window) *right-click*
First corner: *pick* **Other corner:** *pick*
Select objects: *right-click*
<Rotation angle>/Reference: *enter* 30 *right-click*
Command:

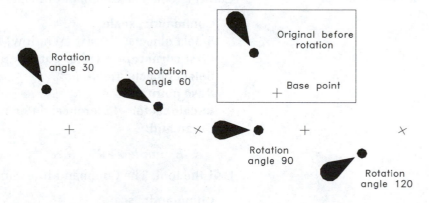

Fig. 6.24 **Rotate**. Example 1

Example 2 – Fig. 6.25

Command: _rotate
Select objects: *pick* the entity (in this case a polyline)

Select objects: *right-click*
<Rotation angle>/Reference: *enter* r (Reference) *right-click*
Reference angle <0>: *enter* 45 *right-click*
New angle: *enter* 60 *right-click*
Command:

Note: The figures given in this example refer to the right-hand drawing of Fig. 6.25.

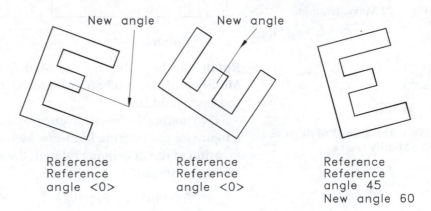

Fig. 6.25 **Rotate**. Example 2

Fig. 6.26 Calling **Scale** from the **Modify** toolbar

Scale

Scale can be called from the **Modify** toolbar (Fig. 6.26), from the **Modify** pull-down menu, by *entering* scale or its abbreviation sc at the Command line.

Example 1 – Fig. 6.27

Call the tool. The Command line shows:

Command: _scale
Select objects: *enter* w (Window) *right-click*
First corner: *pick* **Other corner:** *pick* **3 found**
Select objects: *right-click*
Base point: *pick*
<Scale factor>/Reference: *enter* 1.2 *right-click*
Command:

Example 2 – Fig. 6.28

Call the tool. The Command line shows:

Command: _scale
Select objects: *enter* w (Window) *right-click*
First corner: *pick* **Other corner:** *pick* **5 found**
Select objects: *right-click*
Base point: *pick*

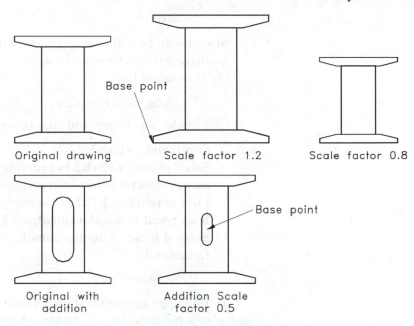

Base point

Original drawing   Scale factor 1.2   Scale factor 0.8

Base point

Original with   Addition Scale
addition   factor 0.5

Fig. 6.27 **Scale**. Example 1

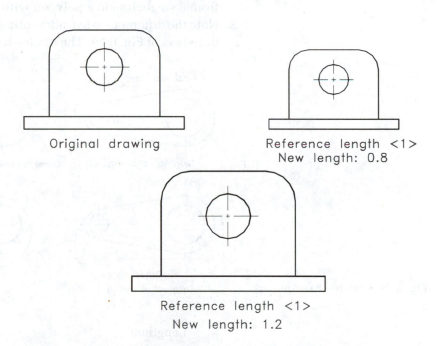

Original drawing   Reference length <1>
                          New length: 0.8

Reference length <1>
New length: 1.2

Fig. 6.28 **Scale**. Example 2

    <Scale factor>/Reference: *enter* r *right-click*
    Reference length <1>: *right-click*
    New length: *enter* 0.8 *right-click*
    Command:

Stretch

Stretch can be called from the **Modify** toolbar (Fig. 6.29), from the **Modify** pull-down menu, by *entering* stretch or its abbreviation s at the Command line.

Example – Fig. 6.29

Call **Scale**. The Command line shows:

Command: _stretch
Select objects to stretch by crossing-window or crossing-polygon...
Select objects: *enter* c (Crossing-window) *right-click*
First corner: *pick* **Other corner:** *pick* **5 found**
Base point or displacement: *pick*
Second point of displacement: *pick*
Command:

Notes

1. When using **Stretch**, the selection of a window must be a crossing or a polygon (fence) window. A polygon window can be anything from a single line to a polygon with many lines.
2. Note the difference when attempting to stretch a circle – lower two drawings of Fig. 6.29. The circles have resisted being stretched.

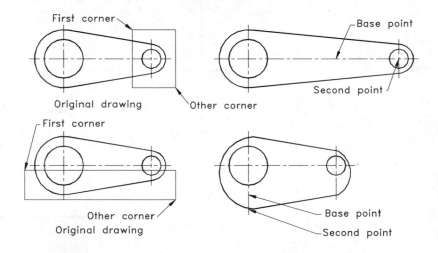

Fig. 6.29 **Stretch** – Example

Lengthen

Fig. 6.30 Calling **Lengthen** from the **Modify** toolbar

Lengthen can be called from the **Modify** toolbar (Fig. 6.30), from the **Modify** pull-down menu, by *entering* lengthen or its abbreviation len at the Command line.

Line, Plines and arcs can be lengthened with the aid of the tool. The prompts for the **Lengthen** tool are:

DElta/Percent/Total/DYnamic and if **DE** is *entered* as a response:
Angle/Delta length

DElta: Lengthens by the given *entered* figure.
Percent: Lengthens by the *entered* figure of percentage.
Total: Lengthens to the *entered* figure, whether larger or smaller.
Cannot be used on a polyline.
DYnamic: Lengthens by *dragging* under mouse control.
Angle: changes the angle of an arc to its centre point.

Trim

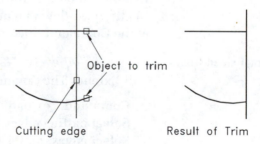

Fig. 6.31 Calling **Trim** from the **Modify** toolbar

Trim can be called from the **Modify** toolbar (Fig. 6.31), from the
Modify pull-down menu, by *entering* trim or its abbreviation tr at the
Command line.

Example 1 – Fig. 6.32

Call **Trim**. The Command line shows:

> **Command: _trim**
> **Select cutting edges: Projmode = UCS, Edgemode = No extend)**
> **Select edges:** *pick* **1 found**
> **Select objects:** *right-click*
> **<Select object to trim>/Project/Edge/<Undo>:** *pick*
> **<Select object to trim>/Project/Edge/<Undo>:** *right-click*
> **Command:**

Object to trim

Cutting edge · · · · · Result of Trim

Fig. 6.32 **Trim**. Example 1

Example 2 – Fig. 6.33

If the **Edge** prompt is chosen a trim can take effect against what
would be an extension of the selecting cutting edge object. Four
examples of the use of **Edge** are given in Fig. 6.33. For each of them
the Command line prompts and responses are the same, as follows:

> **Command: _trim**
> **Select cutting edges: Projmode = UCS, Edgemode = No extend)**
> **Select edges:** *pick* **1 found**
> **Select objects:** *right-click*

<Select object to trim>/Project/Edge/<Undo>: *enter* e (Edge) *right-click*
Extend/No extend<No extend>: *enter* e *right-click*
<Select object to trim>/Project/Edge/<Undo>: *pick*
<Select object to trim>/Project/Edge/<Undo>: *right-click*
Command:

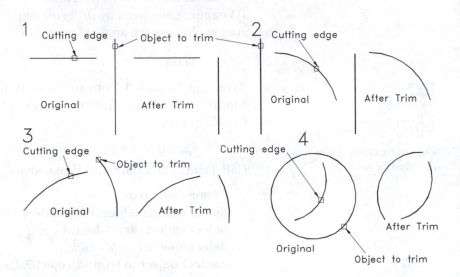

Fig. 6.33 **Trim**. Example 2

Fig. 6.34 Calling **Extend** from the **Modify** toolbar

Extend

Extend can be called from the **Modify** toolbar (Fig. 6.34), from the **Modify** pull-down menu, by *entering* extend or its abbreviation ex at the Command line.

Example 1 – Fig. 6.35

Call **Extend**. The Command line shows:

Command: _extend
Select cutting edges: Projmode = UCS, Edgemode = Extend)
Select edges: *pick* **1 found**
Select objects: *right-click*
<Select object to extend>/Project/Edge/<Undo>: *pick*
<Select object to extend>/Project/Edge/<Undo>: *pick*
<Select object to extend>/Project/Edge/<Undo>: *right-click*
Command:

Note: The similarity between the prompts for **Trim** and **Extend**.

Example 2 – Fig. 6.36

The left-hand pair of drawings of Fig. 6.36 show the use of the **Extend** tool used in the same way as in Example 1 in Fig. 6.35. The

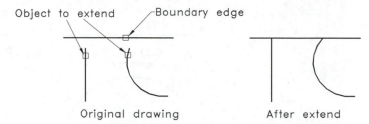

Fig. 6.35 **Extend**. Example 1

right-hand pair of drawings of Fig. 6.36 shows the use of **Extend** using the **Edge** prompt. The entity (object) being extended is taken to an imaginary extension of the selected Boundary edge.

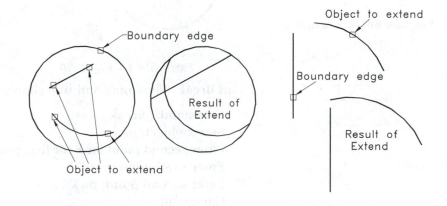

Fig. 6.36 **Extend**. Example 2

Break

Fig. 6.37 Calling **Break** from the **Modify** toolbar

Break can be called from the **Modify** toolbar (Fig. 6.37), from the **Modify** pull-down menu, by *entering* break or its abbreviation br at the Command line.

Example 1 – Fig. 6.38

Call **Break**. The Command line shows:

Command: _break
Select object: *pick*
Enter second point (or F for first point): *pick*
Command:

Notes

1. In this example, the first point *picked* – in response to the **Select object:** prompt is the start point of the break.
2. Remember that, when breaking arcs or circles the default anti-clockwise (ccw) direction must be observed, otherwise the break will not be as intended.

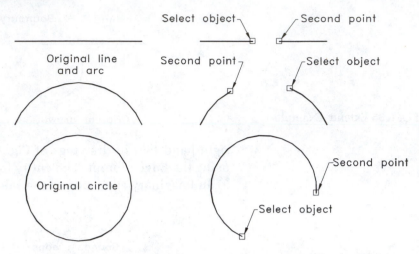

Fig. 6.38 **Break**. Example 1

Example 2 – Fig. 6.39

Call **Break**. The Command line shows:

> **Command: _break**
> **Select object:** *pick*
> **Enter second point (or F for first point):** *enter* f (First) *right-click*
> **Enter first point:** *pick*
> **Enter second point:** *pick*
> **Command:**

Notes

1. When the **or F for first point** prompt is invoked, the **Select object** *picked* point can be anywhere on the entity.
2. Note that in the upper example of Fig. 6.39, the pline is a single entity, so the **Select object** *pick* point can be anywhere on the pline,

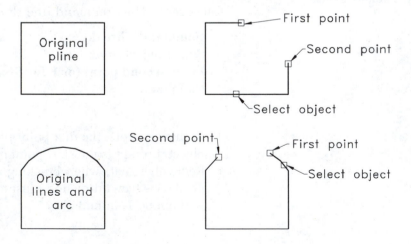

Fig. 6.39 **Break**. Example 2

whereas in the lower example, the arc is an entity apart from the three lines, so the *pick* point must be on the arc.

Chamfer

Fig. 6.40 Calling **Chamfer** from the **Modify** toolbar

Chamfer can be called from the **Modify** toolbar (Fig. 6.40), from the **Modify** pull-down menu, by *entering* chamfer or its abbreviation cha at the Command line.

Example 1 – Fig. 6.41 (Drawing 1)

Drawing 1 of Fig. 6.41 is a rectangle constructed with the tool **Line**. Call **Chamfer**. The Command line shows:

Command: _chamfer
(TRIM mode) Current chamfer Dist1 = 10, Dist2 = 10
Polyline/Distance/Angle/Trim/Method/<Select first line>: *enter*
    d (Distance) *right-click*
Enter first chamfer distance <10>: *enter* 15 *right-click*
Enter second chamfer distance <15>: *right-click*
Command: *right-click*
CHAMFER
(TRIM mode) Current chamfer dist1 = 15, Dist2 = 15
Polyline/Distance/Angle/Trim/Method/<Select first line>: *pick*
Select second line: *pick*
Command:

Example 2 – Fig. 6.41 (Drawing 2)

Drawing 2 of Fig. 6.41 is a rectangle constructed with the tool **Polyline**. Call **Chamfer**. The Command line shows:

CHAMFER
(TRIM mode) Current chamfer dist1 = 15, Dist2 = 15
Polyline/Distance/Angle/Trim/Method/<Select first line>: *enter*
    p (Polyline) *right-click*
Select 2D polyline: *pick*
4 lines were chamfered
Command:

Example 3 – Fig. 6.41 (Drawing 3)

In this example, two lines have been drawn which do not meet. Set **Dist1** and **Dist2** to 0 and the lines are extended to meet. If the lines had crossed or one had extended beyond the other, the result would have been the same – the lines would form a corner join.

Example 4 – Fig. 6.41 (Drawing 4)

No matter how complicated a closed polyline is, when chamfering with the **Polyline** prompt, all corners become chamfered.

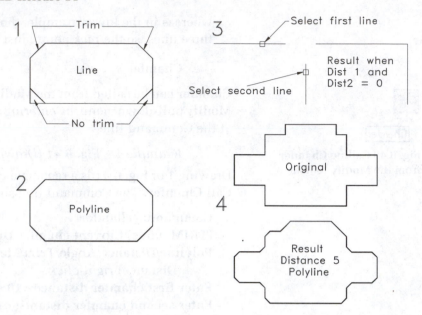

Fig. 6.41 **Chamfer.** Examples

Notes

1. If a chamfer is to be constructed with one distance along the first line to be different to that along the second line the response to the prompt:

    Polyline/Distance/Angle/Trim/Method/<Select first line>:

    will be a (Angle). Then the two distances can be different.
2. Note the upper drawing in the first example above. If the edges are not to be trimmed, the response to the prompt:

    Polyline/Distance/Angle/Trim/Method/<Select first line>:

    will be t (Trim), in which case another prompt appears:

    Trim/No trim/<Trim>: *enter* n (No trim) *right-click*

Fillet

Fig. 6.42 Calling **Fillet** from the **Modify** toolbar

Fillet can be called from the **Modify** toolbar (Fig. 6.42), from the **Modify** pull-down menu, by *entering* fillet or its abbreviation f at the Command line.

Example 1 – Fig. 6.43

The prompts for **Fillet** are similar to those for **Chamfer**, except that instead of settings figures for distances (**Dist1** and **Dist2**) figures for **Radius** must be *entered*.

The four examples of Fig. 6.43 were constructed using similar response examples as for those for the **Chamfer** examples (Fig. 6.41).

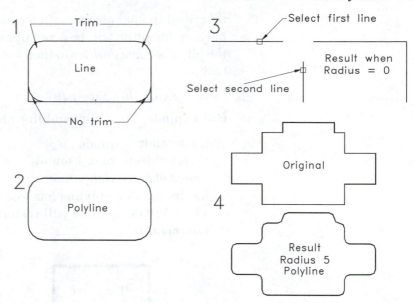

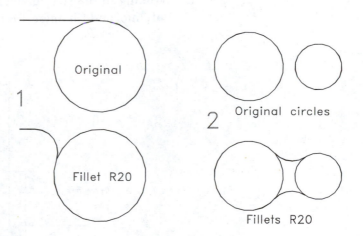

Fig. 6.43 **Fillet**. Examples

Example 2 – Fig. 6.44

It is possible to fillet between circles or arcs, between circles and lines or between arcs. Figure 6.44 shows two examples – the first (Drawing 1) between a circle and a line, the second (Drawing 2) between circles.

Fig. 6.44 **Fillet**. Example 2

Explode

Fig. 6.45 Calling **Explode** from the **Modify** toolbar

Explode can be called from the **Modify** toolbar (Fig. 6.45), from the **Modify** pull-down menu, by *entering* explode or its abbreviation ex at the Command line.

Explode can be used to change many types of AutoCAD constructions into their constituent parts. Some of the uses for the tool will be described in later chapters. In the example given below (Fig. 6.46), only a wide pline will be acted upon by **Explode**. The four parts of the pline become entities in their own right and are changed to **Line** entities.

Example – Fig. 6.46

Call **Explode**. The Command line changes to:

Command: **_explode**
Select objects: *pick* **1 found**
Select objects: *right-click*
Exploding this polyline has lost its information.
The UNDO command will restore it.
Command:

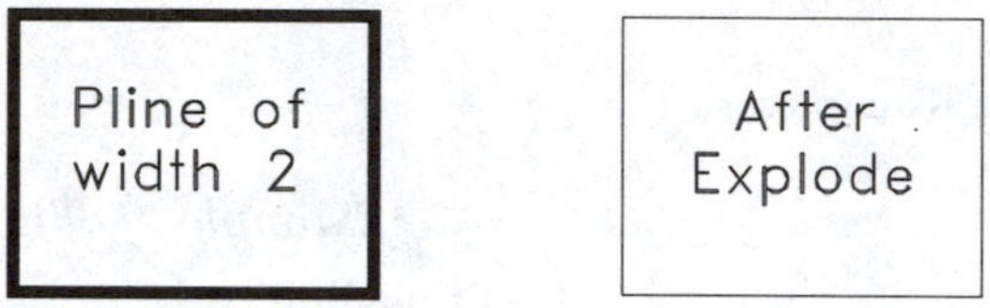

Pline of width 2

After Explode

Fig. 6.46 **Explode**. Example

Exercises

1. Working to the sizes given in Fig. 6.47, copy the drawing. Use **Polyline**, and **Chamfer**. Do not include dimensions.

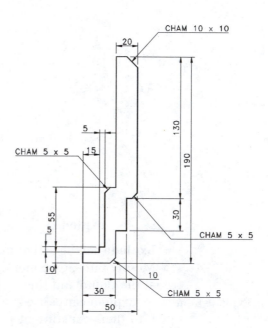

Fig. 6.47 Exercise 1

2. With the aid of the tools **Circle**, **Trim** and **Array** construct the drawing Fig. 6.48. Do not include any dimensions.

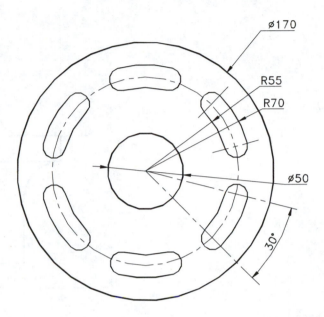

Fig. 6.48 Exercise 2

3. Figure 6.49. With the tools **Polyline** and **Array** construct the given drawing without the dimensions.

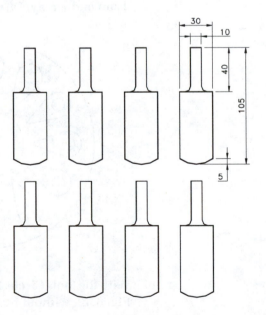

Fig. 6.49 Exercise 3

4. Using the tools **Polyline**, **Chamfer** and **Fillet** construct the outline Fig. 6.50, without including any of the dimensions.

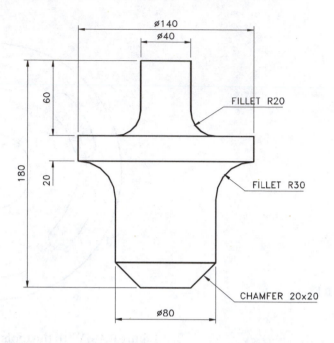

Fig. 6.50 Exercise 4

5. Figure 6.51. Construct the given drawing. Use tools **Circle**, **Line**, **Trim** and **Array**. Do not add the dimensions.

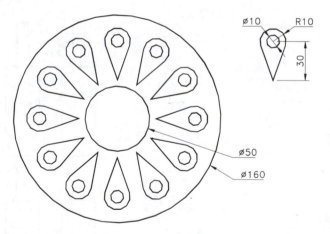

Fig. 6.51 Exercise 5

6. With the tools **Circle**, **Line**, **Trim** and **Array** construct the drawing Fig. 6.52, without including any dimensions.

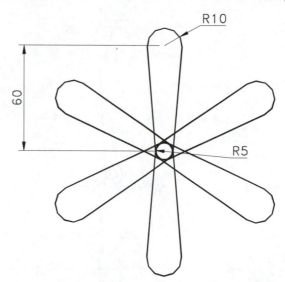

Fig. 6.52 Exercise 6

7. With **Line**, **Circle**, **Trim** and **Array** construct the drawing Fig. 6.53, without including any of the dimensions.

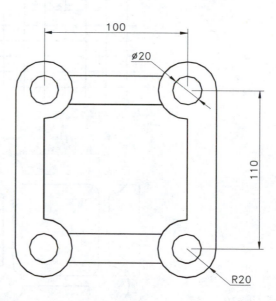

Fig. 6.53 Exercise 7

8. Copy Fig. 6.54 with the aid of **Line**, **Circle**, **Trim** and **Rotate**. Dimensions should not be included.
9. Construct the right-hand drawing of Fig. 6.55 by the use of **Trim** after constructing the lines of the left-hand drawing of Fig. 6.55.
10. Construct the left-hand drawing of Fig. 6.56 using **Circle**, **Line**, **Fillet** and **Trim**. Then **Copy** it twice. **Scale** the first copy to 0.5 times scale and the second copy to 0.75 times scale.

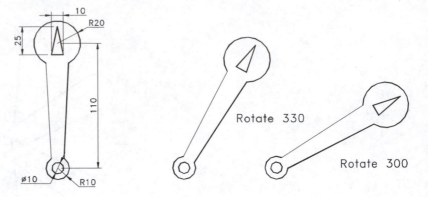

Fig. 6.54 Exercise 8

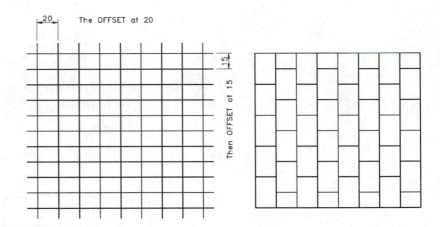

Fig. 6.55 Exercise 8

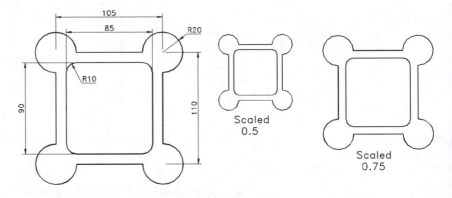

Fig. 6.56 Exercise 10

11. Using **Circle**, **Line**, **Trim** and **Fillet** copy the drawing in Fig. 6.57, without including any dimensions.
12. Figure 6.58. A more difficult exercise. Construct the drawing to the dimensions given.

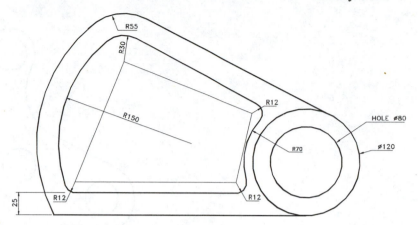

Fig. 6.57 Exercise 11

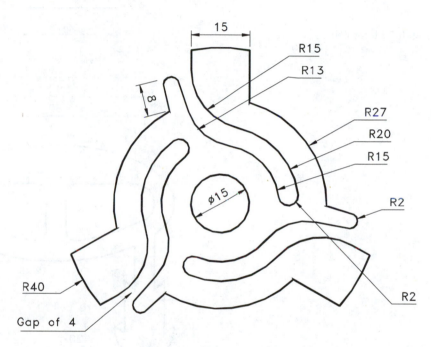

Fig. 6.58 Exercise 12

13. Construct the drawing of a metal plate given in Fig. 6.59 to the sizes shown.
14. Construct the drawing of a plastic handle shown in Fig. 6.60 to the given dimensions.
15. Figure 6.61 is a view of a wooden handle. Construct the view to the given dimensions.

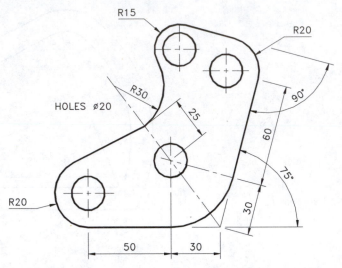

Fig. 6.59 Exercise 13

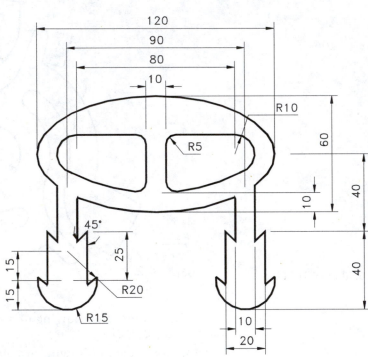

Fig. 6.60 Exercise 14

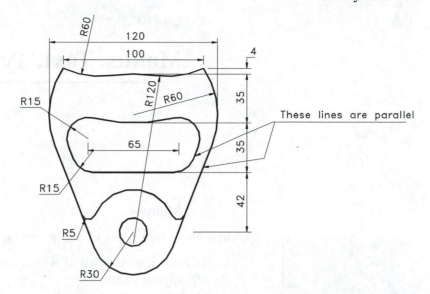

Fig. 6.61 Exercise 15

CHAPTER 7

Menus. Text. Types of drawing

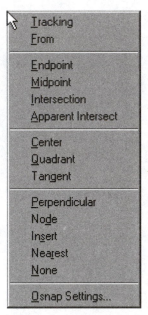

Fig. 7.1 The osnaps menu appearing with **Shift**+*right-click*

Menus

In general two types of menu can be called to the R14 window:

1. Pull-down menus, all of which are shown in Fig. 7.2, and which will appear either:
   (a) With a *left-click* on the menu name from the menu bar.
   (b) By pressing the **Alt** key of the keyboard, together with the initial letter of the menu name. Thus **Alt+F** brings the **File** pull-down menu on screen.
2. Menus or dialogue boxes, which appear with a *right-click*, sometimes in conjunction with pressing the **Shift** key of the keyboard. Those in most common use are:
   (a) The osnap settings menu (Fig. 7.1) appearing with **Shift+***right-click*.
   (b) The **Toolbars** dialogue box, which appears with a *right-click* in any part of any toolbar (not on an icon). Figure 7.3 shows the dialogue box appearing with a *right-click* in the **Modify** toolbar. This facility allows the choice of another toolbar to be called to screen from which tools can be selected.
   (c) The **Button Properties** dialogue box (Fig. 7.4) called to screen when, with the **Toolbars** dialogue box on screen, any tool icon is selected with a *right-click*. This facility can be useful if the tool represented by an icon is either not known, or its uses are not understood.
   (d) The window controls menu, appearing with a *right-click* in any part of the R14 title bar (Fig. 7.5). The R14 window can be acted upon by selection of the window command from the menu.
   (e) The menu (Fig. 7.6) which appears with a *right-click* in the Command window. Note that, from this menu the **Copy History** and **Paste** refer to the history of commands in the Command window. *Left-click* on **Preferences...** and the **Preferences** dialogue box appears.

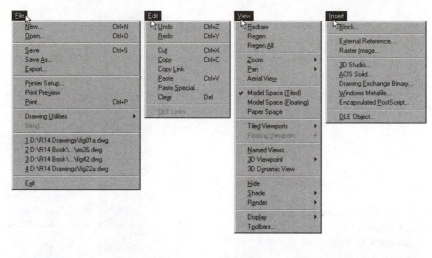

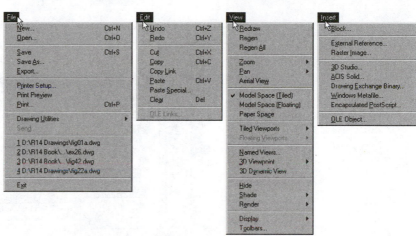

Fig. 7.2 The pull-down menus
as called from the menu bar

The ? icon in some dialogue boxes

Whenever a **?** icon appears at the top right of a dialogue box, a *left-click* on the icon and it another **?** icon appears at the cursor, which can be *dragged* to any feature in the dialogue box. Another *left-click* on the feature brings up a **Help** panel showing details of the use of the chosen feature. An example is given in Fig. 7.7.

Text

In general there are two methods of calling text commands (Fig. 7.8):

Multiline Text: Called when the **Multiline Text** tool icon is selected from the **Draw** toolbar, selected from the **Draw** pull-down menu or by *entering* mtext or mt at the Command line.

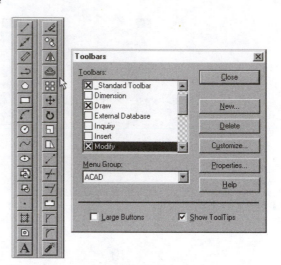

Fig. 7.3 The **Toolbars** dialogue box called on screen with a *right-click* in any toolbar

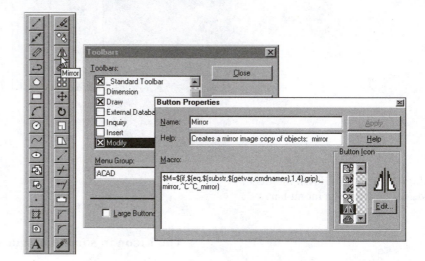

Fig. 7.4 The **Button Properties** dialogue box, called with a *right-click* on a tool icon

Fig. 7.5 The R14 window controls menu called with a *right-click* in the title bar

Dynamic Text: Called from the **Draw** pull-down menu or by *entering* dtext or t at the Command line.

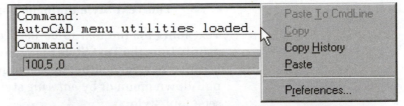

Fig. 7.6 The menu appearing
with a *right-click* in the
Command window

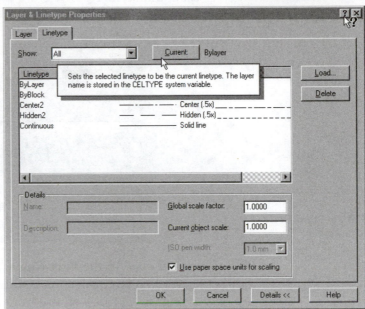

Fig. 7.7 Using the **?** icon in a
dialogue box

Fig. 7.8 Methods of calling text

The Text Style dialogue box

Text fonts for the text to be used can be set in several ways, but mainly from the **Text Style** dialogue box (Fig. 7.9). The dialogue box is called to screen either by selecting **Text Style...** from the **Format** pull-down menu or by *entering* style or st at the Command line. To set a font style:

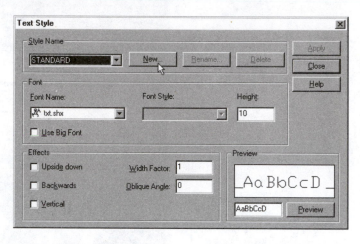

Fig. 7.9 The **Text Style** dialogue box

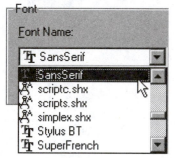

Fig. 7.10 The **Font Name:** popup list

1. *Left-click* in the **Font Name:** box and a popup list appears (Fig. 7.10). A large selection of different font styles are available in R14. Figure 7.11 lists all the font names in popup list.

2. Select a name from the popup list. The name appears in the **Font Name:** box.

3. *Left-click* on the **New...** button and a **New Text Style** box appears (Fig. 7.12). The **Style Name:** box will show **Style 1** (or **2**, **3** etc.). In place of the name **Style**, *enter* the name of the chosen font. Note that if the font has more than one word in its name the words must be separated with a _ dash.

4. *Enter* the required height in the **Height:** box and set check boxes against **Upside Down**, **Backwards**, **Vertical** if necessary. Also *enter* the **Width Factor:** and **Oblique Angle:** if they are to be different from the defaults of 1 and 0.

5. Continue in this manner until all the fonts which may be required have been *entered* into the **Text Style** dialogue box. A *left-click* on the **Font Name:** box will then show all the fonts which have been already loaded.

Multiline text

Call the tool – either from the **Draw** toolbar, from the **Draw** pull-down menu, by *entering* mtext or mt. The Command line shows:

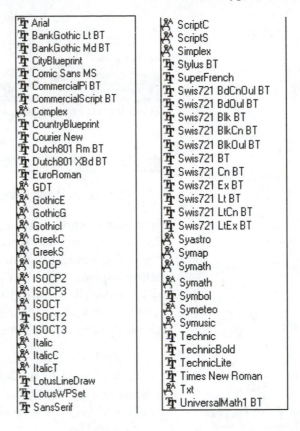

Fig. 7.11 The font names in the popup list

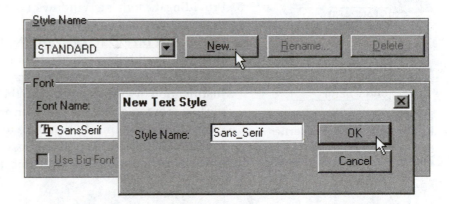

Fig. 7.12 The **New Text Style Box**

Command: _mtext Current text style: TIMES_NEW_ROMAN:
Text height 15
Specify first corner: *pick*
Specify opposite corner or (Height/Justify/Rotation/Style/Width):
pick
Command:

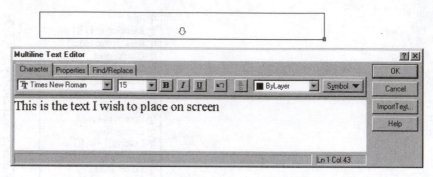

Fig. 7.13 The **Multiline Text Editor**

This is the text I wish to place on screen

As the corners are *picked* a box outline can be *dragged* to the window size in which the text is to be *entered* (upper drawing of Fig. 7.13). When the **opposite corner** has been *picked*, the **Multiline Text Editor** appears on screen (middle illustration of Fig. 7.13). In the editor *enter* the required text, followed by a *left-click* on the **OK** button of the dialogue box. The text appears on screen in the windowed area (bottom line of Fig. 7.13).

Notes

1. The font used in the editor can be changed to one of the fonts already *entered* in the **Text Style** dialogue.
2. The text height can be altered in the height box to the right of the font name box.
3. Providing the font is a Windows True Type font, text can be *entered* in **BOLD**, *ITALIC* or <u>UNDERLINED</u> text, or a combination of all three – ***<u>BOLD,ITALIC,UNDERLINED</u>***.
4. *Left-click* on the **Properties** label of the editor and it will be seen that the fonts already *entered* can be chosen (Fig. 7.14), the **Justification** of the text can be set, the **Width** of the box into which the text is *entered*, and the **Rotation** angle of the text can be altered.
5. At the Command line, in response to the prompts **(Height/Justify/ Rotation/Style/Width)** these settings can be *entered* at the Command line, rather than from the **Multiline Text Editor**.

Fig. 7.14 The popup list of loaded fonts in the **Properties** part of the **Multiline Text Editor**

Dynamic text

This is text which appears on screen as it is typed at the Command line. To place dtext, either select **Single Line Text** from the **Draw** pull-down menu, or *enter* dtext or d at the Command line. The Command line then shows:

Command: _dtext Justify/Style/<Start point>: *pick* a point
Rotation angle <0>: *right-click*

Text: *enter* the required text which appears on the screen. Then press the **Return** key (NOT a *right-click*)

Text: press **Return**

Command:

Note: Justification or Style can be set at the Command line in response to prompts which appear when j (Justify) or s (Style) are *entered* as a response to the first line of prompts.

Examples of text styles

Figure 7.15 shows a few of the many text styles available in R14. The fonts include AutoCAD fonts (those with the file extension ***.shx**) and Windows True Type Fonts (extensions ***.ttf**). The AutoCAD fonts are held in the directory **AcadR14\fonts** and the True Type fonts in **Windows/fonts**. Text such as shown in Fig. 7.15 can be *entered* as Mtext or as Dtext.

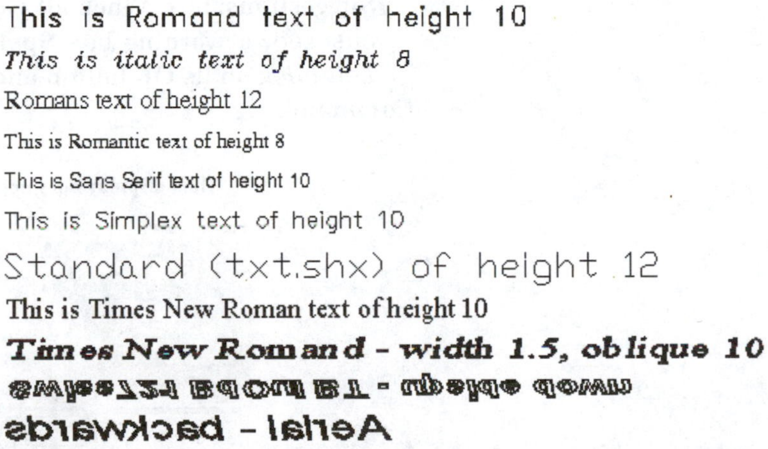

This is Romand text of height 10

This is italic text of height 8

Romans text of height 12

This is Romantic text of height 8

This is Sans Serif text of height 10

This is Simplex text of height 10

Standard (txt.shx) of height 12

This is Times New Roman text of height 10

Times New Romand – width 1.5, oblique 10

emoẞ elqiɔ – 1ɒ mo₹ɒ₹ sɪɹɘ/ɯe

Aerial – backwards

Fig. 7.15 Examples of text styles in R14

Text which includes symbols

Some text, particularly the figures dealing with dimensions or measurements will require symbols to be included either before or after the text. Such symbols (Control Codes and Special Characters) are *entered* using %% calls. The following list shows these control codes:

%%d – Degree symbol. Thus **45%%d** will place 45°.

%%c – diameter symbol. Thus **%%c45** will place Ø45.

%%p – tolerance symbol Thus **45%%p0.5** will place 45±0.5.

%%% – % sign. Thus **45%%%** will place 45%

%%u – underscore. Thus **%%u45** will place <u>45</u>.

Note: In AutoCAD Release 13 Postscript fonts were available, but in R14 the equivalent Windows True Type fonts have taken the place of Postscript fonts.

Spellcheck

Fig. 7.16 The **Spelling** tool from the **Standard** toolbar

Misspelt words in text can be checked and changed with the use of the **Spelling** tool (Fig. 7.16), the icon for which is found in the **Standard** toolbar at the top of the R14 window. The tool can also be called by *entering* spell, or its abbreviation sp at the Command line. When selected the Command line shows:

Command: _spell
Select objects: *pick* the line of text in which the misspelling occurs **1 found**
Select objects: *right-click*
And the **Check Spelling** dialogue box appears (Fig. 7.17). As each word is checked, a correct spelling can be selected from the **Suggestions:** box. When all words in a line of text have been checked, a warning box **Spelling check complete** appears. *Left-click* on its **OK** button and the Command line reverts to:
Command:

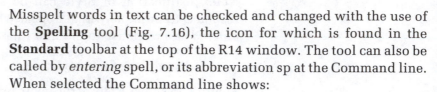

Fig. 7.17 The **Check Spelling** dialogue box

Types of drawing

Two of the common types of 2D (two-dimensional) technical drawings which can be constructed in R14 are introduced in this chapter. By far the most common of these is orthographic projection, which is used extensively in the engineering and building industries. The other one is a pictorial type – isometric.

Orthographic projection

Orthographic projections are the most common form of technical drawings in the engineering and building industries. In general there are two forms of this type of projection – first angle projection and third angle projection. In the USA, third angle orthographic projection is that most commonly used, but elsewhere in the world, both angles of projection will be found in about equal proportions.

The theory behind this form of projection is based upon two imaginary planes, crossing at right angles, one horizontal and the other vertical. Planes crossing at right angles said to be orthogonal to each other, hence the term orthographic. The two planes form four angles – first, second, third and fourth, but it is only the first and third angles which are pertinent to orthographic projection. The left-hand drawing of Fig. 7.18 is a pictorial view of the two planes and the right-hand drawing shows an edge view of the planes, together with arrows showing the directions from which objects placed within the planes are viewed for the purposes of this form of projection.

Figure 7.19 shows the general principles of obtaining a first angle projection of a simple bracket. The object is placed within the first angle of the H.P. and V.P. and is then viewed from the front and from above. What is seen from the directions of viewing is cast onto the planes, a Front view onto the V.P. and a Plan onto the H.P. A second V.P. is introduced onto which an End view is drawn. The three planes are rotated so that they all lie in the same plane – that of the drawing sheet, or in the case of a computer, of the screen of the monitor. Figure 7.20 shows the resulting three views on the rotated planes (left-hand drawing) and the resulting projection when the imaginary planes are withdrawn (right-hand drawing).

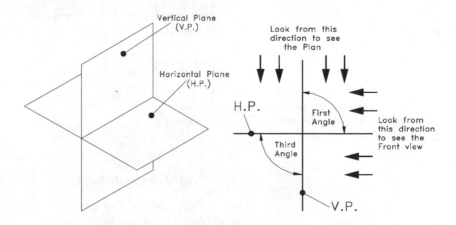

Fig. 7.18 The H.P. and V.P. on which orthographic projection is based

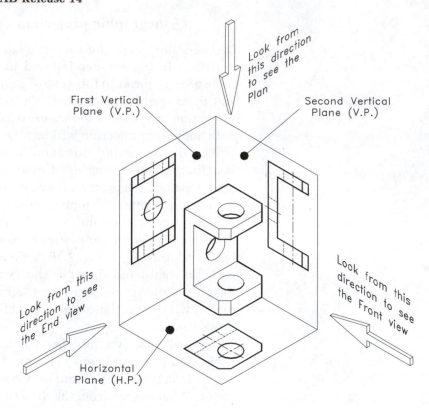

Fig. 7.19 The theory behind
first angle orthographic
projection

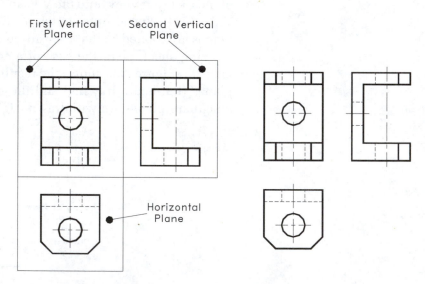

Fig. 7.20 First angle projection
when the planes have been
rotated and then removed

Third angle orthographic projection

Figure 7.21 shows the general principles governing third angle
projection. The object is placed within the third angle of the H.P. and

V.P. and viewed from the front and from above. What is seen is cast upon the planes. A second V.P. allows an End view to be added. The three planes are then rotated so as to lie all in the same plane (Fig. 7.22 left-hand drawing) and the imaginary planes then withdrawn (right-hand drawing of Fig. 7.22).

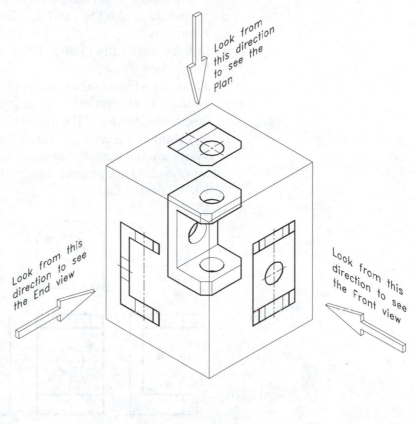

Fig. 7.21 The theory behind third angle orthographic projection

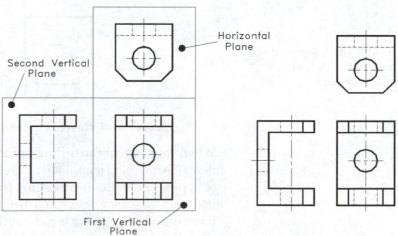

Fig. 7.22 Third angle projection when the planes have been rotated and then removed

First and third angles compared

Note the following differences between first and third angle projections:

1. In first angle, the Plan is below the Front view.
2. In third angle, the Plan is above the Front view.
3. In first angle the Plan and the End view face outwards from the Front view.
4. In third angle, the Plan and End view face inwards towards the Front view.
5. There is no limit to the number of views of a single object that can be drawn. Theoretically there is a maximum of six, but by the insertion of further V.P.s and/or H.P.s, many more than 6 views can be obtained. Figure 7.23 shows the theoretical 6 views.
6. Views are not usually named. Their positions in relation to each other makes naming unnecessary. This rule does not apply to views which are sections.

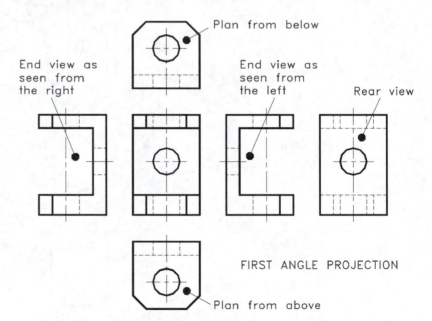

Fig. 7.23 The theoretical six views of an object in first angle projection

Number of views required

When constructing an orthographic projection, the aim should be to describe fully and completely the object being drawn in as few views as is possible without detracting from the fact that it is important to maintain accuracy and to ensure that a full understanding of the meaning of the drawing is not sacrificed. Thus some objects, such as a thin plate may require only one view – a Front view, some may require only two, others three or more.

Lines in technical drawings

R14 contains a large number of different line types. Apart from these, the common line types used in technical drawings for engineering are shown in Fig. 7.24. Note that outlines are normally two or three times the thickness of other lines. A general rule is that outlines in drawings designed for plotting on A3 sheets should be about 0.7 units and other lines about 0.3 units. The **Polyline** tool is of value here.

Outline – thick line

Thin line – for features such as dimension lines, hatching lines, etc.

Centre line – a thin line made up from long and short lines alternating with each other. Should be drawn through all circles, spheres, cylinders and similar features.

Hidden detail – thin lines. A broken dashed line drawn through features not seen from the outside of the object being drawn.

Break line – thin lines drawn at a break in a drawing.

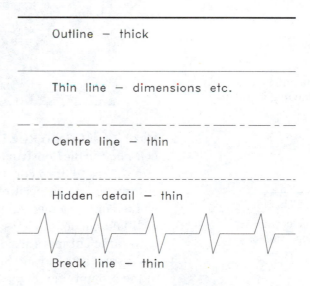

Fig. 7.24 Types of lines in engineering drawings

An example of a third angle orthographic projection

To draw a third angle orthographic projection of the hanger shown in Fig. 7.25 follow the procedures:

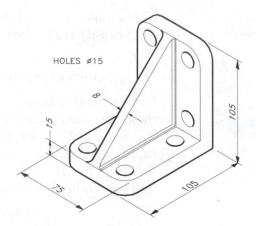

HOLES Ø15

Fig. 7.25 The support for the
third angle orthographic
projection example

1. Open your personal drawing template – Fig. 7.26.

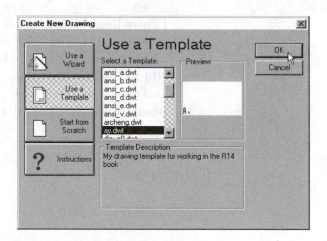

Fig. 7.26 Opening one's
personal drawing template

Construction Line

Fig. 7.27 Select the
Construction Line tool

2. Make Layer **CONSTRUCTION** the current layer – see Fig. 7.28.
3. *Left-click* on the **Construction Line** tool icon from the **Draw** toolbar (Fig. 7.27) and draw construction lines as shown in Fig. 7.28. The arithmetic for the positions of the construction lines should be worked out on a piece of paper beforehand to help in obtaining a well laid out set of views. Attempt equal spacing between views with sufficient space at sides, top and bottom of the drawing sheet.
4. Make sure that **Grid** and **Snap** are on – *double-click* on their names in the prompt line (Fig. 7.29) or *left-click* on **F7** and **F9**.
5. *Left-click* on the **Polyline** tool icon from the **Draw** toolbar (Fig. 7.30). Make Layer 0 the current layer as in Fig. 7.32. Set the **Pline** width to 0.7 and construct the three views based on the already drawn construction lines. (Fig. 7.32). If **ORTHO** is set on (see Fig. 7.29) the plines may be easier to draw. Use the **Arc** prompt of the

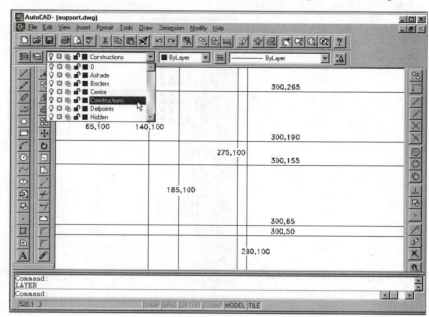

Fig. 7.28 Construction lines for the example

Fig. 7.29 Set **Grid** and **Snap** on

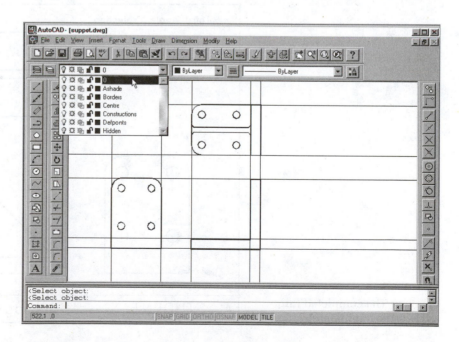

Pline prompts to construct the circles – two half circles based upon **Snap** points. Use the **Fillet** tool to produce the radiused corners.
6. Make the **CENTRE** layer current (Fig. 7.32) and add centre lines, then make the **HIDDEN** layer current and add hidden detail. Then

Fig. 7.30 Select the **Polyline** tool

Fig. 7.31 Adding outlines of the three views of the orthographic projection example

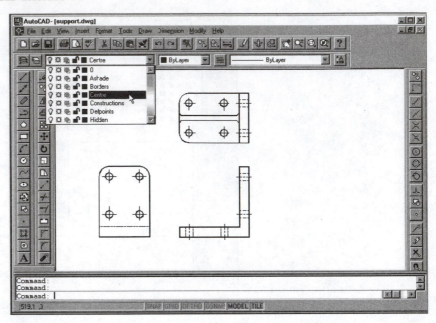

Fig. 7.32 Adding centre lines
to the orthographic projection
example

turn off the **CONSTRUCTION** layer. The resulting drawing now
looks like Fig. 7.33.

7. With the **Polyline** tool set to width 0 add a border line and a title
block area. With text of height 10 add a title and after resetting the
text height to 6 add the angle of projection – Fig. 7.33.

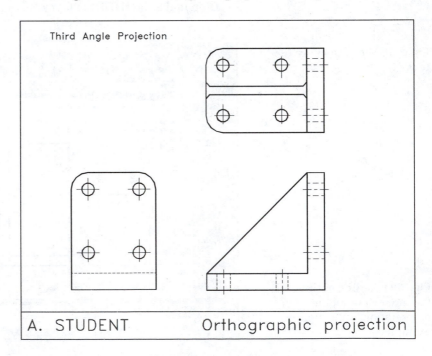

Fig. 7.33 The completed third
angle orthographic projection

Notes

1. In this example the text style is **Romand**, set to a height of 10 (for the title and 6 for the Third Angle Projection label.
2. Dimensions have not been included with the drawing. This is because dimensioning will be dealt with in a later chapter (Chapter 9).

Isometric drawing

The **Grid** and **Snap** settings for constructing isometric drawings are best set in the **Drawing Aids** dialogue box (Fig. 7.34). As can be seen in Fig. 7.34:

Snap is on, **Grid** is on (check boxes with crosses).
Y Spacings for **Snap** (5) and **Grid** (10) have been *entered*.
Isometric Snap/Grid is on (check box with cross).
Left Isoplane is current (check circle showing).

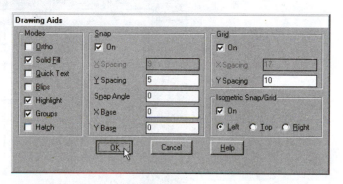

Fig. 7.34 Settings in the **Drawing Aids** dialogue box

Isoplanes

R14 recognises three isoplanes – **Left**, **Top** and **Right**. Isoplanes are shown in Fig. 7.35. The easiest method of setting the required isoplane is to press the **Ctrl** and the **E** key. Repeated pressing of **E** while holding down **Ctrl** toggles between the three isoplanes.

With the settings shown in Fig. 7.36, the R14 window will appear as in Fig. 7.37.

Constructing an isometric drawing

To construct an isometric drawing of the frame shown in the orthographic projection of Fig. 7.37, proceed as follows:

1. Open your personal drawing template.
2. In the **Drawing Aids** dialogue box *enter* settings as shown in Fig. 7.34.

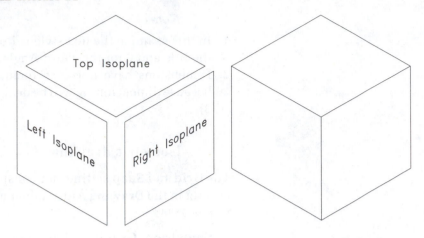

Fig. 7.35 The three **Isoplanes** of R14

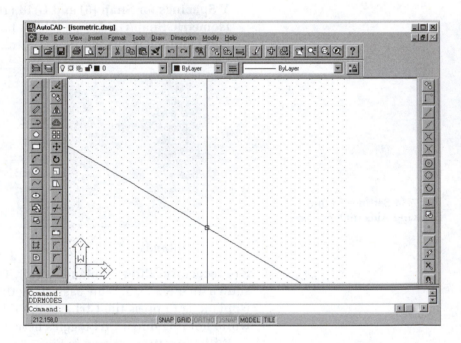

Fig. 7.36 The R14 window set up for isometric drawing

3. Press **Ctrl/E** until **Isoplane Right** shows at the Command Line. Press **Ctrl/D** until relative coordinates show in the Coordinate Window.
4. Select the **Polyline** tool (or *enter* pl *Return*) and, following the relative coordinate figures in the Coordinate Window, draw the outer rectangle of 120 by 100 units.
5. Draw the inside rectangle 15 units inside the outer.
6. **Ctrl/E** to obtain the **Isoplane Top**. With **Polyline** add the lines of the top edge.
7. **Ctrl/E** to obtain Isoplane Left and add plines for the left-hand edge.

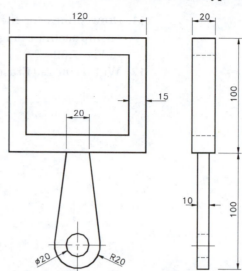

Fig. 7.37 An orthographic
projection of the isometric
drawing example

8.   Add plines for inner edges, amending the Isoplane with **Ctrl/E** as
     necessary. The construction should now look like the left-hand
     drawing of Fig. 7.38.
9.   Construct lines to position the top of the handle and draw another
     line to give the centre of the arc for the bottom of the handle.
10. Guided by the lines (item 9) draw isometric ellipses for the handle
     end and its hole. The construction now appears as in the right-
     hand drawing of Fig. 7.38.

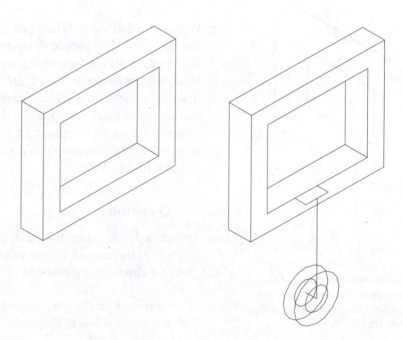

Fig. 7.38 First stages of
constructing the isometric
drawing example

11. Draw plines for the handle edges using the **Osnap Tangent** to ensure accurate tangency to the outer ellipses – left-hand drawing of Fig. 7.39.

12. With **Trim** and **Erase** complete the drawing – right-hand Fig. 7.39.

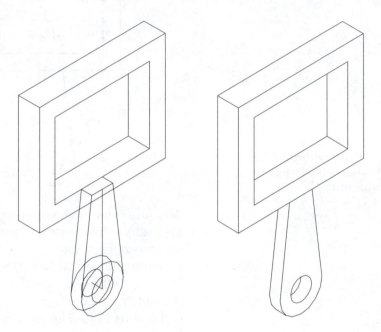

Fig. 7.39 Final stages in the construction of the isometric drawing example

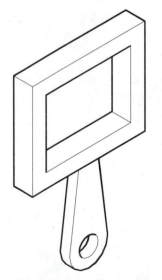

Fig. 7.40 Outer lines of the isometric drawing example widened to width of 1 with **Polyline**

Notes

1. With the aid of the **Polyline Edit** tool, together with the **Break** tool, the outlines of isometric drawings can be thickened as shown in Fig. 7.40, to give an appearance of depth to the drawing.

2. Isometric drawing is not a 3D method, although the resulting drawing may have a 3D appearance. Isometric drawings are a 2D method of constructing pictorial views. True 3D drawing will be described later in Chapters 13 and 14.

3. Figure 7.41 Shows a simple exploded isometric drawing constructed in the R14 window.

Questions

1. What happens when the **Shift** key is pressed and the right-hand button of the mouse is also pressed?

2. What is the quickest method of calling the **Toolbars** dialogue box on screen?

3. Can you explain the purpose of the **?** icon which appears at the top left corner of some dialogue boxes?

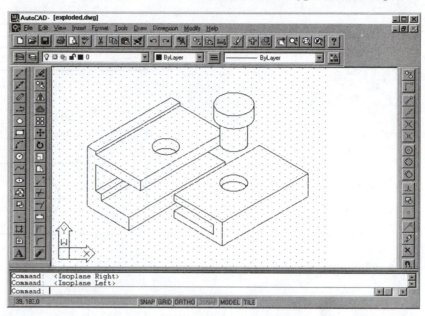

Fig. 7.41 A simple exploded isometric drawing

4. How can you differentiate between an AutoCAD font and a True Type font in the popup lists showing the font selection?
5. If a spelling mistake occurs when *entering* text in R14, what is the best way of putting it right?
6. What happens when **%%c50**, **%%d50** and **50%%%** are *entered* as text in R14?
7. Why is orthographic projection given its name?
8. Can you list the differences between first angle and third angle orthographic projection?
9. How many views can be included in an orthographic projection?
10. How are **Isoplanes** set?

Exercises

1. Figure 7.42 shows a two-view third angle orthographic projection of an engineering component. Construct the lower of the two views and then, working in first angle projection, add a plan and an end view as seen from the left. Dimensions are not required.
2. Construct an isometric drawing of the component shown in Fig. 7.42.
3. Figure 7.43 is a rendering (see Chapter 15) of a slide fitting from a machine. Figure 7.44 is a two-view third angle projection of the slide. Working to the dimensions included with the drawing, construct a three-view, third angle orthographic projection of the slide. The end view should be taken as if looking from the left of the front view. Dimensions should not be included.

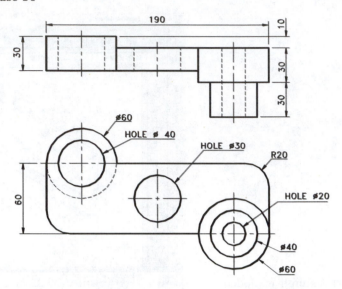

Fig. 7.42 Exercises 1 and 2

Fig. 7.43 A rendering for
Exercise 3

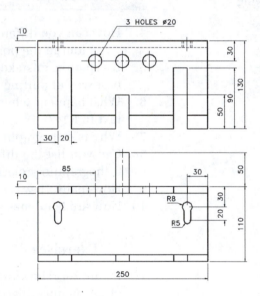

Fig. 7.44 Exercise 3

4. Figure 7.45 is a two-view first angle projection of a component from a machine. Working in third angle projection, construct the front view (the upper of the two views) and from it project a plan and an end view, with the end view seen as if from the left of the front view. Dimensions are not required.

5.   Construct an isometric drawing of the part shown in Fig. 7.45.

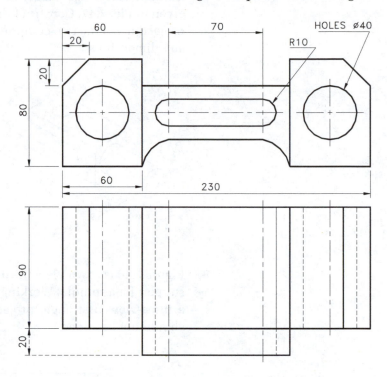

Fig. 7.45 Exercises 4 and 5

6.   An angle bracket is shown in an isometric drawing (Fig. 7.46). Construct an accurate three-view, first angle orthographic projection of the bracket.

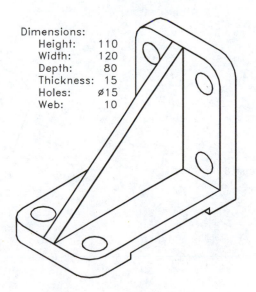

Dimensions:
  Height: 110
  Width: 120
  Depth: 80
  Thickness: 15
  Holes: ø15
  Web: 10

Fig. 7.46 Exercise 6

7. Isometric drawings – labelled **1** and **2** – of two components are given in Fig. 7.47. Construct three-view third angle orthographic projections of the two components. It is not necessary to include any dimensions.

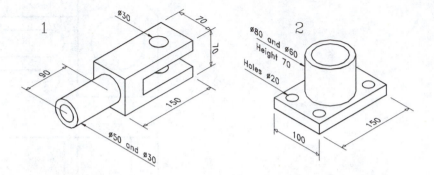

Fig. 7.47 Exercise 7

8. Figure 7.48 is a two-view third angle orthographic projection of a support for a spindle. Working in first angle projection, construct a three-view first angle projection of the support. Dimensions should not be added.

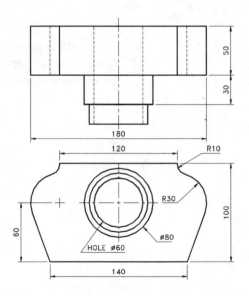

Fig. 7.48 Exercise 8

9. Figure 7.49 is a rendering of a bearing support. The bush in which a spindle is to run is shown in an exploded position. Figure 7.50 is a two-view first angle orthographic projection of the bearing support. Working to the given dimensions construct a three-view orthographic projection of the support, with an end viewed from what you consider to be the side showing the most details. No dimensions required.

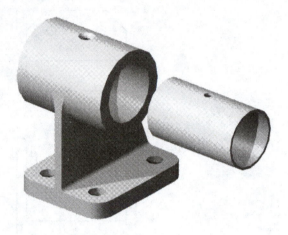

Fig. 7.49 A rendering of the support for exercise 9

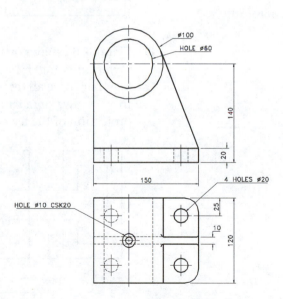

Fig. 7.50 Exercise 9

10. Figure 7.51 shows two parts of a wall support. Part B clips into Part A from the outside, in such a manner that it can revolve through 180°. Construct a three-view third angle orthographic projection of the two parts with Part B assembled in Part A in the horizontal position shown in Fig. 7.51. Dimensions should not be added to your views.

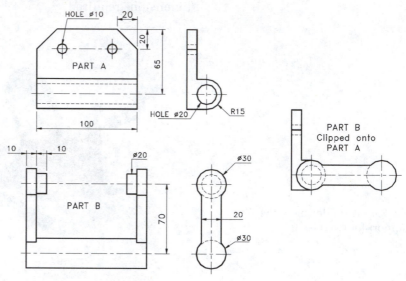

Fig. 7.51 Exercise 10

11. Figure 7.52 shows orthographic views of parts of an assembly. The lower drawing is a front view of the three parts assembled together. With all three parts in the position indicated in the lower front view, construct a three-view first angle orthographic projection of the assembly. No dimensions are necessary.

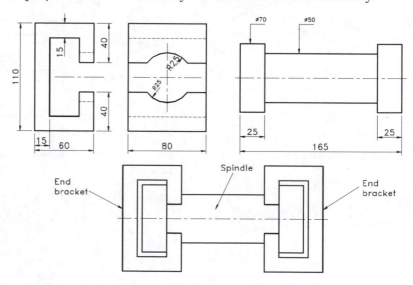

Fig. 7.52 Exercise 11

Plate I A two-view orthographic projection of a two-storey house showing the layers on which the drawing was constructed

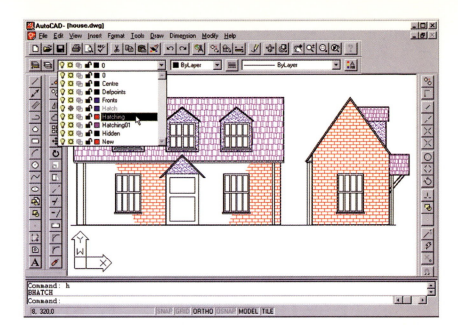

Plate II A three-view orthographic projection of a bracket with a bitmap pasted into the AutoCAD drawing area

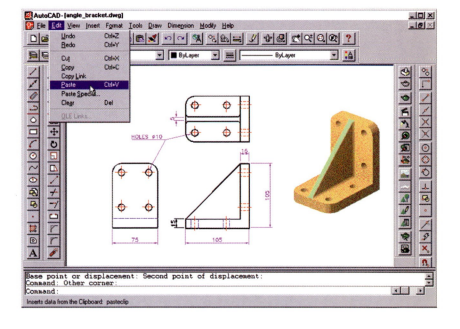

Plate III The drawing from Plate I pasted into a PageMaker document

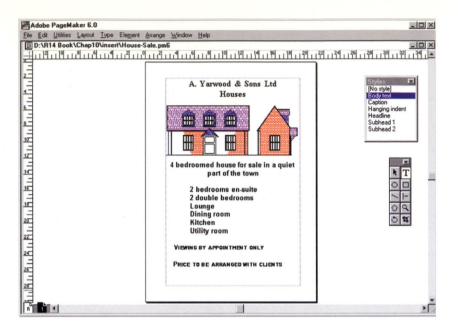

Plate IV A 3D solid model constructed in a four-viewport window (drawing area colour: black; Command window colour: blue)

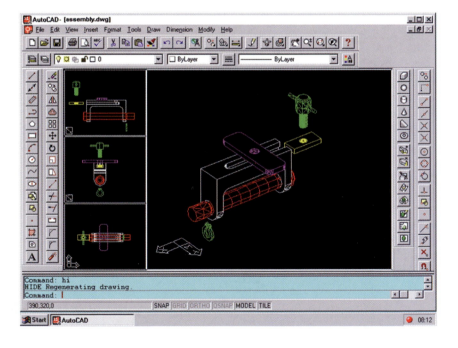

Plate V A 3D solid model of a house in a south-west isometric viewing position

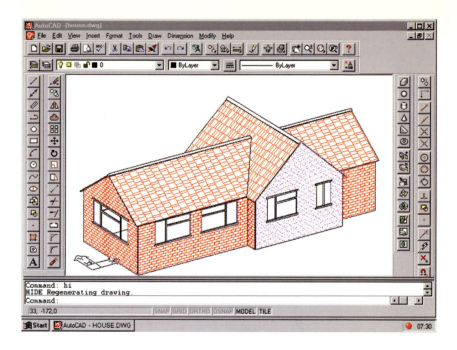

Plate VI A rendered 3D solid model

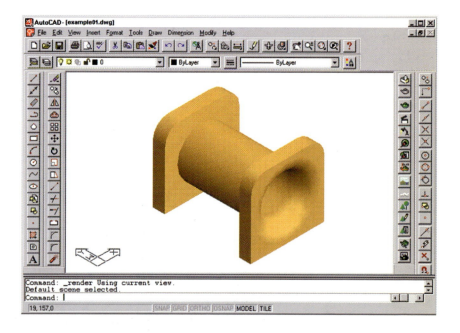

Plate VII A 3D assembly
model rendered against a
sky background

Plate VIII A 3D assembly
model rendered in several
materials

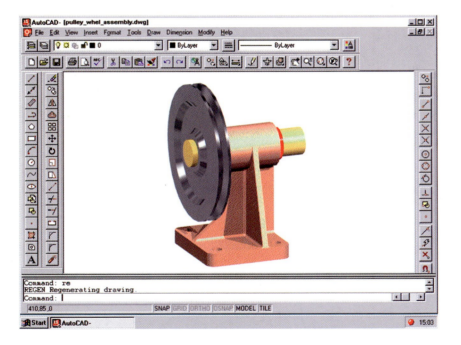

Plate IX An exploded 3D
solid model rendered in
two materials

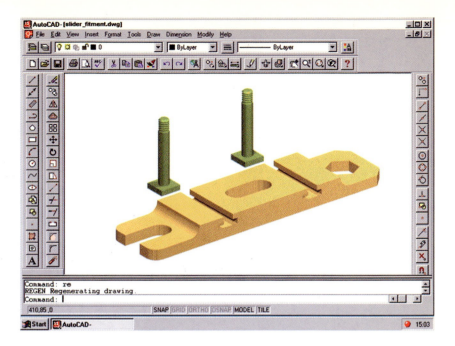

Plate X A 3D assembly
model rendered against a
magenta background;
several materials have
been assigned

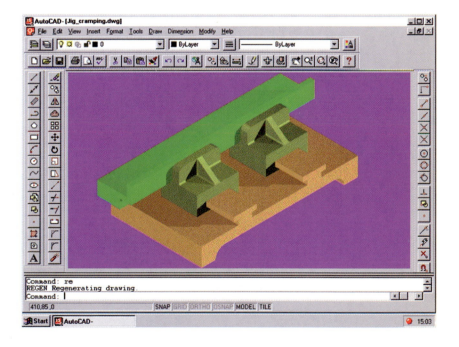

Plate XI A 3D solid model rendered against a blue background; several materials have been assigned

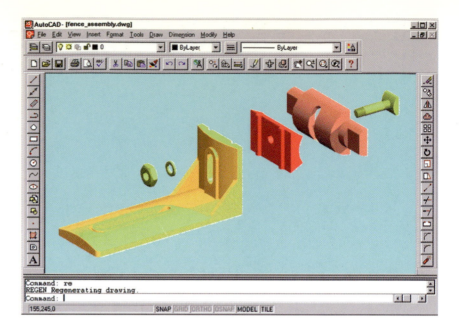

Plate XII A dimensioned three-view orthographic projection of an assembled component; a rendered 3D exploded view of the component is also shown

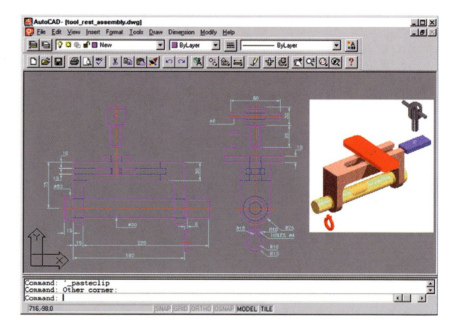

Plate XIII A rendering of a drill tray which has had a material assigned to its surfaces

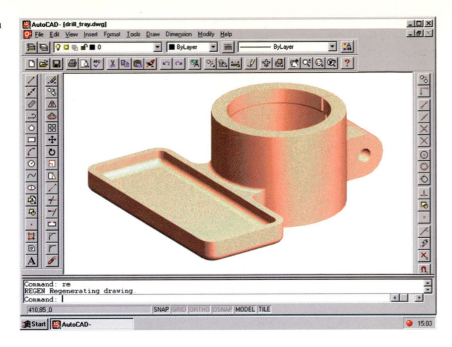

Plate XIV A rendering of a 3D solid model of a microsope part which has had the material **Brass Gifmap** assigned to its surface

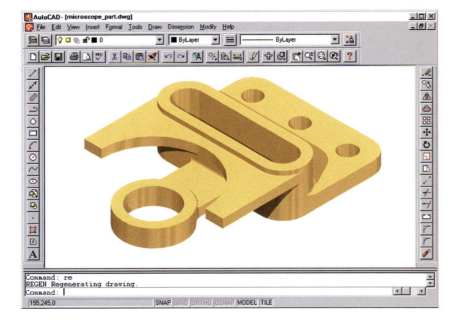

Plate XV   A 3D model of a saw handle rendered with the material **Whiteash** assigned against a blue background

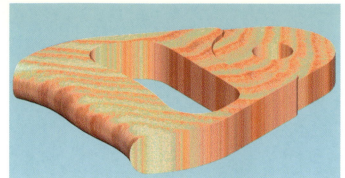

Plate XVI   A rendering of an assembly; different materials have been assigned to the various parts

Plate XVII   A rendering of a gear wheel with its spindle

Plate XVIII   A rendering in several materials against a sky background of parts of a lathe rest

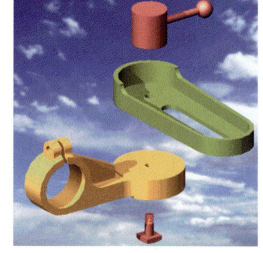

Fig. 7.53 A rendering for
Exercise 12.

Fig. 7.54 Exercise 12

12. Figure 7.53 is a rendering of a V-pulley and spindle in a bearing
block. Figure 7.54 is a two-view, third angle projection of the
assembly. Working to the given dimensions construct a three-
view orthographic projection of the pulley in its bearing block
using any angle of projection you consider to be suitable. No
dimensions are required.

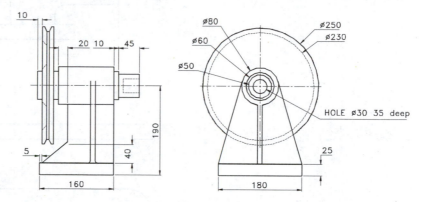

13. Figure 7.55 is a rendering of a pointing device. Figure 7.56 is a
front view and plan of the device. Working to the given dimensions,
construct a three-view, third angle orthographic projection of the
device. Do not include any dimensions.

Fig. 7.55 A rendering for
Exercise 13

14. Construct an isometric drawing of the body of the pointing device shown in Figures 7.55 and 7.56 – the part into which the spindle and the pointer fit.

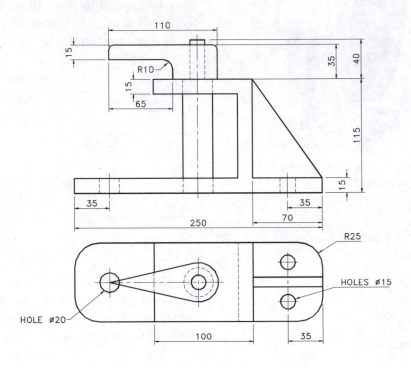

Fig. 7.56 Exercise 13

15. Go back to Fig. 7.52. Construct an isometric drawing of one of the end pieces of the assembly.

CHAPTER 8

Hatching

The Hatch tool

Some details about the using **Hatch** have already been given in Chapter 4.

To call the tool, either *left-click* on the **Hatch** icon in the **Draw** toolbar or on **Hatch...** in the **Draw** pull-down menu, or at the Command line *enter* h. See Fig. 8.1. Any one of these calls brings the **Boundary Hatch** dialogue box on screen (Fig. 8.2).

Do not *enter* hatch, because doing so will bring a number of prompts into the Command window, allowing settings for hatching to be made by *entering* prompt initials and responses. In the majority of cases where hatching is to be used, it can be more easily set up from the **Boundary Hatch** dialogue box.

To hatch an area

Figure 8.3 shows the steps necessary to fill an area with a hatch pattern using the **Boundary Hatch** dialogue box. Two examples are shown on the left of the dialogue box in Fig. 8.3. Proceed as follows:

Fig. 8.1 Methods of calling the **Hatch** tool

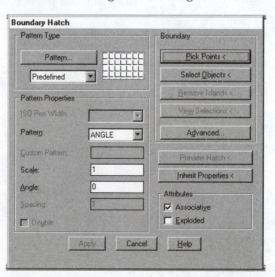

Fig. 8.2 The **Boundary Hatch** dialogue box

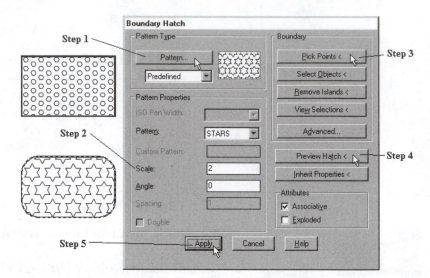

Fig. 8.3 Steps to fill an area with a hatch pattern

1. Call the **Hatch** tool (Fig. 8.1). The **Boundary Hatch** dialogue box appears.
2. **Step 1:** *Left-click* on the **Pattern...** button. The **Hatch pattern palette** box appears showing a range of patterns as icons (Fig. 8.4).

   If the desired pattern is not showing, *left-click* on the **Next** button and a second group of hatch icons appears (Fig. 8.5).
3. Locate the required pattern, *left-click* in its icon. The icon highlights. *Left-click* on the **OK** button, which causes the **Boundary Hatch** box to reappear.
4. **Step 2:** *Enter* the **Scale** required for the pattern in the **Scale:** box. In the upper of the two drawings in Fig. 8.3, the chosen pattern was **HEX** set to a scale of **1** (default scale). In the case of the lower drawing, the pattern was **STARS** set to a scale of **2**.

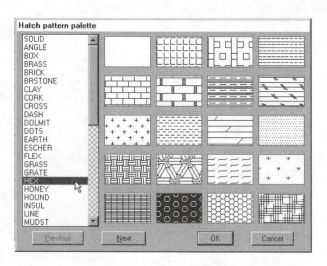

Fig. 8.4 The first of three default **Hatch pattern palette** boxes

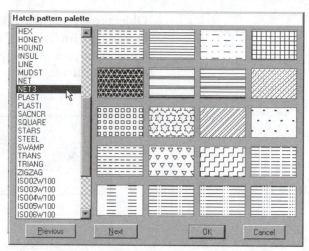

Fig. 8.5 The second of the **Hatch pattern palette** boxes

5. **Step 3:** *Left-click* in the **Pick Points<** button. The dialogue box disappears. *Left-click* in the area to be hatched. The outline of the area highlights to confirm correct choice of area. A *right-click* brings back the dialogue box.

6. **Step 4:** *Left-click* on the **Preview Hatch<** button. The dialogue box again disappears and the picked area is shown with the pattern to the set scale within the picked area. In the centre of the R14 window a message box (Fig. 8.6) appears. *Left-click* on its **Continue** button. The dialogue box reappears on screen.

7. **Step 5:** If satisfied that the hatched area is correct, *left-click* on the **Apply** button. The dialogue box disappears and the area is hatched.

Notes

1. If the preview of the hatching does not show the desired result, when the dialogue box reappears, changes made to the pattern, its scale or its angle will appear when the **Preview Hatch<** button is again used.

2. When selecting an area to be hatched, it must be a closed boundary. If an area is picked which is not closed – even with the slightest gap in the outline – the **Boundary Definition Error** box (Fig. 8.7) will appear. This does not necessarily mean the area cannot be hatched, but that the **Pick Point<** method cannot be used. Try the **Select**

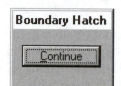

Fig. 8.6 The **Continue** message box

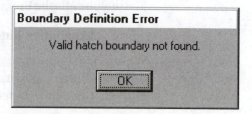

Fig. 8.7 The **Boundary Definition Error** box

Objects< button instead and *pick* each entity (object) forming the boundary. However, unwanted results may occur. Figure 8.8 shows some examples. Although the given examples show obvious gaps, they do indicate what happens no matter how large the gap.

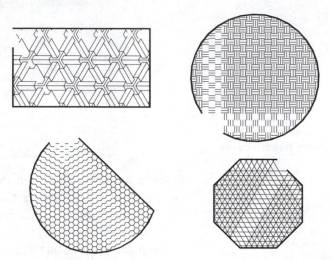

Fig. 8.8 Using **Select Objects<** when a boundary is not closed

3. In R14 **Solid** hatching can be achieved. The first of the names in the list of hatch patterns in the **Hatch patterns palette** is **SOLID**. When that pattern is called, the results will appear as those shown in Fig. 8.9. The three examples given in Fig. 8.9 show selection with the **Advanced Options Boundary Styles** set to the default of **Normal**.

Fig. 8.9 Three examples of **Solid** hatching

4. To set **Boundary Style**, *left-click* on the **Advanced...** button in the **Boundary Hatch** dialogue box. This brings up the **Advanced Options** box. In the **Boundary Style:** area of the box, a *left-click* in the **Style:** box brings a popup list into action (Fig. 8.10). Figure 8.11 shows simple examples of the three advanced styles.
5. Bhatch calls the **Boundary Hatch** dialogue from the Command line.

Associative hatching

When two boundaries, one inside the other, are hatched with different hatch patterns, if the inner boundary and its hatching are moved, the outer hatching accommodates to the move. This is

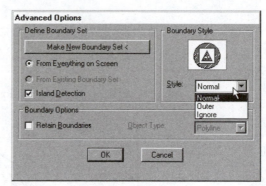

Fig. 8.10 The **Advanced Options** box

Fig. 8.11 Advanced styles of hatching

known as **Associative hatching** (Fig. 8.12). The circle within the **BRICK** hatching has been hatched with the **NET** pattern. Call **Move**. Window the circle and its hatching and the hatch and its boundary can be *dragged* to another position, even outside the **BRICK** area.

When associative hatching is set in the **Object Settings** dialogue box from the **Tools** pull-down menu, both the hatch boundary and hatching become associative.

If a boundary and its hatching are acted upon by the **Stretch** tool the hatching accommodates to the new boundary (Fig. 8.13).

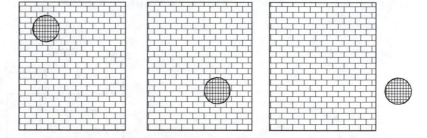

Fig. 8.12 Associative hatching. Using the **Move** tool

Examples of hatching

Hatching is used extensively when constructing working drawings for industries such as engineering and building and the examples which follow are taken from parts of simple engineering drawings or building drawings.

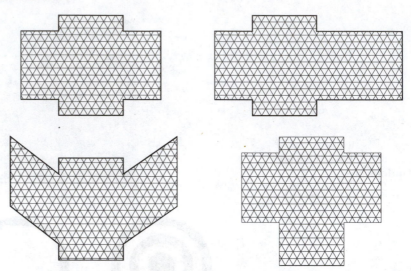

Fig. 8.13 Associative hatching.
Using the **Stretch** tool

Example 1 – Fig. 8.14

Figure 8.14 is a two-view third angle projection of an attachment bracket. The sectional view (left-hand view) is obtained by imagining a vertical plane cutting through the pin and its bracket, its edge signified by the letter **A** with arrows (right-hand view) pointing towards the direction from which the sectional view is to be obtained. The section plane is imagined as cutting through the parts of the assembly and what is in front of the view as seen from the right is thrown away, leaving a view of the cut surface.

The cut surface is then hatched. It is customary to use ANSI31 hatch pattern for this purpose in engineering drawing practice – lines at about 3 or 4 units apart at an angle of 45°.

Figure 8.14 shows examples of some of the rules governing such section hatching:

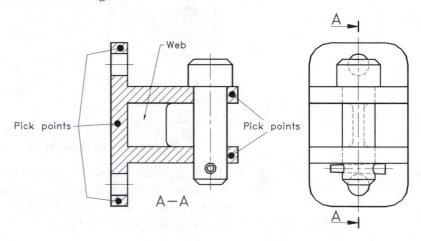

Fig. 8.14 Example 1

1. The edge of the section plane is shown as a centre line ending in thick lines with arrows pointing in the direction from which the sectional view should be seen.
2. The sectional view is labelled with the letters on the section plane line.
3. The arrows on the section plane line carry letters labelling the sectional view.
4. Features such as bolts, nuts, screws, ribs, webs and similar parts are shown in sections as outside views – thus the pin and web in the example are not hatched – i.e. they are shown as outside views.

Example 2 – Fig. 8.16

Figure 8.16 is a section taken through the centre of one of the webs (ribs) of the moveable jig placers of the device shown in Fig. 8.15. The example is given to show that, if several areas in an engineering drawing are adjacent to each other, either alternate angle hatching or hatching at different scales is necessary to distinguish one part from another.

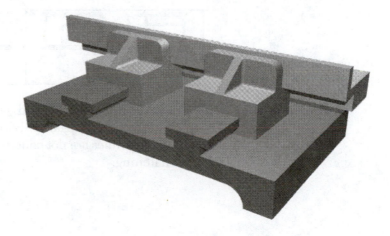

Fig. 8.15 Example 2. A rendering of the assembly from which the section was taken

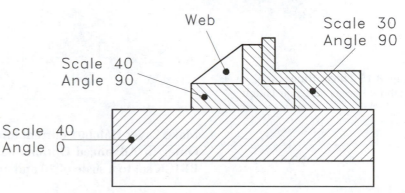

Fig. 8.16 Example 2

Example 3 – Fig. 8.20

This example – the hatching of the front view of a bungalow to show bricks, facing and roof tiles requires the use of several layers.

Fig. 8.17 Example 3 – the set of layers

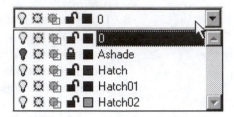

1. Set-up layers as shown in Fig. 8.17. Layer **0** black; Layer **Hatch** blue; Layer **Hatch01** red; Layer **Hatch02** cyan.
2. On layer **0** construct the outline of the front view (Fig. 8.18).

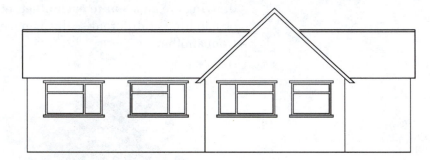

Fig. 8.18 Construction of outlines of front view

3. Make Layer **Hatch** current and, with the aid of the osnap **endpoint** and **AutoSnap**, construct polylines of width 0 as shown in Fig. 8.19. If these lines are not constructed, the windows may be filled with hatching.

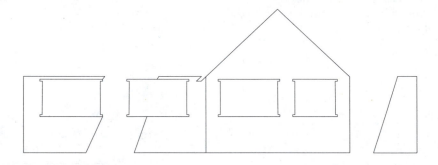

Fig. 8.19 The outlines for hatched areas on Layer **Hatch**

4. Make Layer **Hatch01** current and with the **Boundary Style** set to **Outer** in **Advanced Options** hatch the brickwork using pattern **BRICK** set to a scale of 20 and angle 0.

5. Make Layer **Hatch01** current and with pattern **AR-SAND** set to a scale of 2 and angle 0 hatch the face of the central portion of the view.
6. Make Layer **Hatch02** current and with pattern **AR-SHAKE** set to a scale of 0.7 hatch the two roof areas.
7. Freeze Layer **Hatch**.
   The results are shown in Fig. 8.20.

Fig. 8.20 Example 3

Example 4 – Fig. 8.21

When text is placed within an area to be hatched it automatically sets up its own invisible surround, protecting it, as it were, from becoming covered in the hatch pattern. An example is given in Fig. 8.21.

Fig. 8.21 Example 4

Example 5 – Fig. 8.22

If hatch is *entered* at the Command line, followed by *entering* a **?** and two *right-clicks* an AutoCAD Text window appears showing the names of available patterns and, what can be very useful, the materials they are assumed to represent. Figure 8.22 shows part of the whole text window, which runs to several **Return** key presses.

Example 6 – Figs 8.23 and 8.24

Figure 8.23 is a two-view projection of a two-storey house. The views were constructed using the same techniques as for the

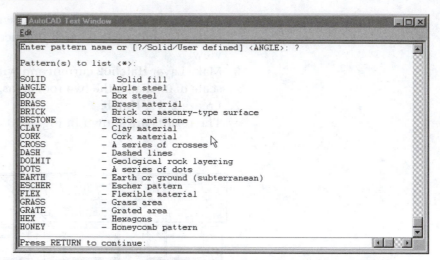

Fig. 8.22 The results of calling hatch from the Command line

Fig. 8.23 Example 6

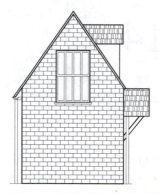

Fig. 8.24 Example 6. Taking advantage of associative hatching to move the window in the end view

Example 3. After constructing the end view, it could be seen that the window was wrongly positioned. It was easily re-positioned because of associative hatching (Fig. 8.24).

Example 7 – Fig. 8.25

For this example, hatch was *entered* at the Command line which showed the following prompts for the right-hand drawing of Fig. 8.25:

Command: *enter* hatch *right-click*
Enter pattern name or (?/Solid/User defined) <DOTS>: *enter* hound *right-click*
Scale for pattern <1>: *enter* 2 *right-click*
Angle for pattern <0>: *right-click*
Select hatch boundaries or press ENTER for direct hatch option: *Return* (press Return key)
Select objects: *right-click*
Retain polyline <Y>: *enter* n (No) *right-click*

From point: *pick*
Arc/Close/Length/Undo/<Next point>: *pick*
Arc/Close/Length/Undo/<Next point>: *pick*
Arc/Close/Length/Undo/<Next point>: *pick*
Arc/Close/Length/Undo/<Next point>: *enter* c (Close) *right-click*

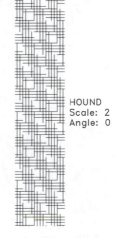

HOUND
Scale: 2
Angle: 0

Fig. 8.25 Example 7

HONEY
Scale: 2
Angle: 0

DOTS
Scale: 2
Angle: 0

Command:

Questions

1.   How is the **Hatch** tool called into use?
2.   What is the difference between the results of *entering* hatch and *entering* bhatch at the Command line?
3.   If there is an existing area filled with a hatch pattern, how can the pattern be copied to the same scale and angle by using one of the buttons in the **Boundary Hatch** dialogue box?
4.   What is the rule about hatching a spindle within a sectional view?
5.   Why is it necessary to ensure that boundaries are closed before they can be filled with hatch patterns?
6.   What are the differences between hatching with **Boundary Style** set to **Normal** compared to when it is set to **Ignore**.
7.   What is meant by Associative Hatching?
8.   What is the effect of using the **Stretch** tool on an area which has been hatched?
9.   There are several ways in which an area can be hatched without showing the boundary of the area. Can you describe two methods?
10. What is the rule about the hatching of adjacent areas?

Exercises

1. Figure 8.26 is a rendering of a pulley wheel. Figure 8.27 shows a two-view first angle projection of the wheel.

    Copy the given front view (the left-hand of the two views) and add a sectional end view on a section plane taken vertically central to the wheel.

    Work to the given dimensions, but do not include them.

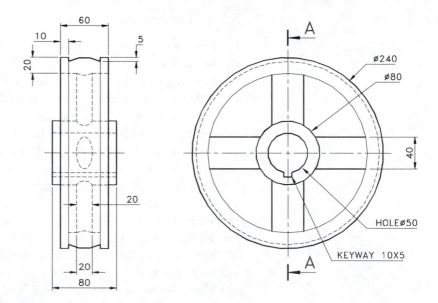

Fig. 8.26 A rendering of the pulley wheel – Exercise 1

Fig. 8.27 Exercise 1

2.   Figure 8.28. Using suitable tools construct the outline pattern shown. Then, using a suitable hatch pattern add hatching to the areas shown.

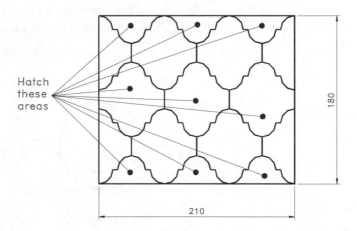

Fig. 8.28 Exercise 2

3.   The construction of Fig. 8.29 makes use of the **Polyline** tool, at least two layers and a couple of hatch patterns. Working to any suitable sizes, construct a similar drawing.

Fig. 8.29 Exercise 3

4.   Figure 8.30 is a rendering of a rotate link from a machine. It consists of a link arm (dimensioned details of which are given in Fig. 8.30) and two spindles, the narrower being 140 long, the thicker being 100 long.

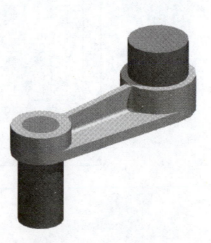

Fig. 8.30 Rendering of rotate link for Exercise 4

With the two spindles in position within the link arm, construct the following views:

(a) A plan – the upper view in Fig. 8.31.
(b) A front sectional view, the section plane to lie central to the holes as seen in the plan.

Do not dimension your drawing.

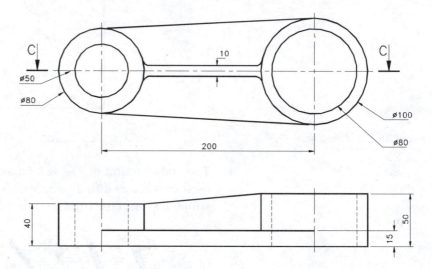

Fig. 8.31 Exercise 4

5.   Using the tools **Polyline**, **Hatch** and **Mirror** and working to sizes of your own choice, copy the pattern given in Fig. 8.32.

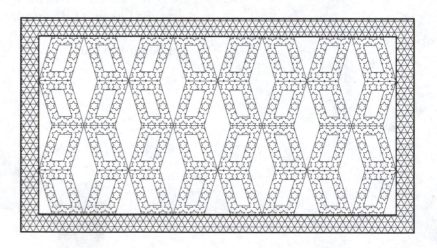

Fig. 8.32 Exercise 5

6. Figure 8.33 is a two-view orthographic projection in first angle of a slide support from a machine. Working to the given dimensions construct the following two views of the support:

(a) The plan.
(b) The sectional view **B-B**.

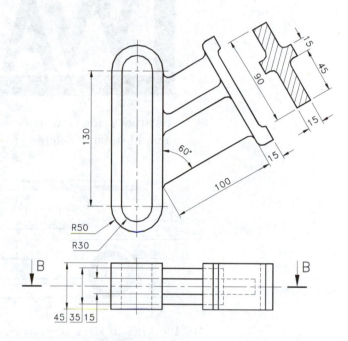

Fig. 8.33 Exercise 6

7. The dimensions shown in the front view of a bungalow in Fig. 8.34 are obviously not the full scale sizes of the building, they are included with the drawing to suggest sizes to which you can work.
   Copy the given view and using suitable hatch patterns add hatching as thought fit.

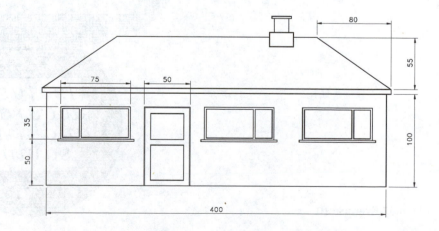

Fig. 8.34 Exercise 7

8. Using **Polyline**, **Arc** and **Hatch** construct the design given in Fig. 8.35.

Fig. 8.35 Exercise 8

9. Construct a side view of a vehicle such as that shown in Fig. 8.36 and add suitable hatching to parts to emphasise its shape.

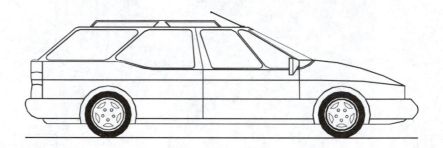

Fig. 8.36 Exercise 9

10. Working to sizes of your own discretion, construct a drawing similar to that shown in Fig. 8.37.

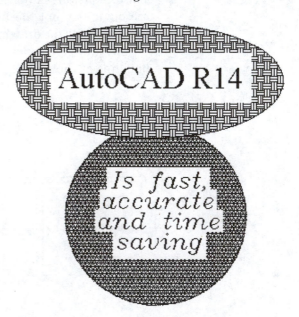

Fig. 8.37 Exercise 10

CHAPTER 9

Dimensions

The Dimension toolbar

To bring the **Dimension** toolbar on screen:

1. *Right-click* in any toolbar already on screen.
2. The **Toolbars** dialogue box appears.
3. Scroll the **Toolbars:** list until the name **Dimension** appears. *Left-click* in its check box. The **Dimension** toolbar then appears (Fig. 9.1).
4. Close the **Toolbars** dialogue box – *left-click* on its close button. Figure 9.2 shows the names of the tools in the toolbar.

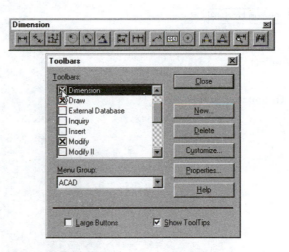

Fig. 9.1 Bringing the **Dimension** toolbar on screen

Setting a dimension style

1. *Left-click* on the **Dimension Style** tool icon in the toolbar (Fig. 9.2). This brings the **Dimension Styles** dialogue box on screen (Fig. 9.3).
2. The dialogue box has three sub dialogue boxes, called by *left-clicks* on the respective buttons in the **Dimension Styles** dialogue box:

Geometry: Figure 9.4. *Left-click* on **Geometry...** button.

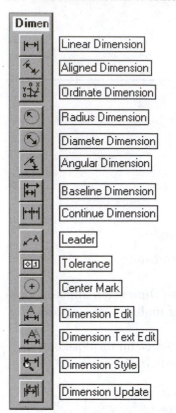

Fig. 9.2 The tools in the **Dimension** toolbar

Fig. 9.3 The **Dimension Styles** dialogue box

Fig. 9.4 The **Geometry** dialogue box

Format: Figure 9.5. *Left-click* on **Format...** button
Annotation: Figure 9.6. *Left-click* on **Annotation...** button.

3. Make settings in each of the three boxes as shown in Figs 9.4 to 9.6. These are the settings which have been used in most of the dimensions for drawings throughout this book. The reader need not necessarily follow all the settings shown, but it is advisable at this stage to make the dimension style settings for one's own purposes and then save them to the template in use. My settings as shown here have been saved to my **ay.dwt** template.

Different methods of linear dimensioning

Figure 9.7 shows eight different methods of dimensioning a front view of a spindle using the **Linear Dimension** tool. The differences

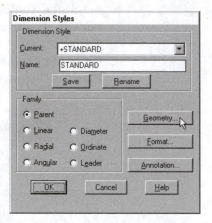

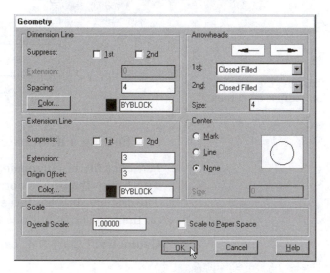

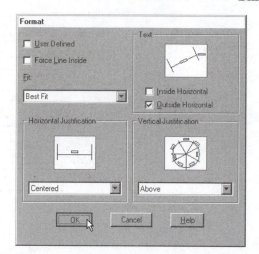

Fig. 9.5 The **Format** dialogue box

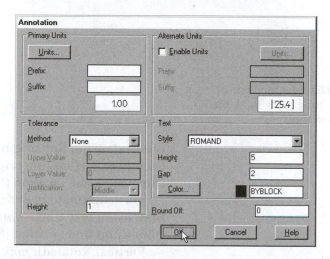

Fig. 9.6 The **Annotation** dialogue box

relate to settings in the three parts of the **Dimension Styles** dialogue box. Thus:

Arrows: Set in the **Geometry** dialogue box.
Position of dimensions: Set in the **Annotation** dialogue box.
Tolerance: Set in the **Tolerance** area of the **Annotation** dialogue box.
Prefix or/and Suffix: Set in the **Primary Units** area of the **Annotation** dialogue box.

Notes

1. When calling, say, **Linear Dimension** from the **Dimension** toolbar, the following sequence of prompts appears at the Command line:

Command:
DIMLINEAR

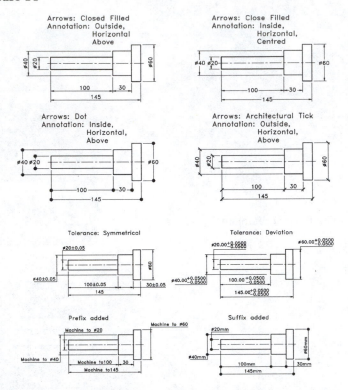

Fig. 9.7 Different methods of dimensioning using the **Linear Dimension** tool

First extension line origin or press ENTER to select: *pick*
Second extension line origin: *pick*
**Dimension line location (Mtext/Text/Angle/Horizontal/
    Vertical/Rotated):** *enter* t (Text) *right-click*
Dimension text < 60>: *enter* %%C60 *right-click*
**Dimension line location (Mtext/Text/Angle/Horizontal/
    Vertical/Rotated):** *pick*
Command:

2. Figures for the dimensions are normally automatically applied.
3. However, in the examples given in Fig. 9.7, the diameter symbol Ø can only be *entered* by using the **Text** prompt in the sequence at the Command Line when dimension tools are used. Then it must be *entered* as **%%c** preceding the figures. This is only necessary when using the **Linear Dimension** tool, not when using the **Diameter** tool.
4. If the Ø symbol is to be included with a suffix or a prefix, it will be necessary to use the **Text** prompt and *enter* the text at the Command Line.

Other tools in the Dimension toolbar

Figure 9.8 shows examples of using some of the other tools from the **Dimension** toolbar.

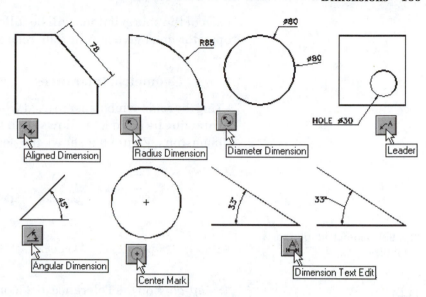

Fig. 9.8 Using other tools from the **Dimension** toolbar

Dimensions from the Command line

Selecting tools from the icons in the **Dimension** toolbar is not the only way of adding dimensions to a drawing. To add a dimension by *entering* responses to prompts at the Command line:

> **Command:** *enter* dim *right-click*
> **Dim:** *enter* hor (Horizontal) *right-click*
> **First extension line origin or press ENTER to select:** *pick*
> **Second extension line origin:** *pick*
> **Dimension line location (Text/Angle):** *pick*
> **Dimension text (145):** either *right-click* to accept, or *enter* new dimension (e.g. %%C145) *right-click*
> **Dim:**

Another dimension can now be added to a drawing.

Other abbreviations when entering from Command line

The abbreviation given above for Horizontal (hor) can be replaced by other dimension abbreviations:

ve:	Vertical
l:	Leader
ra:	Radius
d:	Diameter
al:	Aligned
te:	Similar action to **Dimension Text Edit**
an:	Angular
cen:	Center Mark

Each of the abbreviations will be followed by prompts to which the operator must give appropriate responses.

Geometric tolerances

Using the same symbols as are used when adding geometric tolerances to drawing by hand R14 allows such tolerances to be included with dimensions. Figure 9.9 shows the geometric tolerance symbols

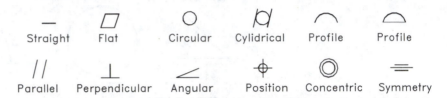

Straight   Flat   Circular   Cylidrical   Profile   Profile

Parallel   Perpendicular   Angular   Position   Concentric   Symmetry

Fig. 9.9 Geometric tolerance symbols

Fig. 9.10 Selecting the **Tolerance** tool from the **Dimension** toolbar

Fig. 9.11 The **Symbol** box

1. *Left-click* on the **Tolerance** tool icon in the **Dimension** toolbar (Fig. 9.10) and the **Symbol** box appears (Fig. 9.11).

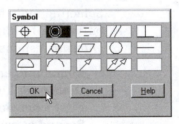

2. *Left-click* on the required symbol and the **Geometric Tolerance** dialogue box appears, with the selected symbol placed in the **Sym** area of the box (Fig. 9.12).

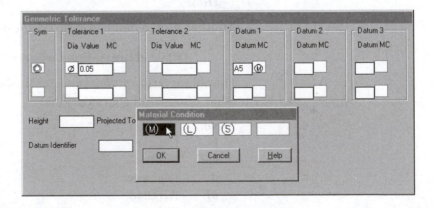

Fig. 9.12 The **Geometric Tolerance** dialogue box

3. *Left-click* in the **Dia** box of the **Tolerance 1** area of the box and a diameter symbol appears (in this example).

4. *Enter* A5 in the **Datum 1** area, followed by a *left-click* in the box to the right of A5. This brings up the **Material Condition** box as shown in Fig. 9.12. *Left-click* on the **M** followed by another on the **OK** button. The **M** appears next to A5.

5. *Left-click* on the **OK** button of the **Geometric Tolerance** dialogue box and the required geometric tolerance appears, being *dragged* at the intersection of the cursor cross hairs. Figure 9.13 shows the tolerance produced by the entries made in this example. *Drag* the tolerance into position next to the dimension to which it belongs and *left-click*.

Fig. 9.13 An example of a geometric tolerance produced in R14

Figure 9.14 shows some examples of geometric tolerances included with dimensions.

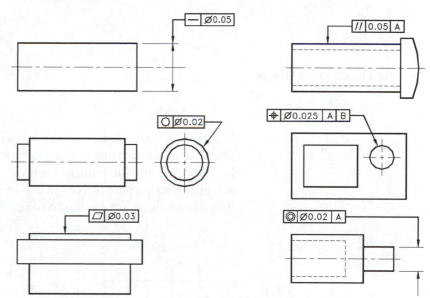

Fig. 9.14 Examples of geometric tolerances

The action of Scale and Stretch on dimensions

In general dimensions in R14 are **associative**. When working to a scale of 1:1 (full size), the dimension automatically appearing when points for a dimension are *picked* is the same as the unit distance between the points or, when dimensioning radius or diameter, the unit radius or diameter of the arc or circle.

Because dimensions are associative, if a drawing is stretched or scaled, dimensions automatically associate with the new scale or stretch of the drawing.

The action of Stretch on dimensions

Figure 9.15 shows the effects of using **Stretch** on the dimensions of the drawing number **1**. Drawing **2** shows stretch applied horizontally, Drawing **3** when stretch is applied vertically and Drawing **4** when stretch is applied to a corner.

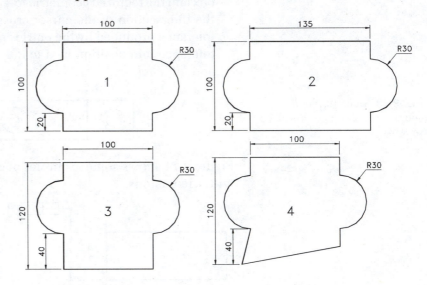

Fig. 9.15 The effects of **Stretch**

Scale

Figure 9.16 shows the effect of scaling a drawing to a larger size and also to a smaller. When scaling in this fashion, the dimensions must be included in the scaling window. The changes in dimensions accommodating themselves to the new scales is due to the fact that R14 dimensions are associative.

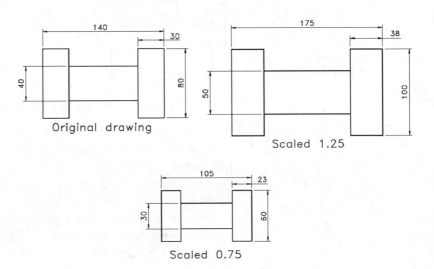

Fig. 9.16 The effect of **Scale** on dimensions

The %% symbols

These have been given earlier (page 127) in this book, but are repeated here because of their importance when adding dimensions to a drawing.

%%c   Ø symbol for diameter.
%%d   ° symbol for degrees.
%%p   ± symbol for tolerances.
%%%   symbol for %.

Questions

1. Will the use of **Stretch** affect a radius dimension?
2. Can you name five of the dimension abbreviations when *entering* dimensions at the Command line?
3. How is the **Dimension** toolbar called to screen?
4. What happens when the **Dimension Style** tool icon is selected?
5. What settings can be made in the **Geometry** dialogue box of **Dimension Styles**?
6. What settings can be made in the **Annotation** dialogue box of **Dimension Styles**?
7. Is it necessary to change the **Linear Dimension** tool when adding horizontal and vertical dimensions to a drawing?
8. For which purposes would the **Leader** dimension tool be used?
9. Can you name the steps needed to add a geometric tolerance to a drawing?
10. What happens when **%%c60 mm** is *entered* for a dimension?

Exercises

If you have saved the drawings resulting from exercises in previous chapters, now is the time to load them and add dimensions.

Exercises 1, 2 and 3 are from drawings which have been constructed inside a grid of 10 unit squares. To construct the drawings, count the number of squares occupied by each part of the drawing, multiply by 10 and take this as the size to which dimensions should be taken.

1. Figure 9.17. Count the number of 10 unit sides for each part of the outline given. Construct the outline and add dimensions.
2. Figure 9.18. Count the number of 10 unit sides for each part of the outline given. Construct the outline and add dimensions.
3. Figure 9.19. Count the number of 10 unit sides for each part of the outline given. Construct the outline and add dimensions.

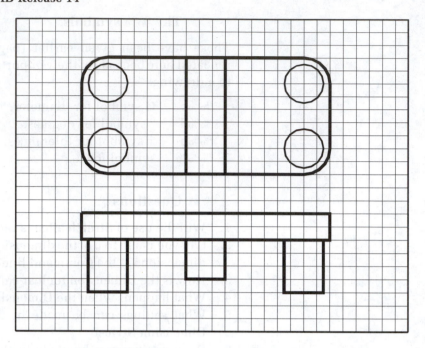

Fig. 9.17 Exercise 1

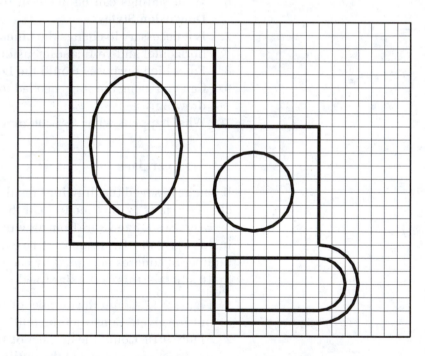

Fig. 9.18 Exercise 2

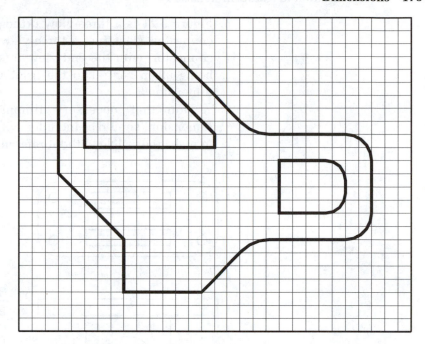

Fig. 9.19 Exercise 3

4. Figure 9.20 is a front view of an arm from a machine. Construct the given drawing and add all dimensions.

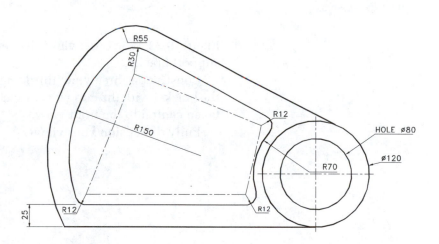

Fig. 9.20 Exercise 4

5. Figure 9.21 is a three-view orthographic projection of a towbar connector. Construct a three-view third angle projection of the connector, with the end view in section, the section plane line being taken central to the front view. Then add all necessary dimensions.

Note that 'necessary dimensions' means that sufficient dimensions should be included with the drawing to enable anyone to make the article without reference to other drawings.

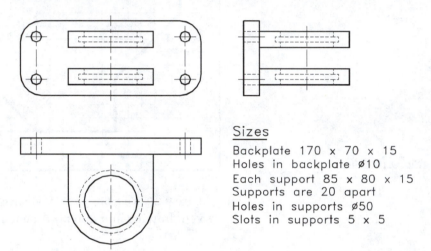

Sizes

Backplate 170 x 70 x 15
Holes in backplate ø10
Each support 85 x 80 x 15
Supports are 20 apart
Holes in supports ø50
Slots in supports 5 x 5

Fig. 9.21 Exercise 5

6. Figure 9.22 is a three-view first angle projection of a spindle support bracket.

Construct a three-view third angle orthographic projection of the bracket with the end view in section, the sectional plane being taken central to the front view.

Fully dimension your views.

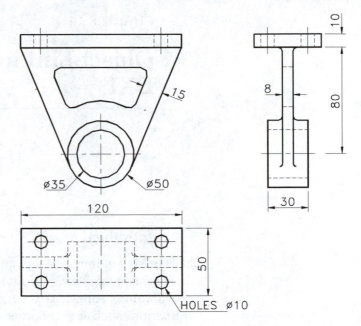

Fig. 9.22 Exercise 6

CHAPTER 10

Object Linking and Embedding. DXF

Introduction

Object linking and embedding allows graphics files from one application to be pasted into another application, or linked with another application. For example an AutoCAD drawing can be pasted into, or linked with applications such as word processing packages, desktop publishing packages and the like. It also means that in R14, graphic images from other applications can be pasted into or linked with AutoCAD.

Embedded graphics

When a graphic object is embedded from one application to another, usually with the **Paste** command (common to all Windows 95 applications), there is no link between the graphic object in the application from which it originated and the graphic into which it has been pasted. Changes subsequently made in the original graphic are not taken into the embedded graphic.

Linked graphics

When a graphic object is linked from one application to another, changes made in the original graphic automatically update in the linked graphic. Thus, if an AutoCAD drawing is linked in a desktop publishing application, any subsequent changes made to the AutoCAD drawing also take place in the linked object.

The Windows Clipboard Viewer

Linking or embedding take place via the Windows **Clipboard Viewer**. The object to be linked or embedded into another application is first pasted in the Clipboard Viewer, from which it can be linked or embedded into other applications. Usually, there is no need to even know that the Clipboard is in use because it functions without having to appear in a window.

If, however, one wishes to see the contents of the **Clipboard Viewer**, *left-click* on its icon and name in the Windows 95 start-up window. Figure 10.1 shows its position in the hierarchy of applications.

Fig. 10.1 Opening the **Clipboard Viewer**

In the examples which follow, some of the illustrations show the Clipboard appearing on screen with the object being acted upon by OLE. This is only to allow the reader to see clearly that the Clipboard is the agent through which the OLE system functions.

Examples of the use of OLE

Example 1 – Fig. 10.3

1. A rendering of an angle bracket is loaded into the Windows 95 **Paint** programme. This graphic is a bitmap (Fig07.bmp) which was produced from a rendering of a 3D model of the angle bracket, itself constructed in R14. See Chapters 13 and 14.
2. *Left-click* on **Select All**, followed by another on **Copy** in the **Edit** pull-down menu of **Paint** (Fig. 10.2). The bitmap is loaded into the **Clipboard Viewer**.
3. Load the drawing **angle_bracket.dwg** into R14.
4. In the **Edit** pull-down menu *left-click* on **Paste**. The bitmap of the rendering appears in the R14 window, complete with handles by which the bitmap can be re-sized (Fig. 10.3). If the cursor is moved inside the area of the rectangle covered by the handles a **Move** cursor appears allowing the bitmap to be moved into position in the R14 window.

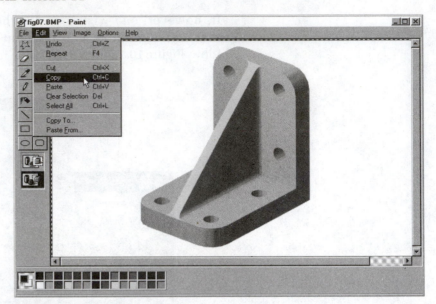

Fig. 10.2 Example 1. A rendering of an angle bracket loaded into **Paint**

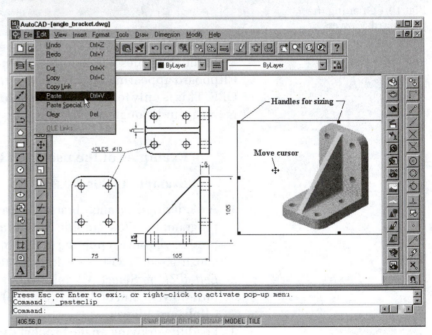

Fig. 10.3 Example 1. The bitmap from **Paint** pasted into R14

5. When the bitmap has been re-sized and moved into position, *left-click* in the R14 window outside the handle and the bitmap is pasted.

Example 2

1. Load the drawing **house.dwg** into R14.

2. *Left-click* on **Copy** in the **Edit** pull-down menu. The Command line shows:

   Command: 'copyclip
   Select objects: *enter* w (Window) right-click
   First corner: *pick* **Other corner:** *pick* **241 found**
   Select objects: *right-click*
   Command:

3. The windowed part of the R14 drawing appears on the **Clipboard** (which does not need to appear, but is shown in Fig. 10.4).

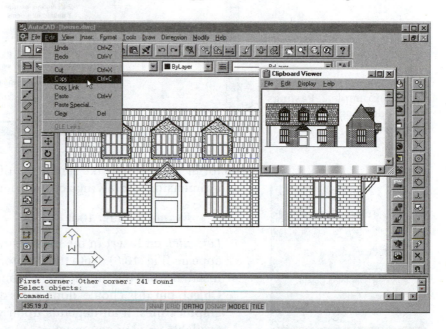

Fig. 10.4 Example 2. Using **Copy** in the drawing in R14

4. Open the application **PageMaker 6.0** with a new A4 sheet loaded portrait fashion.
5. In The **Edit** pull-down menu of **PageMaker**, *left-click* on **Paste**. The R14 drawing appears in the A4 sheet (Fig. 10.5).
6. Text can now be added to the **PageMaker** sheet as appropriate – as shown in Fig. 10.5.

Inserting objects

R14 can insert a variety of graphics from a number of different file types. Only one example of this will be given here, but the reader is advised to experiment with this facility. The ability to be able to insert bitmap files of the types ***.wmf** (Window metafiles) ***.bmp** (bitmap files) ***.pcx** (another type of bitmap file in common use) among others, is a useful facility when one wishes to combine a

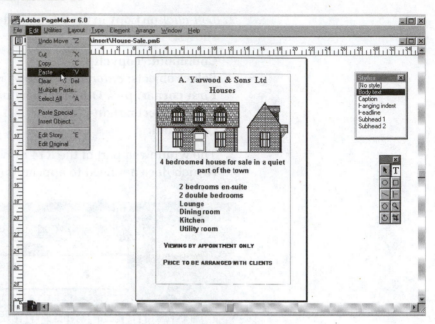

Fig. 10.5 Example 2. **Pasting** the R14 drawing into **PageMaker**

Fig. 10.6 The **Insert** pull-down menu

pictorial photograph-like rendering of a component with detailed and dimensioned drawings of the component.

Example – Fig. 10.8

1. *Left-click* on **Insert** in the menu bar. The **Insert** pull-down menu appears (Fig. 10.6). Note the different types of files which can be inserted from the menu. We are only concerned here with **OLE Object**, but this choice alone gives access to many other types of graphics files. It all depends upon which applications you have available on your computer.

2. The **Insert Object** dialogue box appears (Fig. 10.7). *Left-click* on **Hijaak Image**. Set **Create from File** active – *left-click* in its check circle to turn it on.

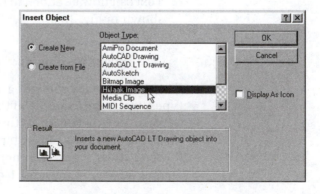

Fig. 10.7 The **Insert Object** dialogue box

3. Another dialogue box appears (Fig. 10.8). *Left-click* on the **Browse...** button. A **Browse** dialogue box then appears from which a file can be selected. *Left-click* on the desired file name, followed by another on the **OK** button, or *double-click* on the file name. The graphics for that file will appear in the R14 window as shown in Fig. 10.8.

4. The graphics will appear in the R14 window with handles and some form of **Move** cursor. These allow the graphic image to be sized and positioned in relation to other features in the drawing.

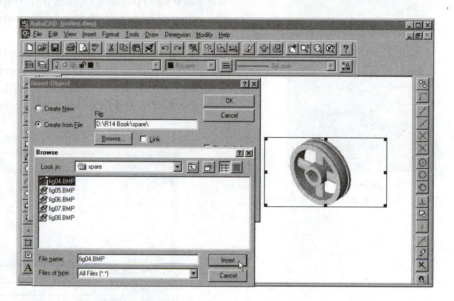

Fig. 10.8 Example

Notes

1. I have chosen **Hijaak Image** because **Hijaak 95** (an application with excellent graphics facilities) is on my computer. Hijaak 95 can deal with practically any known graphics type of file.

2. R14 can both save and open ***wmf** graphics files. These are particularly useful because they are a blend of vector and raster graphics. AutoCAD drawing files are purely vector files – the mathematics for each part of each object has to be stored. ***.bmp** files are raster files – the actual positions of pixels and their colours are stored in the file. Thus ***.wmf** files are particularly useful in storing a blend of both forms of graphics.

DXF files (Drawing Interchange Files)

Exporting a dxf file

DXF files are of great importance throughout all brands of Computer Aided Design software, because they allow the interchange of drawing files between CAD systems from different software manufacturers. Although the format of DXF files is essentially an AutoCAD introduction, it has been taken up and recognised throughout the world as the file type to interchange files between systems.

To save a drawing in DXF format:

1. *Left-click* on **Export...** in the **File** pull-down menu (Fig. 10.9).
2. The **Export Data** dialogue box (Fig. 10.10) appears. A *left-click* in the **Save as type:** box causes a popup list to appear displaying all the types of files which can be exported. It is worthwhile studying this list.
3. Select **AutoCAD R14 DXF (*.dxf)** and *enter* a file name in the **File name:** box, followed by a *left-click* on the **Save** button. The drawing is saved to the *entered* file name with the extension ***.dxf**. The file can now be loaded into any CAD systems as well as into AutoCAD.

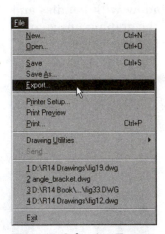

Fig. 10.9 Selecting **Export...** from the **File** pull-down menu

Fig. 10.10 The **Export Data** dialogue box

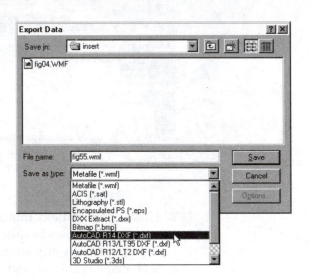

Importing a dxf file

Before a DXF file can be imported into R14, a new drawing must be created which has no settings within its make-up. This is achieved by:

1. *Left-click* on **New** in the **File** pull-down menu.
2. The **Create New Drawing** dialogue box (Fig. 10.11) appears. *Left-click* on the **Start from Scratch** button and in the **Select Default Settings** list, *left-click* again on **Metric**, followed by yet another *left-click* on the **OK** button. The screen clears and the R14 drawing area is without any settings.

An existing DXF file can now be loaded:

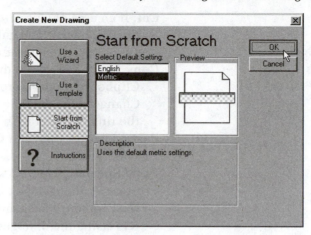

Fig. 10.11 The **Create New Drawing** dialogue box

Command: *enter* dxfin *right-click*

And the **Select DXF File** dialogue box appears (Fig. 10.12), from which a file can be selected. Select the required file, which loads in much the same manner as would an AutoCAD ***.dwg** file.

Note: It must be remembered that if it is attempted to load a DXF file into a drawing area which contains any settings, then the load will fail. It may not fail completely and part of the entities within a drawing may well load, but the whole drawing is unlikely to do so.

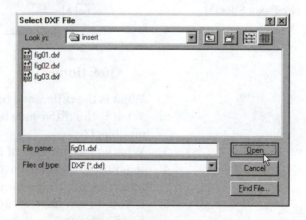

Fig. 10.12 The **Select DXF File** dialogue box

Other commands from the Edit menu

Undo: Undoes the results of the action of the last tool (command used). One can repeatedly undo right back to the beginning of the current drawing session. *Entering* u (for Undo) at the Command line is a much faster option.

Redo: Redoes only the last action undone. Will not redo anything else.

Cut: If an area of a drawing is cut, only that area will appear on the **Clipboard**. The cut area disappears from the drawing.

Copy: An example has already been given.

Copy Link: The whole drawing is automatically placed on the **Clipboard**, from where it can be linked into other applications. Changes then made in the AutoCAD drawing are reflected in the linked drawing in the other application.

Paste: Objects from the **Clipboard** can be pasted into the R14 window.

Paste Special: A *left-click* on this command brings up the **Paste Special** dialogue box (Fig. 10.13). Providing something is on the **Clipboard** from another application, it can be pasted into R14 using the dialogue box.

Clear: Has a similar effect to **Erase**.

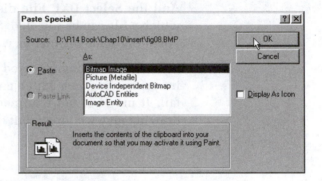

Fig. 10.13 The **Paste Special** dialogue box

Questions

1. What is the difference between the uses for **Copy** and **Copy Link**?
2. What is the difference between embedding an object and linking an object?
3. What is the purpose of the Windows **Clipboard Viewer**?
4. If a bitmap object is pasted into an R14 drawing, can the drawing be printed with the bitmap appearing in the printout?
5. If you do not have an application such as **Hijaak 95** loaded into your computer, is it possible to paste Hijaak images into an R14 drawing?
6. A DXF file can only be loaded into a new drawing. What is meant by a new drawing with respect to loading a DXF file?
7. DXF files used to be known as Data eXchange Files. Why is the new name Drawing Interchange files a better description of the file type?
8. To load a DXF file, what must be *entered* at the Command line?

9. What happens if an attempt is made to import a DXF file into a drawing area which has previously made settings, such as drawing limits?
10. What is the purpose of the command **Cut** from the **Edit** pull-down menu?

Exercises

If you have saved any of your drawings in answer to exercises set in earlier chapters, practise saving them as DXF files and then re-loading them into R14. Better still, if you have access to another CAD system, try loading the DXF files from R14 into this CAD system.

CHAPTER 11

Blocks and Inserts

Introduction

Any AutoCAD drawing (File name extension ***.dwg**) can be inserted into any other AutoCAD drawing. In addition, any part of an AutoCAD drawing can be saved as a separate drawing file and if necessary inserted into another AutoCAD drawing. The two tools which make these tasks possible are **Make Block** and **Insert Block**. In addition, another tool, the command **wblock** can be used to create a file from a drawing or part of a drawing.

Libraries of symbols

Libraries of symbols on disks (floppy and/or CD-ROM) can be purchased for the construction of circuits such as those used in electrical engineering, mechanical engineering etc. The symbols,

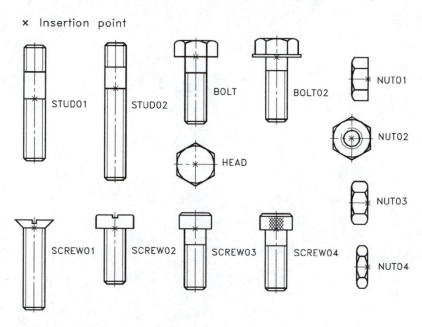

Fig. 11.1 A small library of engineering fixings

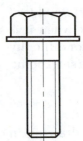

Fig. 11.2 Stage 1 of making a block

Fig. 11.3 Stage 2 of making a block

Fig. 11.4 The **Block Definition** dialogue box

usually in the form of British Standards or ISO symbols, are stored in drawing files and some disks will contain libraries of thousands of such symbols. The reader can build up such libraries for him/herself. As an example, Fig. 11.1 shows a small library of fixings such as are common in engineering. Each stud, bolt etc. has its own name. On disk each symbol would be represented by a file with the extension ***.dwg**.

To add to the library, each symbol is created as follows:

1. Construct the drawing of the symbol (Fig. 11.2).
2. Call **Make Block** (Fig. 11.3). The **Block Definition** dialogue box appears (Fig. 11.4)

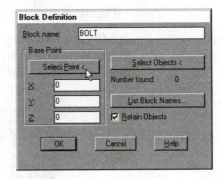

3. *Enter* the **Block name:** – in this example **BOLT**. *Left-click* on the **Select Point<** button. The Command line shows:

   Command: _bmake Insertion base point: *pick* a suitable point

   The dialogue box reappears. *Left-click* on the **Select Objects<** button. Window the objects to be made into a block (Fig. 11.5).
4. The dialogue box again reappears. *Left-click* on the **OK** button and the block is saved.

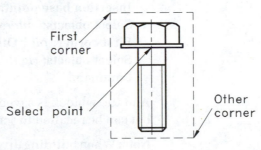

Fig. 11.5 Stage 3 of making a block

Notes

1. The block saved by the above method is saved in the drawing in which the block had been drawn. A *left-click* on the **List Block Names...** button in the dialogue box shows this – see Fig. 11.6.

Fig. 11.6 The **Block Names in This Drawing** box

2. Make sure that the point selected in response to **Select Point** is at a point which enables easy positioning of the block when it is inserted into the drawing. Failure to do so may make for difficulty when the block is inserted. It is usually best to select at a snap point.

Written or wblocks

Blocks can only be saved and re-inserted within the drawing in which they were saved. If part of a drawing or a symbol is to be inserted into another drawing it must be saved independently of the drawing of which it was part. To do this use the **wblock** command as follows.

Command: *enter* w (for wblock) *right-click*

The **Create Drawing File** dialogue box appears. Select a suitable directory in which to save the file and *enter* a file name in the **File name:** box, followed by a *left-click* on the **OK** button (Fig. 11.7).

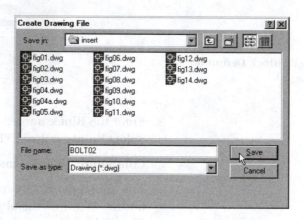

Fig. 11.7 The **Create Drawing File** dialogue box

Block name: *right-click* (but another name could be *entered* here)
Insertion base point: *pick*
Select objects: *enter* w (Window) *right-click*
First corner: *pick* **Other corner:** *pick* **11 found**
Select objects: *right-click*
Command:

And the wblock is saved to the file name. The drawing disappears, but can be recalled to screen by *entering* oops at the Command line.

Note: When building up your own libraries use the **wblock** command system because it makes independent drawing files.

Insert Block

Fig. 11.8 The **Insert Block** tool

Insertion of drawings

To insert a drawing into another drawing use the **Insert Block** tool (Fig. 11.8). When the tool icon is selected, the **Insert** dialogue box appears on screen (Fig. 11.9).

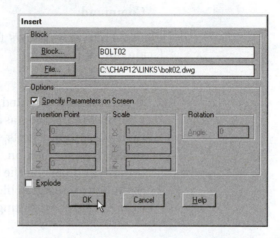

Fig. 11.9 The **Insert** dialogue box

1. *Left-click* on the **File...** button. The **Select Drawing File** dialogue box appears, from which the name of the required drawing can be selected. The selected file name appears in the **File...** box. *Left-click* on the **OK** button.
2. The block drawing appears on screen being *dragged* at its insertion point by the cursor cross hairs (Fig. 11.10). The Command line shows:

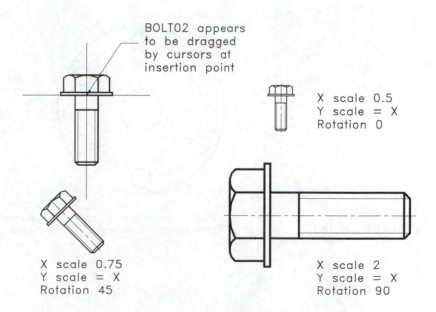

Fig. 11.10 Inserting a block

Command: _ddinsert
Insertion point: *pick* **X scale factor <1>/Corner/XYZ:** *right-click*
      accepts scale of 1)
Y scale factor (default = X): *right-click* (accepts default of 1)
Rotation angle <0>: *right-click* (accepts 0)
Command:

Figure 11.10 also shows the results of amending the default of 1 (scale) and 0 (rotation).

Notes

1. When a block is inserted, it appears as a drawing which can be acted upon by **Modify** tools as a single entity. Blocks can be exploded into their constituent parts, either by setting the **Explode** box in the **Insert** dialogue box on (tick in box), or by using the **Explode** tool (**Modify** toolbar) on the block after it has been inserted.
2. Although an inserted block can be scaled with its Y scale different to its X scale, the resulting insertion will obviously become distorted.

Examples of blocks and inserts

Example 1 – Fig. 11.11

A two-view third angle projection of part of a clutch device has been drawn and the two blocks **HEAD** and **BOLT02** have been inserted in place. The use of the blocks from the small library shown in Fig. 11.1 saves time in completion of the drawing.

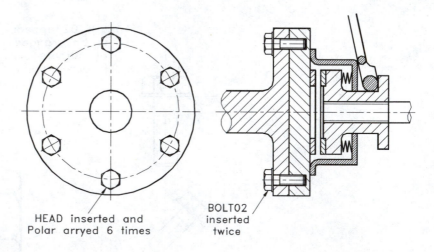

Fig. 11.11 Example 1

HEAD inserted and
Polar arryed 6 times

BOLT02
inserted
twice

Example 2 – Fig. 11.12

This example again uses a block from the library shown in Fig. 11.12. The upper of the two drawings Fig. 11.12 shows a sectional view of a pair of coupled pipes. The lower drawing shows that two bolts have been inserted. The washers were added after the insertions.

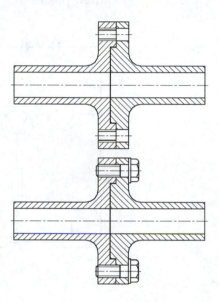

Fig. 11.12 Example 2

Example 3

Figure 11.13 shows a small library of electrical and electronics symbols. Each of the drawings of the symbols have been saved as

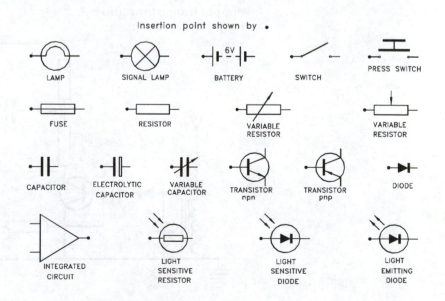

Fig. 11.13 Example 3 – a small library of electrical and electronics symbols

wblocks to form a library of files in *.dwg format on a disk. Figure 11.14 shows two simple circuits constructed by the insertion of the appropriate symbol drawings in position. Conductor lines, donuts at intersection points in the circuits and any symbols not included in the library were added after the symbols had been inserted in their required positions.

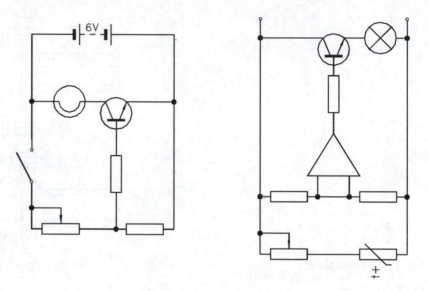

Fig. 11.14 Example 3

Example 4 – Fig. 11.15

Using the same library of electrical and electronics circuit symbols as for the previous example, Fig. 11.16 is a circuit drawing for a simple transistor radio set.

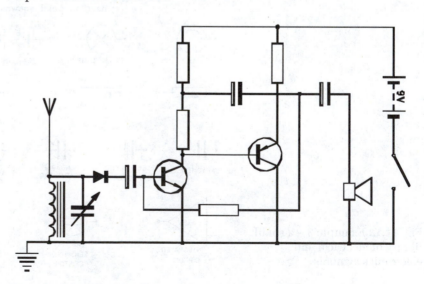

Fig. 11.15 Example 4

Example 5

Figure 11.16 is a small library of symbols for building plans. Using the symbols from the library for insertion in a building plan drawing, Fig. 11.17 shows the layout of rooms in a two-storey building.

The outline of the two storeys was first constructed and then the symbols inserted as required.

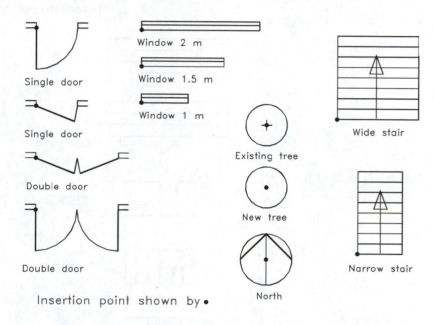

Fig. 11.16 Example 5. A small library of building plan symbols

Insertion point shown by ●

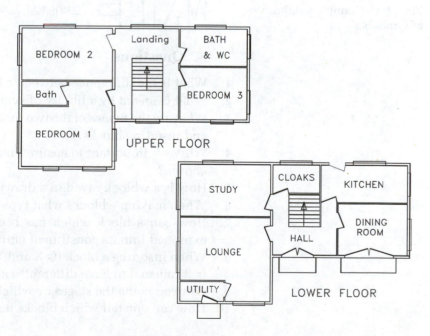

Fig. 11.17 Example 5

Example 6

Figure 11.18 shows a number of pneumatic circuit symbols and Fig. 11.19 a pneumatics circuit constructed from the insertion from the library. The circuit Fig. 11.19 shows one which controls the depth of drilling possible with the drill head to which the circuit is connected.

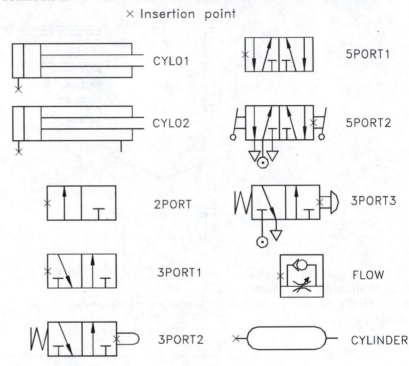

Fig. 11.18 Example 6. Library of symbols

Questions

1. What is the difference between a block and a wblock?
2. What is meant by a library of symbols?
3. What are the names of the two tools usually used for constructing and inserting blocks.
4. Why is it important to ensure that an insertion point is carefully chosen?
5. How is a wblock saved in a drawing into which it was inserted?
6. When making wblocks what type of file are they saved to?
7. How can a block which has been inserted into a drawing be exploded into its constituent entities?
8. When inserting a block its X and Y scaling can be different. Why is it unusual to have different scales for the two axes?
9. Can you name the stages by which a wblock is created?
10. How can one tell which blocks have been inserted in a drawing?

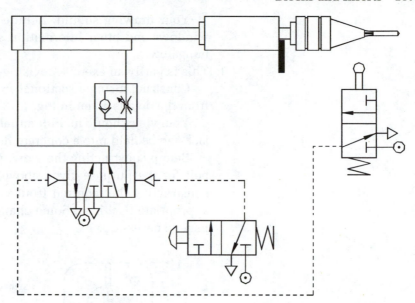

Fig. 11.19 Example 6

Exercises

1. Construct your own small library of nuts, bolts, studs etc. by copying the drawings in Fig. 11.1.
2. Construct a small electrical and electronics symbols library similar to that given in Fig. 11.13.
3. Construct a small library of building drawing symbols similar to that given by Fig. 11.16. Then design and create a building plan drawing for a bungalow based on the information given by the layout of Fig. 11.20.

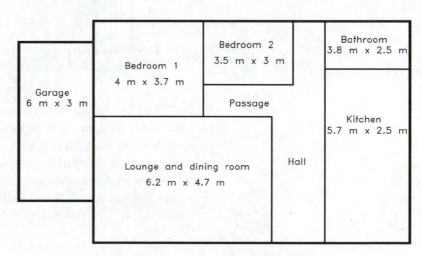

Fig. 11.20 Exercise 3   Outline of a two bedroom bungalow

Your drawing should include outer walls, partitions, doors, windows and other information suited to the design of a small bungalow.

4. This is partly an exercise revising work from earlier chapters.

Construct a single sectional front view of the assembled jack from the details given in Fig. 11.21.

Your view should include suitable bolts by which the base of the jack can be held into a concrete floor.

Before constructing the view, prepare a drawing of a suitable bolt for the purpose given above, save your drawing and, after constructing the required front view insert copies of the bolt at appropriate positions. Some changes in the front view or inserts may be necessary.

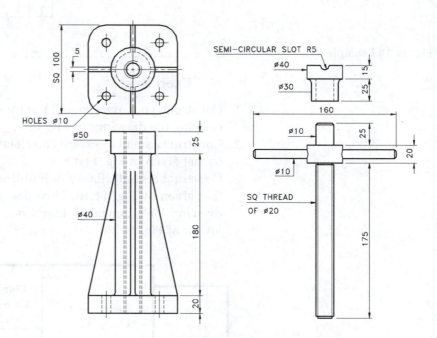

Fig. 11.21 Exercise 4

5. Figure 11.22 is a plate of thickness 20, which is to be fixed in position with 5 bolts, with washers to another plate, the bolts passing through the Ø10 holes.

Construct two views of the plate – that given as a front view and a plan. Include appropriate holding bolts in the plan view. Do not show the plate to which the existing plate is to be bolted.

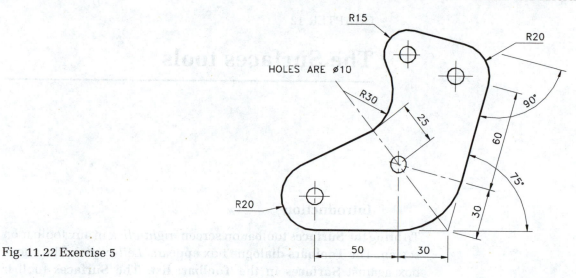

Fig. 11.22 Exercise 5

CHAPTER 12

The Surfaces tools

Introduction

To bring the **Surfaces** toolbar on screen, *right-click* in any toolbar on screen. The **Toolbars** dialogue box appears. *Left-click* in the check box against **Surfaces** in the **Toolbar:** list. The **Surfaces** toolbar appears (Fig. 12.1). The names of the tools in the toolbar are shown in Fig. 12.2.

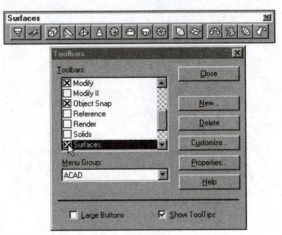

Fig. 12.1 Opening the **Surfaces** toolbar from the **Toolbars** dialogue box

The 2D Solid tool

The tool in the toolbar (**2D Solid**) is a 2D tool. All the others are three-dimensional tools (3D). **2D Solid** is used to fill surfaces with the colour to which the current layer is operating. The filling only takes place if the set variable **Fill** is ON. To set the variable:

> **Command:** *enter* fill *right-click*
> **On/OFF <OFF>:** *enter* on *right-click*
> **Command:**

To fill an area with a solid colour, the order in which points are *picked* or *entered* are important because the filling only occurs in triangles. Examples are given in Fig. 12.4. The upper of the three sets of drawings in Fig. 12.3 shows the order in which points are *picked* to achieve filling as shown in the central sets of drawings. The lower set shows what happens when the variable **Fill** is set OFF. To solid fill the right hand of the three outlines, *left-click* on the tool icon, or *enter* so (Fig. 12.3):

> **Command: _solid First point:** *pick* or *enter* coordinates
> **Second point:** *pick* or *enter* coordinates
> **Third point:** *pick* or *enter* coordinates
> **Fourth point:** *pick* or *enter* coordinates
> **Third point:** *pick* or *enter* coordinates
> **Fourth point:** *pick* or *enter* coordinates
> **Third point:** *pick* or *enter* coordinates
> **Fourth point:** *right-click*
> **Command:**

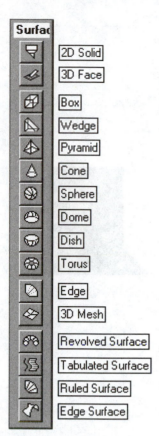

Fig. 12.2 The tools in the **Surfaces** toolbar

Fig. 12.3 Selecting the **2D Solid** tool

Drawing in three dimensions

The coordinate system of AutoCAD allows models to be constructed in 3D (three dimensions). Such models are usually referred to as 3D models, or as 3D solid models. So far in this book, we have

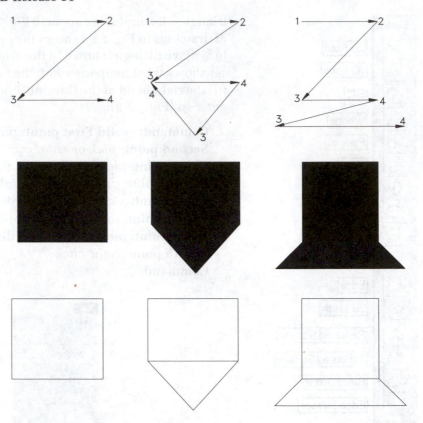

Fig. 12.4 Examples of the use of **2D Solid**

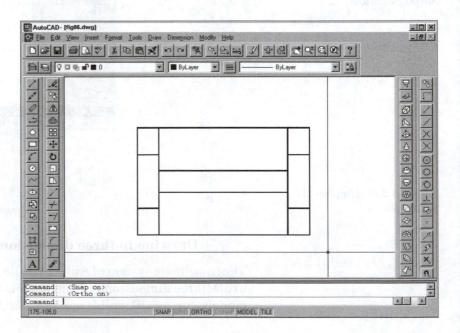

Fig. 12.5 A 3D model as seen in the R14 window in plan view

concentrated on working in 2D – in terms of the coordinates X and Y. The third coordinate, which gives height to a 3D solid, is the Z coordinate. The direction of the Z coordinate is imagined as coming out of the screen perpendicularly towards the computer operator. As an example, Fig. 12.5 shows a plan view of a 3D model as seen in the drawing area of the R14 window. Figure 12.6 shows the model in a pictorial view with the directions of the three coordinates axes X, Y and Z.

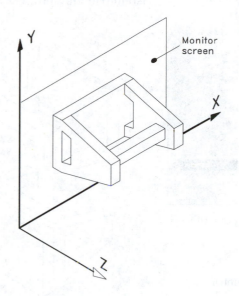

Fig. 12.6 The 3D model from Fig. 12.5 in a pictorial view which includes the directions of the coordinate axes

Notes

1. The Z axis is vertical to the screen, with **+ve X** towards the operator and **–ve X** away from the operator.
2. Coordinate entries can be made in terms of X,Y,Z. Usually the coordinate point *x,y,z* = 0,0,0 is at the bottom left-hand corner of the drawing area (but not always). Using *x,y,z* coordinates allows points to be determined anywhere in 3D space in relation to the R14 drawing area.
3. All tools in the **Surfaces** toolbar, except **2D Solid**, are 3D tools.

The Isometric viewpoints

There are several methods by which, once a 3D model has been constructed, it can be viewed so as to see it in a pictorial view. One such method is to use the **Isometric** viewpoints, which can be selected from the **3D Viewpoint** sub-menu of the **View** pull-down menu (Fig. 12.7). Taking the 3D model shown in Fig. 12.6, Fig. 12.8

shows the four isometric viewpoints. The **SW Isometric** viewpoint can also be obtained as follows:

> **Command:** *enter* vpoint *right-click*
> **Rotate/<View point>: 0,0,1** *enter* -1,-1,1 *right-click*
> **Regenerating drawing**
> **Command:**

Figure 12.8 shows the **Vpoint** figures corresponding to the four isometric viewpoints.

Fig. 12.7 Selecting one of the isometric views

Fig. 12.8 The isometric viewpoints

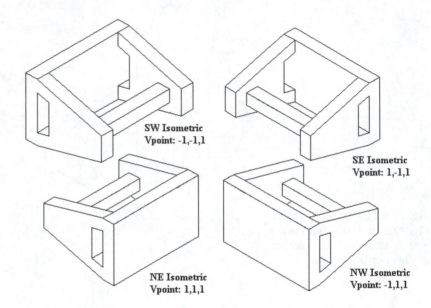

SW Isometric
Vpoint: -1,-1,1

SE Isometric
Vpoint: 1,-1,1

NE Isometric
Vpoint: 1,1,1

NW Isometric
Vpoint: -1,1,1

Notes

1. Another method of obtaining a pictorial view is:

   Command: *enter* vp *right-click*

   And the **Viewpoint Presets** dialogue box appears (Fig. 12.9). Settings in the dialogue box can either be made by *entering* figures in the **From X Axis:** and **From XY Plane:** boxes, or by *clicking* in the two compasses.
2. Do not confuse the two Command line entries **vp** and **vpoint**.

The Hide tool

Another tool in frequent use when constructing 3D models will be the **Hide** tool. The tool can be called either from the **View** pull-down menu, by selection of the **Hide** tool from the **Render** toolbar, or by *entering* hi (or hide) at the Command line (Fig. 12.10). All that is

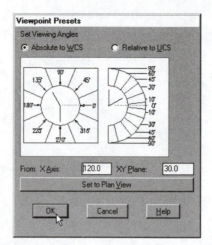

Fig. 12.9 The **Viewpoint Presets** dialogue box

required is to call the tool. All lines behind front-facing 3D meshes will be hidden – hidden line removal.

Command: *enter* hi *right-click*

The 3D models in Figures 12.6 and 12.8 have been acted upon by the **Hide** tool.

Filters in connection with 3D constructions

The 3D filters **.x**, **.y**, **.z**, **xy**, **.xz** and **.yz** are of value for determining **x,y,z** coordinate points for some purposes. As an example, the line from **x,y,z** = 50,100 to 100,150,100 could be determined as follows:

Command: *enter* l (Line) *right-click*
From point: *enter* 50,100 *right-click*
To point: *enter* .xy *right-click*
of *enter* 100,150 *right-click* **(need Z)** *enter* 100 *right-click*
To point:

Fig. 12.10 Calling **Hide**

Examples of using tools from the Surfaces toolbar

Each of the tools can be called either from their tool icons in the toolbar, from the **Surfaces** sub-menu in the **Draw** pull-down menu or, by *entering* the tool name at the Command line.

Example 1: 3dface – Fig. 12.12

This example was made up from four 3dfaces. The first – left-hand face – was created by:

Command: _3dface First point: *pick* 100,250
Second point: *pick* 100,120

Fig. 12.11 The **3D Face** tool icon

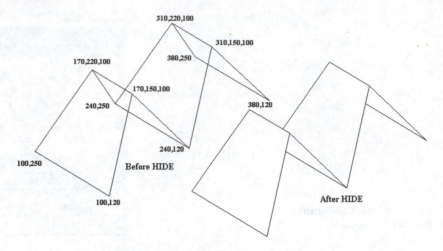

Fig. 12.12 Example 1

Third point: *enter .xy right-click of pick* 170,150 **(need Z)** *enter* 100 *right-click*
Fourth point: *enter .xy right-click of pick* 170,220 **(need Z)** *enter* 100 *right-click*
Third point: *right-click*
Command:

The other faces were created in a similar manner. See Fig. 12.12 for the coordinates of the corners of each 3dface. A 3dface is a solid mesh frame, behind which lines can be hidden with the aid of the **Hide** tool.

Example 2: 3dface – Fig. 12.13

This example shows a simple trough made up from three 3dfaces, the uprights being 250 × 50 and the base being 250 x 60. Using the

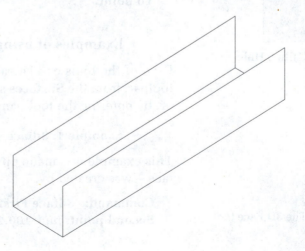

Fig. 12.13 Example 2

same procedures as for the first example, the reader is advised to construct the trough.

Example 3: Box – Fig. 12.15

Fig. 12.14 Calling the **Box** tool

This tool constructs a cube or cuboid consisting of six 3D faces. Call the tool and the Command line shows.

Command: ai_box
Corner of box: *pick* a point or *enter* coordinates
Length: *pick* or *enter* figure (for Length)
Cube/<Width>: *enter* c (for Cube) or *enter* a figure (for Width)
Height: *enter* figure (for Height)
<Rotation angle>/Reference: *enter* figure
Command:

Figure 12.15 shows three boxes drawn with the aid of **Box**, one of which is a cube.

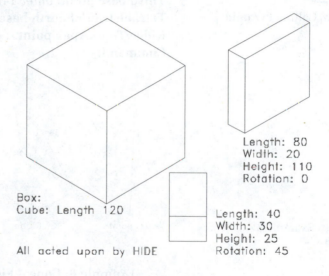

Fig. 12.15 Example 3 – **Box**

Box:
Cube: Length 120

Length: 80
Width: 20
Height: 110
Rotation: 0

Length: 40
Width: 30
Height: 25
Rotation: 45

All acted upon by HIDE

Example 4: Wedge – Fig. 12.17

Fig. 12.16 Calling **Wedge**

Command: ai_wedge
Corner of Wedge: *pick* or *enter* coordinates
Length: *enter* 100 *right-click*
Width: *enter* 50 *right-click*
Height: *enter* 120 *right-click*
Rotation angle about Z axis: *enter* 0 *right-click*
Command:

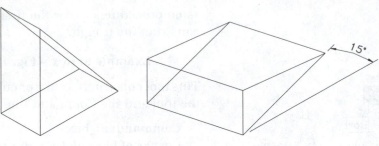

Length: 100
Width: 50
Height:120
Rotation about Z axis: 0

Length: 150
Width: 100
Height: 50
Rotation about Z axis: 15

Fig. 12.17 Example 4 – **Wedge**

Example 5: Pyramid – Fig. 12.19

Fig. 12.18 Calling **Pyramid**

Command: ai_pyramid
First base point: *enter* 70,240 *right-click*
Second base point: *enter* 140,240 *right-click*
Third base point: *enter* 140,170 *right-click*
Tetrahedron/<Fourth base point>: *enter* 70,170
Ridge/Top/<Apex point>: *enter* 105,205,120 *right-click*
Command:

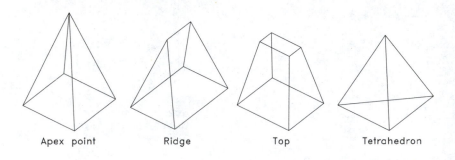

Apex point   Ridge   Top   Tetrahedron

Fig. 12.19 Example 5 –
Pyramid

Example 6: Cone – Fig. 12.21

Fig. 12.20 Calling **Cone**

Command ai_pyramid
Base center point: *enter* 120,250 *right-click*
Diameter/<radius> of base: *enter* 40 *right-click*
Diameter/<radius> of top <0>: *right-click*
Height: *enter* 100 *right-click*
Number of segments <16>: *right-click*
Command:

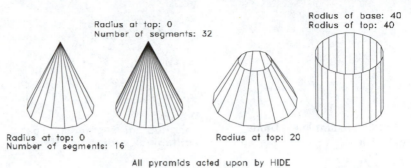

Radius at top: 0
Number of segments: 32

Radius of base: 40
Radius of top: 40

Radius at top: 0
Number of segments: 16

Radius at top: 20

All pyramids acted upon by HIDE

Fig. 12.21 Example 6 –
Pyramid

Example 7: Cone – Fig. 12.23

Command: ai_sphere
Center of sphere: *enter* 150,225 *right-click*
Diameter/<radius>: *enter* 50 *right-click*
Number of longitudinal segments: <16>: *right-click*
Number of latitudinal segments: <16>: *right-click*
Command:

Fig. 12.22 Calling **Sphere**

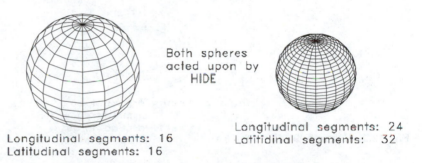

Both spheres
acted upon by
HIDE

Longitudinal segments: 16
Latitudinal segments: 16

Longitudinal segments: 24
Latitidinal segments: 32

Fig. 12.23 Example 7 – **Sphere**

Example 8: Dome and Dish – Fig 12.26

Command: ai_dome
Center of dome: *enter* 115,225 *right-click*
Diameter/<radius>: *enter* 50 *right-click*
Number of longitudinal segments <16>: *right-click*
Number of latitudinal segments <8>: *right-click*
Command:

The command sequence for a **Dish** is the same as that for a **Dome**.

Fig. 12.24 Calling **Dome**

Fig. 12.25 Calling **Dish**

Both surfaces
acted upon by
HIDE

Fig. 12.26 Example 8 – **Dome**
and **Dish**

Dome:
Longitudinal segments: 16
Latitudinal segments: 8

Dish:
Longitudinal segments: 24
Latitudinal segments: 16

Example 9: Torus – Fig. 12.28

Fig. 12.27 Calling **Torus**

Command: ai_torus
Center of torus: *enter* 145,210 *right-click*
Diameter/<radius> of torus: *enter* 145,210 *right-click*
Diameter/<radius> of tube: *enter* 10 *right-click*
Segments around tube circumference <16>: *right-click*
Segments around torus circumference <16>: *right-click*
Command:

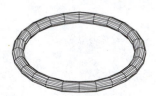

Segments around tube
   circumference: 16
Segments around torus
   circumference: 16

Segments around tube
   circumference: 24
Segments around torus
   circumference: 24

Fig. 12.28 Example 9 – **Torus**

Example 10: Edge – Fig. 12.30

Fig. 12.29 Calling **Edge**

Command: _edge
Display/<Select edge>: *pick* and edge which is to be hidden
Display/<Select edge>: *pick* and edge which is to be hidden
Display/<Select edge>: *pick* and edge which is to be hidden

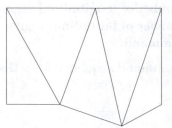
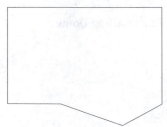

Fig. 12.30 Example 10 – **Edge**

A surface mesh created with 3dface

The same mesh with edges removed

Display/<Select edge>: *pick* and edge which is to be hidden
Display/<Select edge>: *right-click*
Command:

Example 11: 3D Mesh – Fig. 12.32

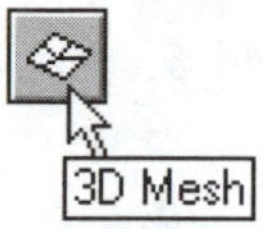

Command: _3dmesh
Mesh Msize: *enter* 4 *right-click*
Mesh Nsize: *enter* 4 *right-click*
Vertex (0, 0): *enter* 70,260 *right-click*
Vertex (0, 1): *enter* 70,140 *right-click*
Vertex (0, 2): *enter* 120,165,50 *right-click*
Vertex (0, 3): *enter* 120,245,50 *right-click*
Vertex (1, 0): *enter* 170,260 *right-click*
Vertex (1, 1): *enter* 70,140 *right-click*
Vertex (1, 2): *enter* 220,165,50 *right-click*
Vertex (1, 3): *enter* 220,245,50 *right-click*
Vertex (2, 0): *enter* 270,140 *right-click*
Vertex (2, 1): *enter* 265,260 *right-click*
Vertex (2, 2): *enter* 310,245,50 *right-click*
Vertex (2, 3): *enter* 310,165,50 *right-click*
Vertex (3, 0): *enter* 365,140 *right-click*
Vertex (3, 1): *enter* 365,260 *right-click*
Vertex (3, 2): *enter* 405,245,50 *right-click*
Vertex (3, 3): *enter* 405,165,50 *right-click*
Command:

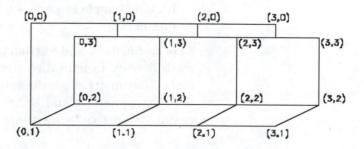

Fig. 12.31 Calling **3D Mesh**

Fig. 12.32 Example 11 – **3D Mesh** – before **Hide**

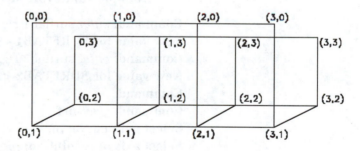

Fig. 12.33 Example 11 – **3D Mesh** – after **Hide**

Fig. 12.34 Calling **Revolved Surface**

Example 12: Revolved surface – Fig 12.35

Command: *enter* surftab1 *right-click*
New value for SURFTAB1 <6>: *enter* 32 *right-click*
Command: *enter* surftab2 *right-click*
New value for SURFTAB2 <6>: *enter* 2 *right-click*
Command:
Command: _revsurf
Select path curve: *pick*
Select axis of revolution: *pick*
Start angle <0>: *right-click*
Included angle (+=ccw, – = cw) <Full circle>: *right-click*
Command:

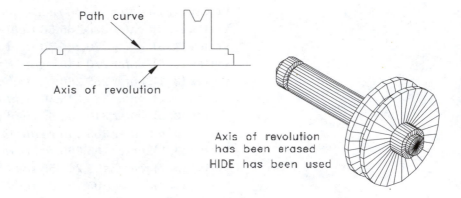

Fig. 12.35 Example 12 – **Revolved Surface**

Example 13: Revolved surface – Fig 12.36

Command: *enter* surftab1 *right-click*
New value for SURFTAB1 <32>: *enter* 16 *right-click*
Command: *enter* surftab2 *right-click*
New value for SURFTAB2 <2>: *enter* 12 *right-click*
Command:
Command: _revsurf
Select path curve: *pick*
Select axis of revolution: *pick*
Start angle <0>: *right-click*
Included angle (+=ccw, – = cw) <Full circle>: *right-click*
Command:

Note on Surftab1 and Surftab2: These two set variables control the mesh density in both directions when using some of the **Surface** tools. They may need settings different to their default settings of 6. Both Examples – 12 and 13 have had both Surfab settings amended to suit the surface being produced.

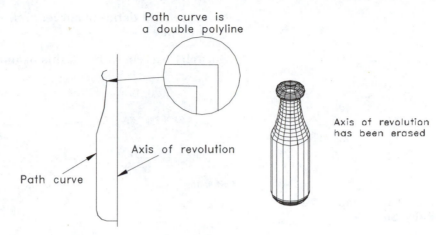

Fig. 12.36 Example 13 –
Revolved Surface

Example 14: Tabulated Surface – Fig. 12.38

Command: _tabsurf
Select path curve: *pick*
Select direction vector: *pick*
Command:

Fig. 12.37 Calling **Tabulated
Surface**

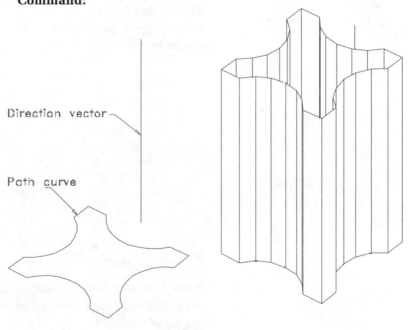

Fig. 12.38 Example 14 –
Tabulated Surface

Fig. 12.39 Calling **Ruled
Surface**

Example 15: Ruled Surface – Fig. 12.40

Command: _tabsurf
Select first defining curve: *pick*

Select second defining curve: *pick*
Command:

Surftab1 was set to 16 for this example.

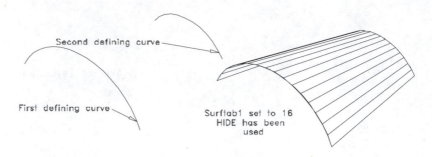

Fig. 12.40 Example 15 –
Ruled Surface

Example 16: Edge Surface – Fig. 12.42

Fig. 12.41 Calling **Edge
Surface**

Command: _edgesurf
Select edge 1: *pick*
Select edge 2: *pick*
Select edge 3: *pick*
Select edge 4: *pick*
Command:

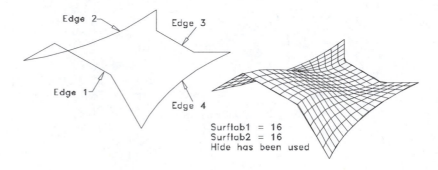

Fig. 12.42 Example 16 – **Edge
Surface**

Questions

1. How is the **Surfaces** toolbar called to screen?
2. One of the tools in the **Surfaces** toolbar is not a 3D tool. What is the name of this tool?
3. How many coordinate axes does one work in when constructing a 3D model?
4. In which menu are the **Isometric Viewpoints** found?
5. What is the purpose of the **Hide** tool?
6. What is meant by the term '3D filters'?

7. There is no **Surfaces** tool for cylinders. How then are surface cylinders constructed?

8. When constructing a surface with many faces, the **3D Face** tool can be used. However, many lines may occur in the resulting surface. How are such lines erased, without affecting the 3D Face as a mesh surface behind which other constructions can be hidden?

9. One problem when using the **Tabulated Surface** tool is that, when the **Hide** tool is used, there is no upper surface to the resulting solid. How could this be remedied?

10. What is the major difference between obtaining a surface using **Ruled Surface** and one obtained by using **Edge Surface**?

Exercises

None of the exercises given below have had dimensions included. When constructing the models from the information given with the drawings, all sizes can be estimated. The exercises are given here to allow the reader to experiment with the **Surfaces** tools and the size of the resulting 3D model is not, at this stage, important.

1. The 3D model shown in Fig. 12.43 was constructed with the aid of the three tools from **Surfaces** as indicated in the text associated with the illustration. Working to any convenient sizes construct a similar model.

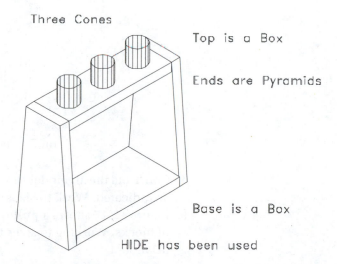

Fig. 12.43 Exercise 1

2. The 3D model shown in Fig. 12.44 was constructed entirely with the tool **3D Face**. Working to sizes of your choice construct a similar 3D model.

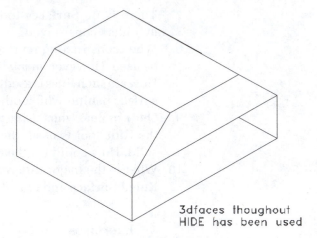

Fig. 12.44 Exercise 2

3dfaces thoughout
HIDE has been used

3. Using your own discretion regarding sizes, construct a 3D model
   similar to that shown in Fig. 12.45.

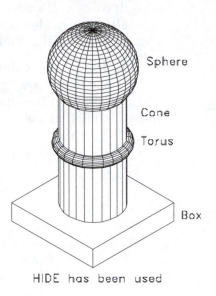

Sphere

Cone

Torus

Box

Fig. 12.45 Exercise 3

HIDE has been used

4. Construct the 3D model shown in Fig. 12.46 with the aid of the tools
   as indicated. Work to sizes of your own judgment.
5. Figure 12.47 shows a pulley with its spindle mounted in a couple
   of blocks. Working to sizes to your own discretion make a similar
   3D model.

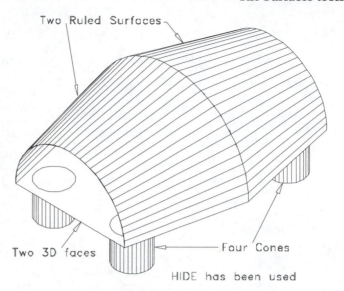

Two Ruled Surfaces

Two 3D faces

Four Cones

HIDE has been used

Fig. 12.46 Exercise 4

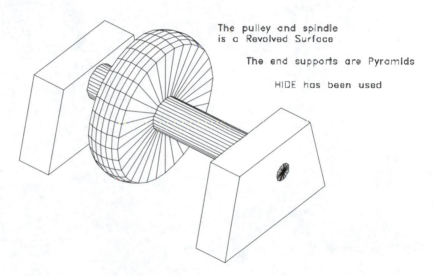

The pulley and spindle
is a Revolved Surface

The end supports are Pyramids

HIDE has been used

Fig. 12.47 Exercise 5

6. Figure 12.48 shows the stages in the construction of the **Patch curve** for a vase to be constructed with the aid of the **Revolved Surface** tool.

You may find it necessary to read parts of the next chapter **The Solids tools** before being able to construct the **Path curve** for this model.

Figure 12.49 shows the outline of the vase constructed from the path curve shown in Fig. 12.48. Working to any convenient sizes construct a similar vase.

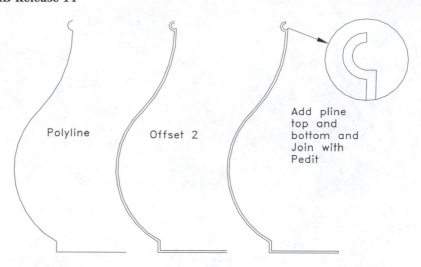

Fig. 12.48 The **Path Curve** for
Exercise 6

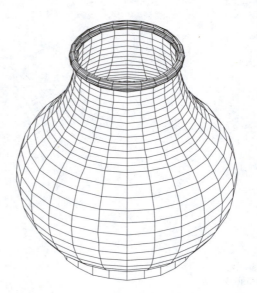

Fig. 12.49 Exercise 6

7. The left-hand drawing of Fig. 12.50 shows a surface formed by the
    3D Face tool. The right-hand drawing shows unwanted edges
    removed from the surface.

    Figure 12.51 shows the resulting surface used as part of a 3D
    model. Working to any convenient sizes construct a similar model.

9. The left-hand drawing of Fig. 12.52 shows four adjoining arcs from
    which the surface shown in the right-hand drawing of Fig. 12.52
    was formed.

    Working to sizes of your own choice construct the surface
    shown.

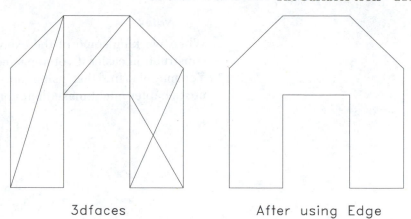

3dfaces   After using Edge

Fig. 12.50 Surface for
Exercise 7

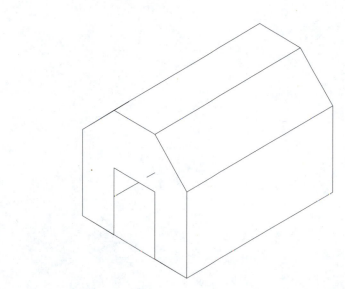

Fig. 12.51 Exercise 8

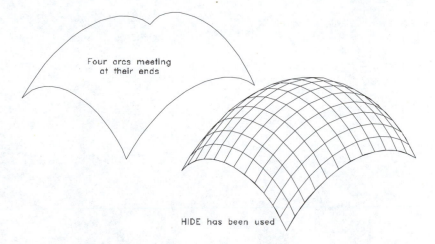

Four arcs meeting
at their ends

HIDE has been used

Fig. 12.52 Exercise 9

Notes

1. When working some of the exercises given you may find their construction easier if you repeatedly use the 3D filter **.xy**.
2. You may also find that, using some of the methods explained in the next chapter might make their construction easier to complete.

CHAPTER 13

The Solids tools

Introduction

Before describing the use of the **Solids** tools, two other toolbars contain tools which are of some importance when constructing 3D solids. These are the **Modify II** toolbar and the **UCS** toolbar.

Tools from the Modify II toolbar

Call the toolbar from the **Toolbars** dialogue box (Fig. 13.1). There are only five tools in the toolbar which concern us here, although Fig. 13.2 shows a sixth.

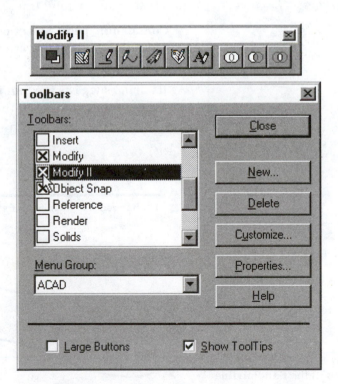

Fig. 13.1 Calling the **Modify II** toolbar from the **Toolbars** dialogue box

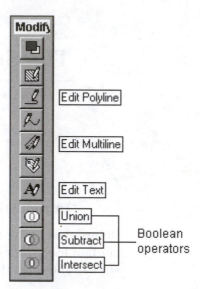

Fig. 13.2 The **Modify II** toolbar with the names of six of its tool icons

Edit Polyline

The tool can be called either from the **Modify II** toolbar or from the **Modify** pull-down menu. It can also be called by *entering* pe (or pedit) at the Command line:

> **Command: _pedit Select polyline:** *pick*
> **Close/Join/Width/Edit vertex/Fit/Spline/Decurve/Ltype gen/Undo/ eXit/<X>:**

As its name suggests the tool is for the editing of polylines. Figure 13.4 gives some samples of the various editing functions.

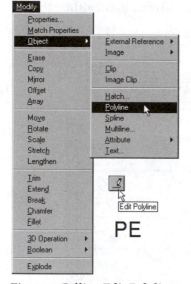

Fig. 13.3 Calling **Edit Polyline**

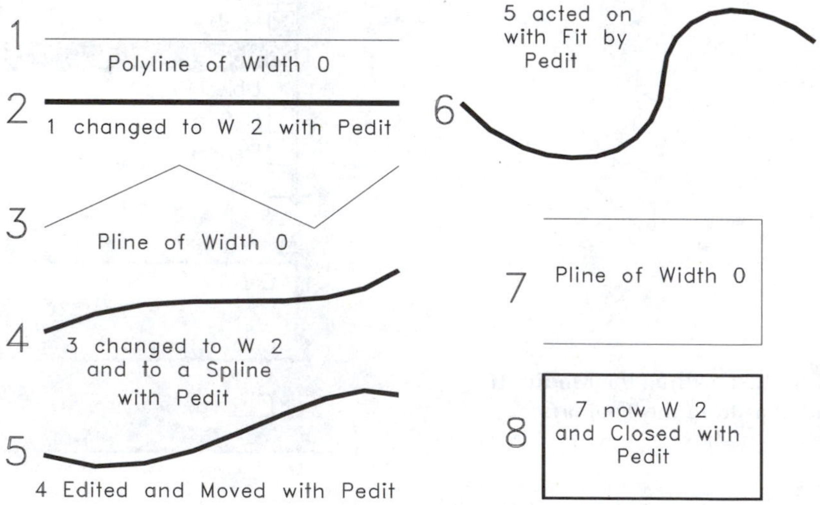

Fig. 13.4 Some of the editing functions of the **Edit Polyline** tool

For the purposes of using the **Solids** tools, perhaps the **Join** and **Close** prompts of **pedit** are among those of the most importance. It should be noted that *entering* pe at the Command line is the quickest method of calling the tool.

Edit Text

Fig. 13.5 Calling **Edit Text**

The tool can also be called from the **Modify II** toolbar or from the **Modify** pull-down menu. *Entering* ddedit will also bring the tool into action:

Command: _ddedit
<Select an annotation object>/Undo: *pick* the text to be edited

When the text to be edited is *picked*, the **Edit Text** box appears. Figure 13.6 shows the sequence involved in editing text that requires to be changed.

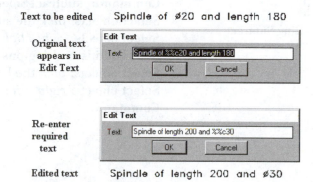

Fig. 13.6 Using the **Edit Text** tool

The Boolean operators

These are of particular importance in the construction of 3D models involving the use of the **Solids** tools.

Example: Union – Fig. 13.8

Fig. 13.7 Calling **Union**

Call the tool, either from the **Modify II** toolbar, from the **Modify** pull-down menu, or by *entering* uni (or union) at the Command line:

Command: _union
Select objects: *pick* one of the boxes **1 found**
Select objects: *pick* the other box **1 found**
Select objects: *pick* the cylinder **1 found**
Select objects: *right-click*
Command:

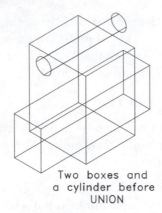
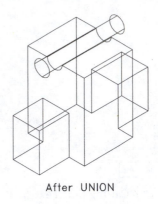

Fig. 13.8 **Union** – Example

Two boxes and
a cylinder before
UNION

After UNION

Example: Subtract – Fig. 13.10

Call the tool, either from the **Modify II** toolbar, from the **Modify** pull-down menu, or by *entering* su (or subtract) at the Command line:

Fig. 13.9 Calling **Subtract**

> **Command: _subtract Select solids and regions to subtract from...**
> **Select objects:** *pick* the smaller of the two boxes **1 found**
> **Select objects:** *right-click*
> **Select solids and regions to subtract...**
> **Select objects:** *pick* the larger of the two boxes **1 found**
> **Select objects:** *right-click*
> **Command:**

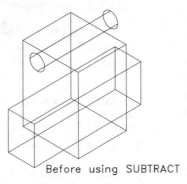
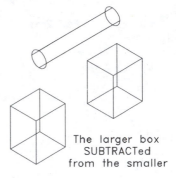

Fig. 13.10 **Subtract** – Example

Before using SUBTRACT

The larger box
SUBTRACTed
from the smaller

Example: Intersect – Fig. 13.12

Call the tool, either from the **Modify II** toolbar, from the **Modify** pull-down menu, or by *entering* int (or intersect) at the Command line:

Fig. 13.11 Calling **Intersect**

> **Command: _intersect**
> **Select objects:** *pick* the larger box **1 found**
> **Select objects:** *pick* the cylinder **1 found**
> **Select objects:** *right-click*
> **Command:**

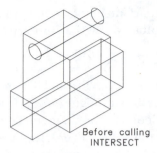 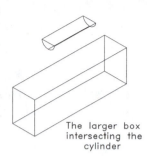

Fig. 13.12 **Intersect** – Example

Before calling
INTERSECT

The larger box
intersecting the
cylinder

The User Coordinate System (UCS)

We have so far used the R14 window with the coordinate system in what is known as the **WORLD** coordinate system, in which the Z axis is perpendicular to the screen. With the aid of the **UCS** the operator can set the X,Y,Z coordinate system at any angle he/she desires to facilitate the construction and viewing of 3D solids. The tools for the UCS are held in the **UCS** toolbar (Fig. 13.13), but can also be called from the **Tools** pull-down menu (Fig. 13.14). The tools can also be seen in the sequence of prompts appearing when ucs is *entered* at the Command line:

Command: *enter* ucs *right-click*
Origin/ZAxis/3point/OBject/View/X/Y/Z/Prev/Restore/Save/Del/ ?/<World>:

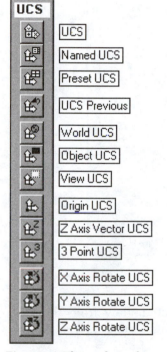

Fig. 13.13 The tools in the
UCS toolbar

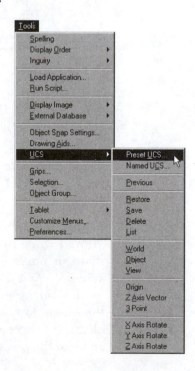

Fig. 13.14 The **UCS** tools from
the **Tools** pull-down menu

A comparison between the prompts and the names of the tools from the toolbar show the similarity.

Preset UCS

Left-click on the **Preset UCS** tool icon in the **UCS** toolbar. The **UCS Orientation** dialogue box appears (Fig. 13.15). A *left-click* in any one of the icons in the dialogue box sets the UCS to the named position — **Top**, **Back**, **Left**, **Front**, **Right** etc. Figure 13.16 shows the directions of viewing to achieve these UCS settings.

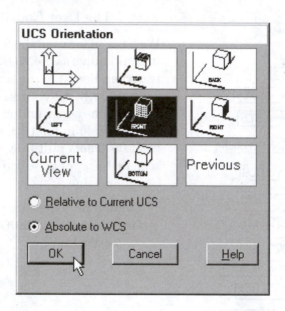

Fig. 13.15 The **UCS Orientation** dialogue box

Notes

1. The UCS will only change to a selected view from the **UCS Orientation** if the **ucsfollow** set variable is ON, or set to 1, as follows:

   Command: *enter* ucsfollow *right-click*
   New value for UCSFOLLOW <0>: *enter* 1 *right-click*
   Command:

2. Figure 13.16 shows the directions in which a 3D solid will be viewed when the **Presets** are selected from the **UCS Orientation** dialogue box.
3. When a new UCS is selected, the X,Y axes will be horizontal and vertical on the screen, with the +veZ axis coming perpendicular to the screen towards the operator. The whole coordinate system is changed to accommodate the new orientation. The orientation of some of the presets is shown in the views of Fig. 13.17.

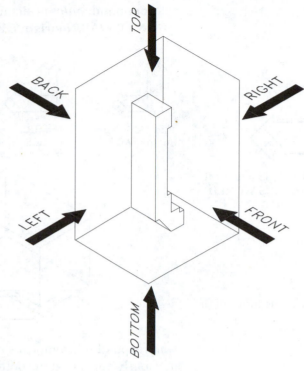

Fig. 13.16 The viewing
directions for the **UCS Presets**

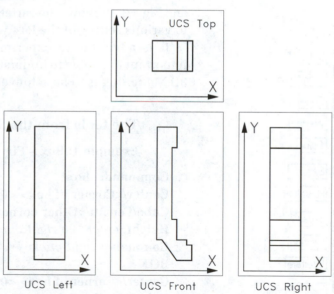

Fig. 13.17 The X,Y orientation
of some of the **UCS Presets**

The UCS icon

If the **UCS icon** is not showing somewhere on the screen *enter*
ucsicon at the Command line:

Command: *enter* ucsicon *right-click*
ON/OFF/All/Noorigin/ORigin/<ON>:

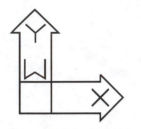

Fig. 13.18 The UCS icon as it appears in the UCS **WORLD**

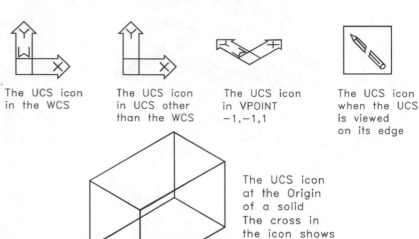

The UCS icon in the WCS

The UCS icon in UCS other than the WCS

The UCS icon in VPOINT −1,−1,1

The UCS icon when the UCS is viewed on its edge

The UCS icon at the Origin of a solid The cross in the icon shows the origin (0,0,0)

Fig. 13.19 Various forms of the UCS icon

and respond to prompts as needed. Figure 13.18 shows the icon as it usually appears at the bottom left-hand corner of the R14 window and Fig. 13.19 shows the variety of forms the icon can take according to various setting of the R14 window.

It is advisable to experiment with settings in the UCS. It is important to be able to understand how the UCS works if successful 3D Modelling is to be achieved.

The tools from the Solids toolbar

Example 1: Box – Fig. 13.22

Command: _box
Center/<Corner of box> <0,0,0,>: *enter* 120,260 *right-click*
Cube/Length/<Other corner>: *enter* 150,160 *right-click*
Height: *enter* 100 *right-click*
Command: *right-click*
BOX
Center/<Corner of box> <0,0,0,>: *enter* 150,260,80 *right-click*
Cube/Length/<Other corner>: *enter* 210,260,80 *right-click*
Height: *enter* 20 *right-click*
Command: *right-click*
BOX
Center/<Corner of box> <0,0,0,>: *enter* 150,260 *right-click*
Cube/Length/<Other corner>: *enter* 210,160 *right-click*

Solid

	Box
	Sphere
	Cylinder
	Cone
	Wedge
	Torus
	Extrude
	Revolve
	Slice
	Section
	Interfere
	Setup Drawing
	Setup View
	Setup Profile

Fig. 13.20 The tools in the **Solids** toolbar

Fig. 13.21 Calling **Box**

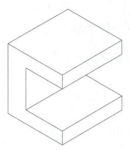

Fig. 13.22 **Box** – Example 1

Fig. 13.23 Calling **Sphere**

Height: *enter* 20 *right-click*
Command: *select* 3D Viewpoint SE Isometric
VPOINT Rotate/<View point> 0,0,1 <1,-1,1>:
Command: *enter* uni (Union) *right-click*
Select objects: *pick* one box
Select objects: *pick* another box
Select objects: *pick* the third box
Select objects: *right-click*
Command: *enter* hi (Hide) *right-click*
Regenerating drawing
Command:

Example 2: Sphere – Fig. 13.24

Command: _sphere
Center of sphere <0,0,0>: *enter* 140,190,50 *right-click*
Diameter <Radius> of sphere: *enter* 50 *right-click*
Command: *enter* co (Copy) *right-click*
Select objects: *pick* the sphere **1 found**
Select objects: *right-click*
<Base point or displacement>>/Multiple: *pick* centre of sphere
Second point of displacement: *enter* 375,190 *right-click*
Command: _box
Center/<Corner of box>: *enter* 140,205,35 *right-click*
Cube/Length/<Other corner>: *enter* 375, 175,35
Height: *enter* 30 *right-click*
Command: *select* 3D Viewpoint SE Isometric
VPOINT Rotate/<View point> 0,0,1 <1,-1,1>:
Command: *enter* uni (Union) *right-click*
Select objects: *pick* one sphere
Select objects: *pick* the box
Select objects: *pick* the other sphere
Select objects: *right-click*

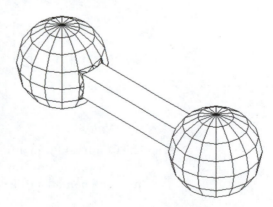

Fig. 13.24 **Sphere** – Example 2

Command: *enter* hi (Hide) *right-click*
Regenerating drawing
Command:

Example 3: Cylinder – Fig. 13.26

Command: _cylinder
Elliptical/<Center point> <0,0,0,>: *enter* 250,210 *right-click*
Diameter/<Radius>: *enter* 60 *right-click*
Center of other end/<Height>: *enter* 120 *right-click*
Command:
Select **Front** from the **UCS Orientation** dialogue box
Command: _cylinder
Elliptical/<Center point> <0,0,0,>: *enter* 250,60 *right-click*
Diameter/<Radius>: *enter* 40 *right-click*
Center of other end/<Height>: *enter* 150 *right-click*
Command: *enter* ucs *right-click*
Origin/ZAxis/3point/OBject/View/X/Y/Z/Prev/Restore/Save/Del/
    ?/<World>: *enter* w *right-click*
Command: *enter* m (Move) *right-click*
Move the second cylinder to be central to the first
Command: *enter* su (Subtract) *right-click*
Select solids and regions to subtract from...
Select objects: *pick* the larger cylinder **1 found**
Select objects: *right-click*
Select solids and regions to subtract...
Select objects: *pick* the smaller cylinder **1 found**
Select objects: *right-click*
Command:

Now place the solid in SE Isometric viewing position and **Hide**.

Fig. 13.25 Calling **Cylinder**

Fig. 13.26 Example 3 – **Cylinder**

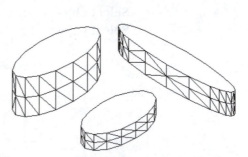

Fig. 13.27 Example 3. Some elliptical cylinders

Notes

1. The Command line prompts will not be included with most of the examples from now on. They are, in any case, similar to those for the same named surface tools described in Chapter 12.

2. The figures for the responses to the Command line prompts will be included with the drawings for each example.

Example 4: Cone – Fig. 13.29

The radii, elliptical point, height and apex figures for the cones are given with Fig. 13.29.

Fig. 13.28 Calling **Cone**

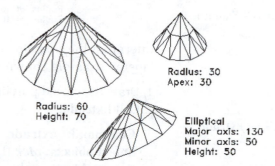

Fig. 13.29 **Cone** – Example 4

Example 5: Wedge – Fig. 13.31

The prompts for this solid require figures for the corners of the base of the wedge and its height to be *entered*. Note that the point of the wedge is at the **Other corner** position. The corner points and height figures for this example are given with Fig. 13.31.

Fig. 13.30 Calling **Wedge**

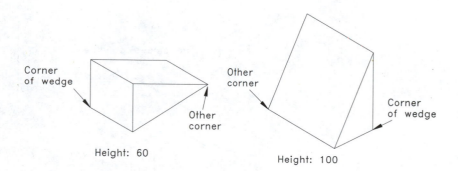

Fig. 13.31 **Wedge** – Example 5

Example 6: Torus – Fig. 13.33

The prompts for this solid require the center of the torus and the radii of torus and tube to be *entered*. These are shown in Fig. 13.33.

Example 7: Extrude – Fig. 13.35

Fig. 13.32 Calling **Torus**

This tool allows 3D solids to be extruded from closed polylines. If the polyline is not closed a warning appears at the Command line

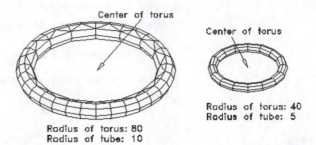

Fig. 13.33 **Torus** – Example 6

Fig. 13.34 Calling **Extrude**

informing the operator that the extrusion cannot be formed. The tapered example shown in Fig. 13.35 was constructed as follows:

1. Draw the closed polyline outline.
2. Call **Extrude**:

    Command: _extrude
    Select objects: *pick* the polyline
    Select objects: *right-click*
    Path/<Height of extrusion>: *enter* 45 *right-click*
    Extrusion taper angle: *enter* 10 *right-click*
    Command:

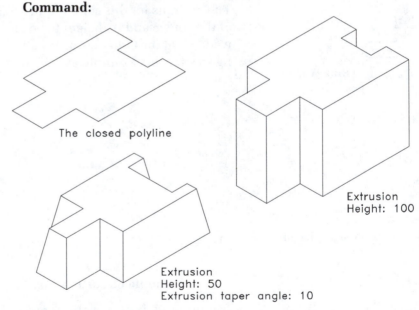

Fig. 13.35 Example 7 – **Extrude**

Example 8: Extrude – Fig. 13.36

If the **Path** prompt is accepted in the **extrude** Command line sequence, the extrusion will follow a line, pline or arc. In the example Fig. 13.36, the path arc was created while in the **Front UCS** selected from the **UCS Orientation** dialogue box.

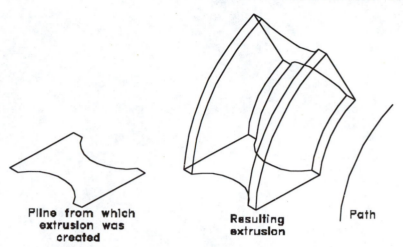

Fig. 13.36 Example 8 –
Extrude

**Pline from which
extrusion was
created**

**Resulting
extrusion**

Path

Example 9: Revolve – Fig. 13.38

This tool allows solids of revolution to be formed from polylines.
When the polyline has been formed:

Command: _revolve
Select objects: *pick* the pline
Select objects: *right-click*
Axis of revolution – Object/X/Y/<Start point of axis>: *pick* or
    enter coordinates *right-click*
Angle of revolution <full circle>: *right-click*
Command:

Fig. 13.37 Calling **Revolve**

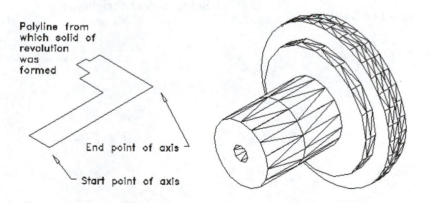

Polyline from
which solid of
revolution
was
formed

End point of axis

Start point of axis

Fig. 13.38 Example 9 –
Revolve

Example 10: Revolve – Fig. 13.39

In this example the **Angle of revolution** was *entered* as 180 for both
the solids. The left-hand half of Fig. 13.39 shows the two plines from
which the half solids of revolution on the right were formed.

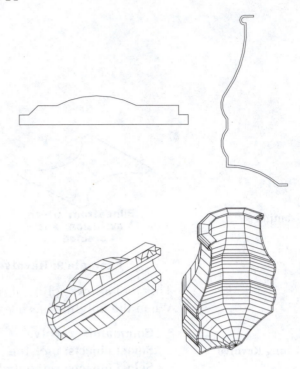

Fig. 13.39 Example 10 –
Revolve

Fig. 13.40 Calling **Slice**

Example 11: Slice – Fig. 13.41

Command: _slice
Select objects: *pick* the extrusion
Select objects: *right-click*

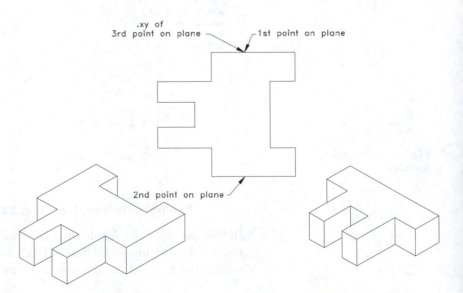

Fig. 13.41 Example 11 – **Slice**

Slicing plane by Object/Zaxis/View/XY/YZ/ZX/<3 points>: *pick* first point
2nd point on plane: *pick* 2nd point
3rd point on plane: *enter* .xy **of** *pick* 3rd point
(need Z): *enter* 1 *right-click*
Both sides/<Point on desired side of the plane>: *pick* to side of extrusion wished to be seen
Command:

Example 12: Section – Fig. 13.44

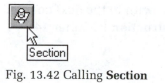

Fig. 13.42 Calling **Section**

This example shows a section plane cut through a 3D solid constructed from extrusions which have been acted upon by the Boolean operators **Subtract** and **Union**. When **Section** is used it creates a section outline from the section cut made through a 3D solid. Figure 13.43 shows three points on the section plane of the solid. Figure 13.44 shows the solid after **Hide** and the section plane removed and hatched.

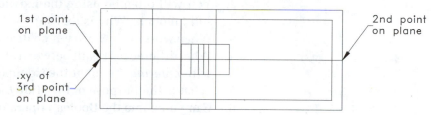

Fig. 13.43 The three points for a section plane

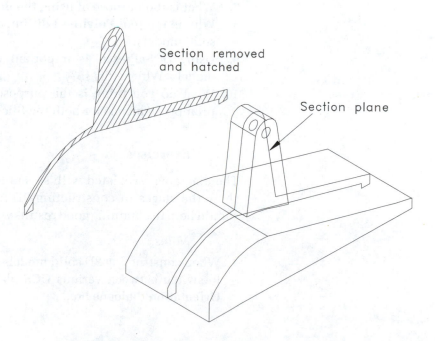

Fig. 13.44 Example 12 –
Section

When the tool is called the Command line shows:

Command: _section
Select objects: *pick* the 3D solid
Section plane by Object/Zaxis/View/XY/YZ/ZX/<3 points>: *pick*
    1st point
2nd point on plane: *pick* 2nd point
3rd point on plane: *enter* .xy **of** *pick* 3rd point
(need Z): *enter* 1 *right-click*
Command:

Note: The remaining tools in the **Solids** toolbar – **Setup Drawing**, **Setup View** and **Setup Profile** will be dealt with in the next chapter which deals with **Further 3D model construction** (Chapter 14).

Questions

1. There seems to be similarities between the tools from the **Surfaces** toolbar and those from the **Solids** toolbar. What are the differences?
2. You will often be using the **Extrude** tool when constructing 3D solid models. Why is this so?
3. When working in 3D in which direction does the +veX axis point?
4. What differences result between *entering* vp at the Command line with *entering* vpoint at the Command line?
5. What is the purpose of the **Hide** tool?
6. Can you name the Boolean operators?
7. What is the purpose of using the Boolean operators?
8. Why is the tool **Polyline Edit** important when constructing 3D solid models?
9. Using UCS Presets is important when constructing 3D solid models. Why is this so?
10. What do you think is the purpose of including **Object** in the prompts sequence for both the **Slice** and **Section** tools?

Exercises

The diagrams associated with several of the exercises given below show the stages in constructing 3D models. The following notes should help in obtaining good results when attempting the exercises.

Notes

1. When constructing 3D solid models in R14 it is usually necessary to switch between various **UCS** planes with the aid of the **UCS Orientation** dialogue box.

2. When switching between **UCS** planes it is necessary to **Zoom** to 1 (scale 1:1), otherwise the model tends to fill the drawing area.

3. In setting a UCS plane with 3 points, whether to obtain a new plane, or to **Slice** or **Section** an object, when using the filter **.xy**, only the figure 1 (one) need be *entered* in response to the **(need Z)** prompt.

4. Rather than work out the exact position for the Z axis coordinate position when working in other than the **World UCS**, it is often easier to switch to the **World UCS** and **Move** the solid, or part to its required position.

5. The Boolean operators **Union** and **Subtract** will frequently be needed during constructions of 3D solid models. The **Intersect** Boolean tool is less likely to be used, but it is advisable for the reader to practise its use to understand how it functions.

6. Use the Isometric **3D Viewpoints** as frequently as required to see how one's constructions are proceeding.

The Exercises

1. Figure 13.45 shows the sequence of operations for constructing the half bearing shown in Fig. 13.46. The construction commences with a change to the **FRONT UCS** (steps 1 to 4), then switching to the **World UCS** in order to **Move** and **Copy** parts. Figure 13.46 shows the completed 3D model after **Hide** in the **SW Isometric** viewing position.

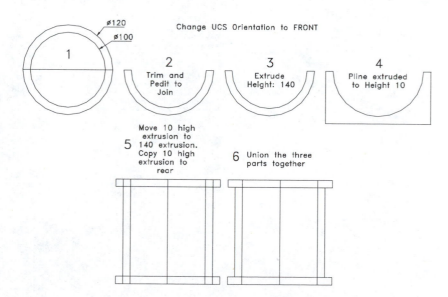

Fig. 13.45 Sequence of
construction for Exercise 1

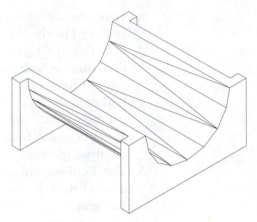

Fig. 13.46 Exercise 1

2. Figure 13.47 shows the steps in constructing the 3D soli model for this exercise. The construction starts in the **World UCS** and changes to the **Left UCS** when necessary. The Boolean operators **Union** and **Subtract** are used in several of the steps of construction.

   The final stage, number 8 in the series of drawing shows the completed model after **Hide** in the **SW Isometric** viewing position.

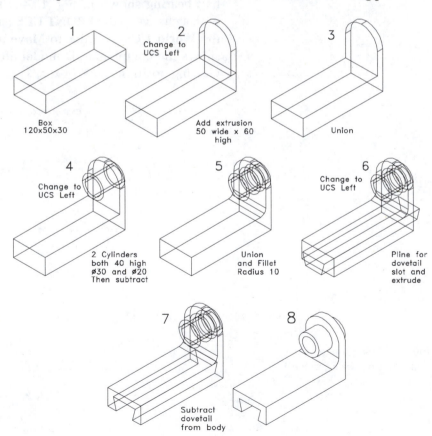

Fig. 13.47 The steps in the construction for Exercise 2

3. Figure 13.48 shows the 3D model which has been constructed in answer to Exercise 2 acted upon by the two tools **Slice** and **Section**. The Section resulting from the use of the tool has been removed from its position central to the solid and the hatched. The hatching has then been moved to the sliced surface.

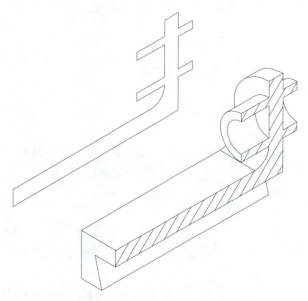

Fig. 13.48 Exercise 3

4. Figures 13.49 and 13.50.
   (a) Change the UCS to **UCS Front**.
   (b) Construct a closed polyline to the dimensions given in Fig. 13.49.
   (c) **Revolve** around the axis of revolution.
   (d) Change the UCS to **UCS Right**.
   (e) Construct a **Cylinder** of **Radius** 15 and **Height** 20.
   (f) Change UCS to **UCS Front**.
   (g) **Move** the cylinder into correct position.

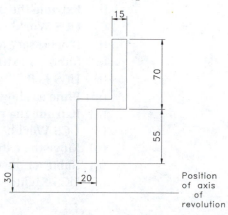

Fig. 13.49 Dimensions for Exercise 4

(h) Change UCS to **UCS Right**.

(i) **Polar Array** the cylinder 6 times.

(j) Set **3D Viewpoint** to **SE Isometric**.

(k) **Subtract** the cylinders from the solid of revolution.

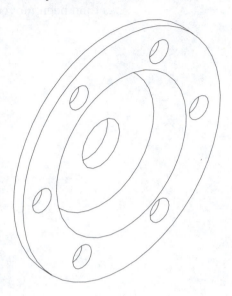

Fig. 13.50 Exercise 4

5. Figure 13.52 shows a 3D solid model of half of a coupling. The model was constructed as follows:

(a) **UCS World**.

(b) **Cylinder** – Radius 60; Height 120.

(c) **Cylinder** – Radius 30; Height 120.

(d) **Subtract** smaller from larger cylinder.

(e) **UCS Front**.

(f) If necessary **Move** the solid to a better position vis-a-vis grid points.

(g) **Pline** as shown in Fig. 13.51 (left-hand drawing).

(h) **Extrude** the pline – Height 140.

(i) **UCS World**.

(j) If necessary **Move** the extrusion.

(k) **Subtract** extrusion from solid.

(l) **UCS Left**.

(m) **Pline** as shown in Fig. 13.51 (right-hand drawing).

(n) **Extrude** the pline – Height 140.

(o) **UCS World**.

(p) **Move** the extrusion.

(q) **Subtract** the extrusion for the solid.

(r) **UCS Right**.

(s) **Cylinder** – Radius 10; Height 140.
(t) **UCS World**.
(u) **Move** cylinder.
(v) **Subtract** cylinder from solid.
(w) **3D Viewpoint** SW Isometric.

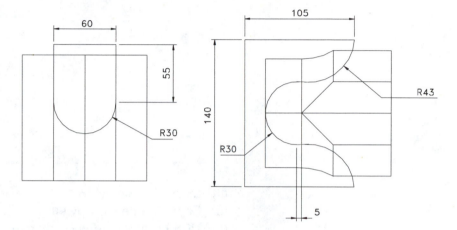

Fig. 13.51 Steps 7 and 13 for
Exercise 5

Notes

1. The illustrations Figures 13.50 and 13.52 have been constructed using the **Setup Drawing**, **Setup View** and **Setup Profile** tools from the **Solids** toolbar. The use of these tools is described in the next chapter.
2. When using the **Subtract** tool it is usually better to make the solid being subtracted larger in some directions than is necessary.
3. After changing the **UCS** planes, always **Zoom** to All or to Scale 1 (or both) to get back to a sensible size for the solid being constructed.

Fig. 13.52 Exercise 5

6. This model of a flange coupling was constructed as follows:

(a) **UCS World**.
(b) Construct the pline Fig. 13.53.

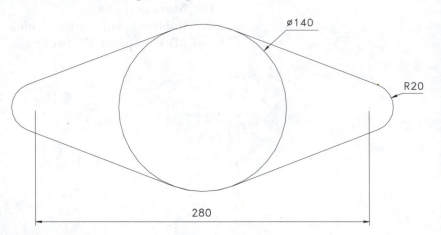

ø140

R20

280

Fig. 13.53 The pline from
which the base and top were
extruded

(c) **Extrude** – Height 15.
(d) **Copy**, **Rotate** copy by 90°.
(e) **UCS Front** and **Move** copy vertically up by 135 units.
(f) **UCS World**.
(g) **Cylinder** – Radius 68; Height 150.
(h) **Union** – cylinder to both extrusions.
(i) **Cylinder** – Radius 60; Height 150.
(j) **Subtract** cylinder from solid.
(k) **3D Viewpoint** SW Isometric.
(l) **Hide**.

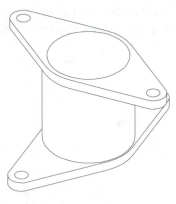

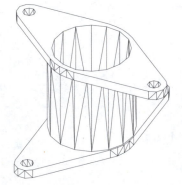

Fig. 13.54 Exercise 6 – after
Setup Profile

Fig. 13.55 Exercise 6 – after
Hide

CHAPTER 14

Further 3D model construction

Profile only drawings from 3D models

1. Load or construct a 3D solid model. As an example, Fig. 14.1 is an exploded 3D solid model of a spindle and a gear wheel which fits in the splines of the spindle.

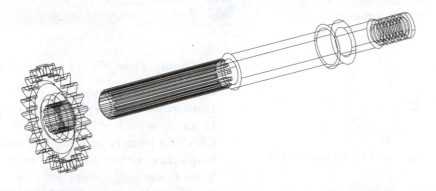

Fig. 14.1 A 3D solid model drawing loaded into R14

Fig. 14.2 Calling **Setup Drawing**

2. Call the **Setup Drawing** tool. The R14 drawing area changes to a **Paper Space** layout (Fig. 14.3).

3. Because we are working in an R14 drawing area set up for an A3 drawing sheet:

   Right-click to bring the Command line back to:
   Command: *enter* limits *right-click*
   On/OFF<Lower left corner> <0.0>: *right-click*
   Upper right corner <12,9>: *enter* 420,297 *right-click*
   Command: *enter* z (Zoom) *right-click*
   All/Center/Dynamic/Extents/Previous/Scale (X/XP)/<Realtime>:
   enter a (All) *right-click*
   Regenerating paperspace.
   Command:

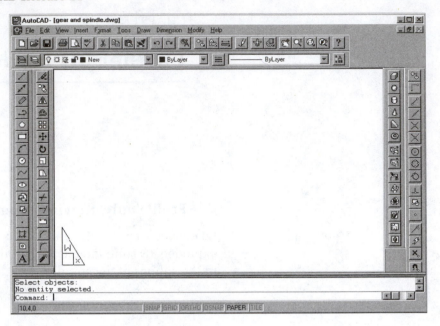

Fig. 14.3 The **Paper Space** drawing area resulting from calling **Setup Drawing**

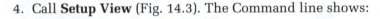

Fig. 14.4 Calling **Setup View**

Fig. 14.5 Calling **Setup Profile**

4. Call **Setup View** (Fig. 14.3). The Command line shows:

   Command: _solview
   Ucs/Ortho/Auxiliary/Section/<eXit>: *enter* u (Ucs) *right-click*
   Enter view scale:<1>: *right-click*
   Clip first corner: *pick* top left corner
   Clip other corner: *pick* bottom right corner
   View name *enter* plan *right-click*
   Ucs/Ortho/Auxiliary/Section/<eXit>: *right-click*
   Command:

   and the R14 window appears as in Fig. 14.6.

5. Go back to **Model Space** in which the 3D model was first loaded:

   Command: *enter* ms (MSpace) *right-click*
   MSPACE
   Command:

   The MSpace ucsicon appears at the bottom left corner replacing the PSpace icon.

6. Call **Setup Profile** (Fig. 14.5):

   Command: solprof
   Select objects: *pick* the two parts of the 3D solid model
   Select objects: *right-click* **2 found**
   Display hidden profile lines on separate layer <Y>: *right-click*
   Project profile lines onto a plane <Y>: *right-click*

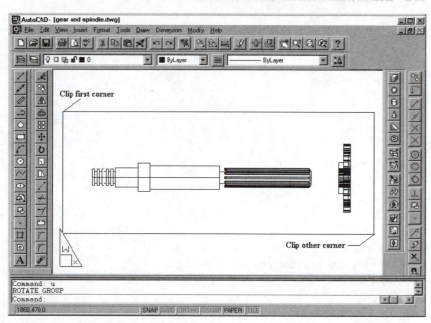

Fig. 14.6 The view after **Setup View** has been applied

Delete tangential edges \<Y\>: *right-click*
One solid selected
Command:

7. Set **3D Viewpoint** SW Isometric.
8. *Left-click* in the **Layer Control** window. The layer popup list appears as in Fig. 14.7.
9. Make the layer **Pv-1b** (or similar) current and turn OFF all other layers. The profile only drawing appears as in Fig. 14.8.

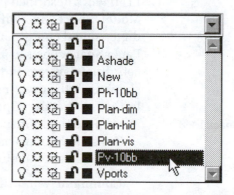

Fig. 14.7 The **Layer Control** popup list after **Setup Profile**

Two profiles making an orthographic projection

Figure 14.9 shows two profiles, one inserted into a drawing containing the first, the two views forming a two-view first angle orthographic projection.

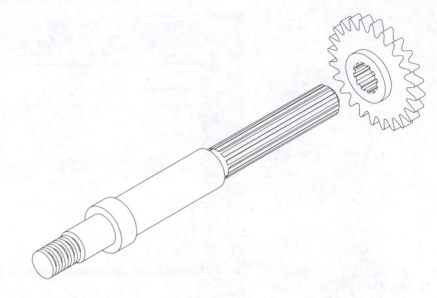

Fig. 14.8 The profile only drawing resulting from the use of **Setup Profile**

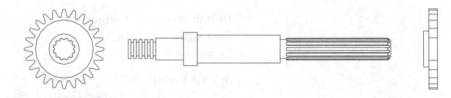

Fig. 14.9 Two profiles making up an orthographic projection

Paper Space (PSpace) and Model Space (MSpace)

In all work described in previous chapters we have been working in **Model Space**, in which constructions can be based on a three dimensional coordinate system in terms of X,Y,Z. If one switches to **Paper Space** constructions can only be carried out in a two dimensional coordinate system in terms of X,Y. If the UCS icon is on and thus showing in the drawing area, **PSpace** is differentiated from **MSpace** by the fact that the PSpace UCS icon is showing (Fig. 14.10), whereas in MSpace the MSpace UCS icon will be showing (Fig. 14.11).

Fig. 14.10 The **PSpace** UCS icon

To switch between MSpace (Tilemode value 1) and PSpace (Tilemode value 0) either:

> **Command:** *enter* tilemode
> **New value for TILEMODE <1>:** *enter* 0 *right-click*
> **Regenerating drawing**
> **Command:**

Fig. 14.11 The **MSpace** UCS icon

Or select **Model Space** for MSpace, or either **Model Space [Floating]** or **Paper Space** for PSpace from the **View** pull-down menu (Fig.

14.12). There is a difference between the two possible selections for PSpace, which will be understood from later pages.

Viewports

Viewports are said to be **tiled** because they fit against each other in **MSpace** much like tiles do on a wall. A variety of settings for viewports are available. A choice from the setting can be made from the **View** pull-down menu (Fig. 14.13) by selecting **Layout...** from the **Tiled Viewports** command of the **View** pull-down menu (Fig. 14.13). This causes the **Tiled Viewport Layout** dialogue box to appear (Fig. 14.14) from which a selection can be made. Figure 14.14 shows that the **Four Left** layout has been selected and Fig. 14.15 shows a 3D model in such a layout.

The purpose of working in a tiled viewport layout is to enable the operator to see his/her construction from various directions as it proceeds. In Fig. 14.15, each viewport is set to a different 3D Viewpoint as set from the **View** pull-down menu (Fig. 14.16). The top left viewport was set to **Front**, the centre left viewport set to **Right**, the bottom left viewport set to **Top** and the main viewport set to **SE Isometric**. These settings enable the operator to work in any of the viewports and be able to see the results from all directions.

Fig. 14.12 Setting **PSpace**

Fig. 14.13 Selecting **Layout...** from the **View** pull-down menu

Fig. 14.14 Selecting a **Tiled Viewport** layout

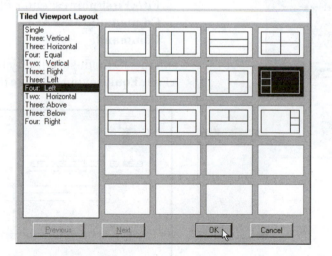

Setting up in Paper Space

Select **Model Space [Floating]** from the **View** pull-down menu. The PSpace screen appears with only the UCS icon showing. The Command Line shows:

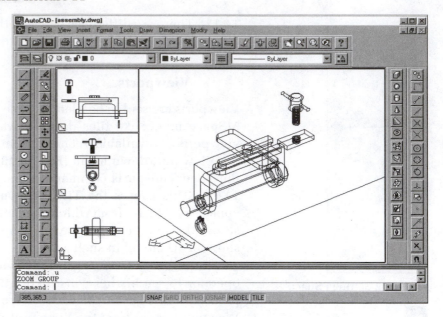

Fig. 14.15 A 3D solid model drawing in a **Four left** tiled viewport layout

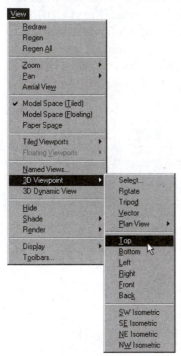

Fig. 14.16 Setting 3D Viewpoints for a tiled viewport layout

Fig. 14.17 The **Four Equal** viewport setting from using **MVIEW**

Command:
Regenerating paperspace
_MVIEW
ON/OFF/Hideplot/Fit/2/3/4/Restore/<First point>: *enter* 4 *right-click*
Fit/<First point>: *enter* f (Fit) *right-click*
Command: _MSPACE
Command:

and the 3D model originally in MSpace (Fig. 14.15) is now fitted into a **Four Equal** layout. Change the viewports to different **3D Viewpoints**

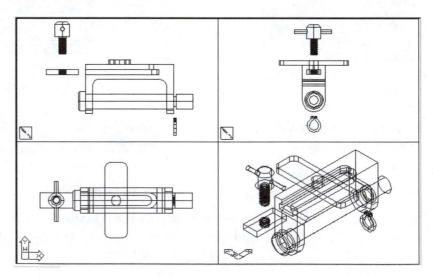

and Fig. 14.17 shows the resulting R14 drawing area. Now switch to **PSpace**:

Command: *enter* ps (PSpace) *right-click*

and the result will appear as in Fig. 14.18.

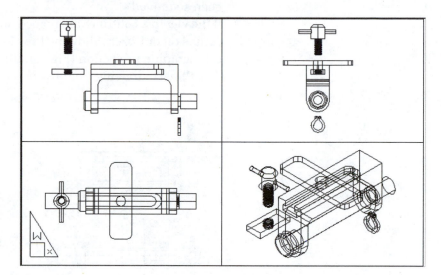

Fig. 14.18 The **PSpace** R14 drawing area

Notes

1. In **MSpace**, the drawing area of Fig. 14.17 consisted of four viewports, allowing settings such as **Zoom**, **Pan**, **3D Viewpoints** etc. to be made in any of the viewports, in **PSpace** there is always a single viewport, even though there appears to be more as in Fig. 14.18. To check this try drawing lines in both the **MSpace** and **PSpace** viewports.

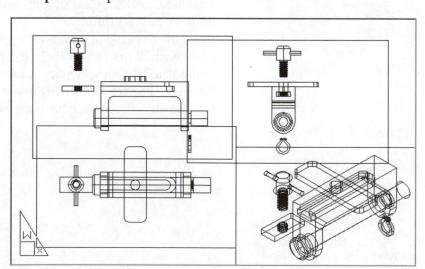

Fig. 14.19 Moving viewport outline in **PSpace**

2. In **PSpace**, the viewport borders from **MSpace** can be moved together with their contents, allowing positioning of the four views of Fig. 4.18 as if in an orthographic projection. Call **Move**, *click* on a viewport edge and move the viewport outline and its contents. Figure 14.19 shows the results after all four viewport outlines have been so moved.

3. If the viewport outlines are placed on a new layer, that layer can be turned off or frozen, allowing the views to appear almost as if in an orthographic projection (Fig. 14.20).

4. The **PSpace** drawing can now be plotted or printed.

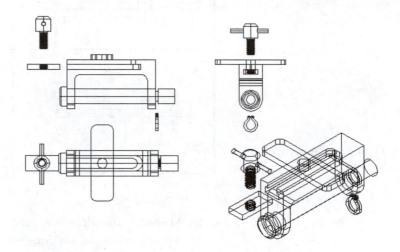

Fig. 14.20 After placing viewport outlines on a new layer and freezing that layer

Using Setup Profile

1. Load or construct a new 3D solid model. Figure 14.21 shows such a model drawing – part of a microscope stand. It has been acted upon by **Setup Profile**.

2. Place the drawing in a four-viewport **MSpace** window.

3. Place each of the viewports in a different **3D Viewport** setting.

4. **Setup Profile** each viewport in turn.

5. Change to **PSpace** and **Move** the viewport boundaries to place each view in an orthographic position relating to the others.

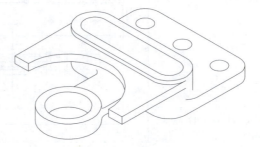

Fig. 14.21 A profiled view of a part from a microscope stand

6. Turn off all layers except those named **Pv-1b** or similar (The **v** means visible). There will be four of them, one for each viewport.
7. Turn off the layer on which the viewport boundaries are stored. The result is as shown in Fig. 14.22.

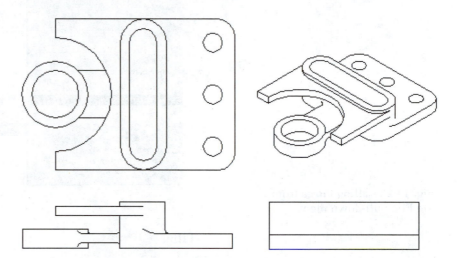

Fig. 14.22 The **PSpace** four-view result

Other tools for constructing 3D models

Purge

When constructing 3D models the **Purge** tool should be used before finally saving the model drawing to file. Purging can save considerable file space on disk. As an example, the four-viewport drawing Fig. 14.17 before **Purge** was saved to file and showed 319 kbytes. After **Purge** (in each of the four viewports) the file size was 181 kbytes.

The tool can be called either from the **File** pull-down menu (Fig. 14.23) or by *entering* pu (or purge) at the Command line. The following shows a typical purging:

Command: *enter* pu *right-click*
Purge unused Blocks/Dimstyles/LAyers/LTypes/SHapes/STyles/
    Mlinestyles/All: *enter* a (All) *right-click*
Purge block OVERHEAD? <N>: *enter* y (Yes) *right-click*
Purge layer DEFPOINTS? <N>: *enter* y (Yes) *right-click*
Purge layer HIDDEN? <N>: *enter* y (Yes) *right-click*
Purge layer CENTRE? <N>: *enter* y (Yes) *right-click*
No unreferenced linetypes found.
No unreferenced text styles found.
No unreferenced shape files found.
No unreferenced dimension styles found.

No unreferenced mlinestyles found.
Command:

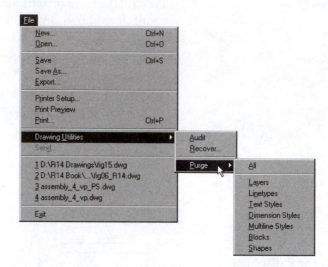

Fig. 14.23 Calling **Purge** from
the **File** pull-down menu

Fillet

The **Fillet** tool from the **Modify** toolbar can be equally as well used
when constructing a 3D model as for 2D work. Figure 14.24 shows
the effects of using the tool on a simple 3D model.

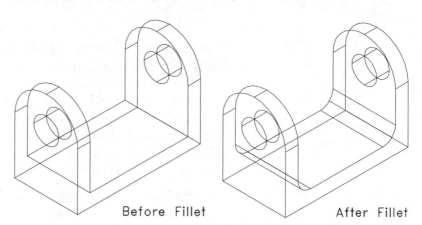

Fig. 14.24 Using **Fillet**

Before Fillet   After Fillet

Chamfer

As with **Fillet** the **Chamfer** tool from the **Modify** toolbar can also be
used when constructing 3D models. Figure 14.25 shows the results
of using the tool on a simple 3D model.

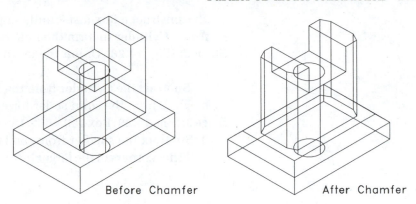

Fig. 14.25 Using **Chamfer**   Before Chamfer   After Chamfer

An example of a 3D model

Figure 14.26 is a **Profile** only drawing of a 3D model of a drill tray from a drilling machine. The model drawing was constructed as follows:

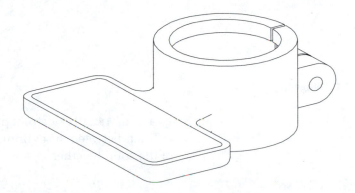

Fig. 14.26 A Profile drawing of
a drill tray

Stage 1: (Fig. 14.27) In the **Front UCS** draw pline outlines for the cylindrical body and the clamping bars. **Revolve** the pline outline for the body and **Extrude** the outlines for the clamps.

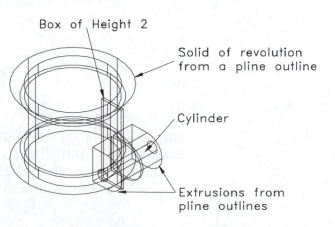

Fig. 14.27 **Stage 1** of
constructing the 3D model of a
drill tray

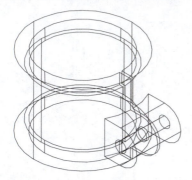

Construct a **Box** just 2 units high between the two clamp jaws. Add a **Cylinder** to form the hole between the clamp jaws.

Stage 2: (Fig. 14.28) **Union** the cylindrical body and the two clamp jaws.

Subtract the **Cylinder** from the clamp jaws. **Subtract** the box of height 2 from the solid so far formed.

Stage 3: (Fig. 14.29) **Box** $150 \times 65 \times 15$, with another $130 \times 45 \times 10$ inside it. **Subtract** the smaller from the larger box.

Fillet corners of the larger box radius 15 and of inner box radius 5.

Fig. 14.28 **Stage 2**

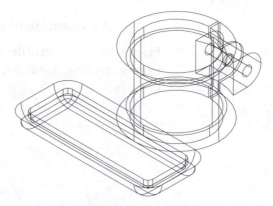

Fig. 14.29 **Stage 3**

Stage 4: (Fig. 14.30) Construct pline outlines of height 10 to fit snugly as fillets between the cylindrical body and the tray. **Union** all parts of the solid together.

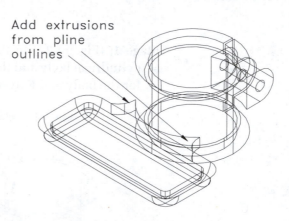

Add extrusions from pline outlines

Fig. 14.30 **Stage 4**

Stage 5: (Fig. 14.31) Now call **Hide**.

Stage 6: (Fig. 14.26) Call **Setup Drawing**, **Setup View** and **Setup Profile** and profile the 3D model. Turn the **Pv** layer off to produce the profile model as shown in Fig. 14.26 above.

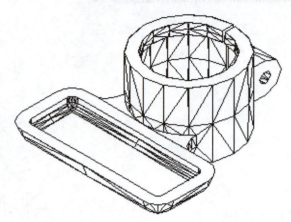

Fig. 14.31 **Stage 5**

Sectioning the example

1. Place in **World UCS**.
2. **Zoom** 1.
3. Call **Slice** and slice the 3D model through its centre.
4. Call **Section** and construct a section plane in line with the slice line.
5. Pace in **Front UCS**.
6. **Zoom** 1.
7. **Hatch** the section outline.
8. Place in **UCS World**.
9. **Zoom** 1.
10. **Move** the hatch to the section plane outline line using **Snap** set on.
11. Place in **3D Viewpoint** SW Isometric (Fig. 14.32).
12. **Change** hatching onto a new layer.
13. **Setup Drawing**.
14. **Setup Profile** (Fig. 14.33).
15. Freeze all layers except the **Pv** one and the layer holding the hatching. (Fig. 14.33).

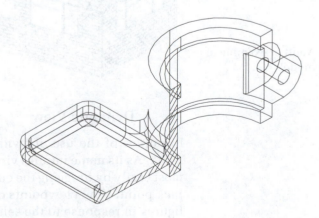

Fig. 14.32 The 3D model
before **Profile**

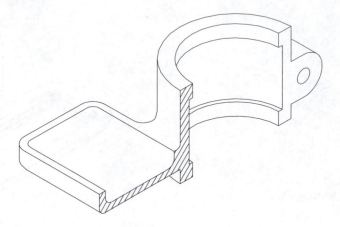

Fig. 14.33 The completed
example

Another example of a 3D model

Figure 14.34 is a 3D solid model drawing of a bungalow. The model
consists of a series of boxes of height 1 which have been joined
together with the Boolean operator **Union**. Each outer surface of the
model was outlined with **Polyline**, the outlines were then hatched
with appropriate hatch patterns.

The model is complete, in that no matter from which viewpoint
the model is viewed, a complete bungalow view is seen.

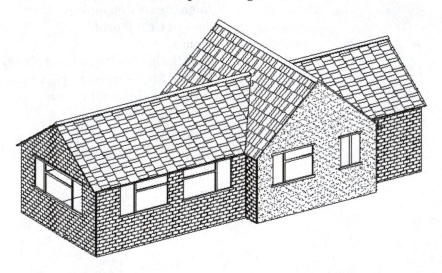

Fig. 14.34 Another example of
a 3D solid model

Dynamic View

Examples of the use of **Dynamic View** are given in Figs 14.36 –
14.42. As its name implies viewpoints can be selected dynamically,
most easily by *dragging* the cursor hairs around the model selection
pick point. New viewpoints can also be selected by the *entering* of
figures in response to the selection of prompts.

Fig. 14.35 Calling **Dynamic View** from the **View** pull-down menu

Experiment with **Dynamic View**, which is of particular value because its use enables 3D perspective views to be obtained. Once in perspective – with the aid of the **Distance** prompt, the view remains in perspective, so unless it is required, do not use the **Distance** prompt until other prompt responses have been completed. The tool (command) can be called either from the **View** pull-down menu (Fig. 14.35) or by *entering* dv (or dview) at the Command line:

> **Command: _dview**
> **Select objects:** in this example *pick* the 3D solid model **1 found**
> **Select objects:** *right-click*
> **CAmera/TArget/Distance/POints/PAn/TWist/CLip/Off/Undo/<eXit>:**
>   **TArget view**
> When the response to the **Dview** prompts is **Target**:
> **CAmera/TArget/Distance/POints/PAn/TWist/CLip/Off/Undo/<eXit>:**
>   *enter* ta *right-click*
> **Toggle angle in/Enter angle from XY plane <-32>:**

Either *enter* an angle figure, when another prompt appears asking for the angle in the **XY plane from X axis**, or, as shown in Fig. 14.36 toggle the required target position by moving the cursor hairs. The ghosted model moves its view with the toggling action.

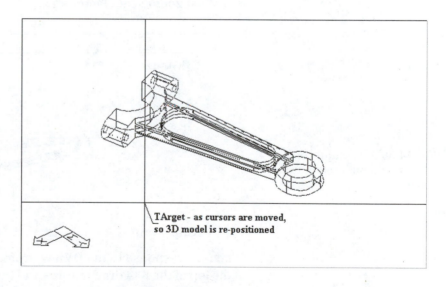

Fig. 14.36 An example of using the **TArget** prompt from **Dview**

TArget - as cursors are moved, so 3D model is re-positioned

TWist view

A similar toggling can be used when the response is **TWist**:

> **CAmera/TArget/Distance/POints/PAn/TWist/CLip/Off/Undo/<eXit>:**
>   *enter* tw *right-click*
> **New view twist <0.00>:**

A rubber band line becomes attached from the cursor hairs to the model and the twisting is toggled by moving the cursor hairs. Or, a figure can be *entered*. See Fig. 14.37.

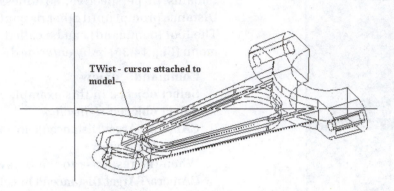

Fig. 14.37 An example of using the **TWist** prompt from **Dview**

Zoom view

When the response is **Zoom**, a slider appears at the top of the R14 drawing area. As the slider is adjusted under mouse control, the model zooms larger or smaller. Alternatively a zoom figure can be *entered* as a response:

Adjust zoom scale factor <1>:

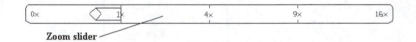

Zoom slider

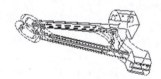

Fig. 14.38 An example of using the **Zoom** prompt from **Dview**

Clip View

When the response to the **DView** prompts is **CLip**, a slider appears at the top of the R14 drawing area and the Command line changes to:

Back/Front/OFF: *enter* b *right-click*

Moving the slider under mouse control alters the clipping plane, an example is shown in Fig. 14.39. If the response is f (for Front) the clipping takes place from the other end of the model.

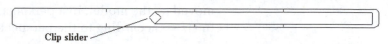

Clip slider

Fig. 14.39 An example of
using the **Clip** prompt from
Dview

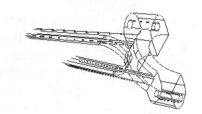

Hide view

Responding with the **Hide** response, hidden lines are removed from
the model (Fig. 14.40).

Fig. 14.40 An example of
using the **Hide** prompt from
Dview

Distance view

When the response to the **Dview** prompts is **Distance**, a distance
slider appears at the top of the R14 drawing area. It is advisable to
first *enter* a distance of, say 400, then respond with distance a second
time before setting the distance from the slider. As the slider is

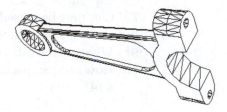

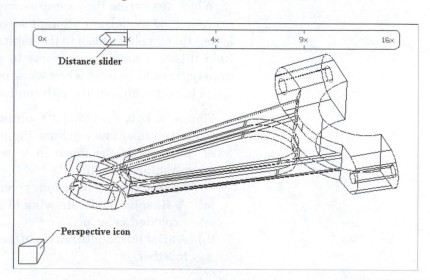

Distance slider

Perspective icon

Fig. 14.41 An example of
using the **Distance** prompt
from **Dview**

moved so the model, in a perspective view, increases, or decreases in size – according to the perspective distance. See Fig. 14.41.

Questions

1. What is the purpose of using the **Setup Profile** tool?
2. Why should the **Purge** tool be used before saving a 3D model drawing to file?
3. Why is it often good practice to use a three or four viewport set up when constructing a 3D model drawing than to construct the drawing in a single viewport?
4. What is the essential difference between **MSpace** and **PSpace**?
5. Can viewports and their contents be moved when working in **MSpace**?
6. When working in **PSpace** can viewports and their contents be copied?
7. Can they be erased?
8. Can they be rotated?
9. What are the differences between using **Dview** and using **Vpoint**?
10. How can perspective views of a 3D model drawing be obtained in R14?

Exercises

Each of the four questions below shows an exploded 3D model of some form of engineered device, together with fairly detailed dimensioned orthographic projections. Each of the exploded 3D drawings is a profile of a 3D solid model drawing.

When answering the exercises, either attempt the whole of the exploded 3D models, or attempt selected parts of the models. It is hoped that you have been in the habit of saving answers to exercises from this and previous chapters to personal disks, because your drawings could be used when working through the examples in the next chapter which deals with rendering of 3D models.

1. Figure 14.42 is a profiled 3D solid model drawing of a fence from a small circular saw machine. Figure 14.43 shows the dimensions of the parts of the fence in a two-view exploded third angle orthographic projection.

    Working to the dimensions given in Fig. 14.43 construct either:
    (a) A 3D solid model drawing of all the parts of the fence in an exploded view, or:
    (b) A 3D solid model drawing of the fence with the parts assembled together, or:

(c) Taking a part, or parts of your own choice, construct a 3D solid model of any part or parts.

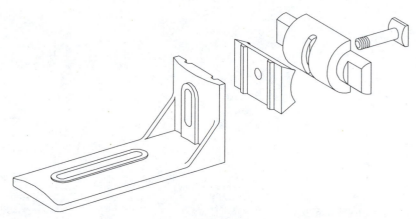

Fig. 14.42 Exercise 1

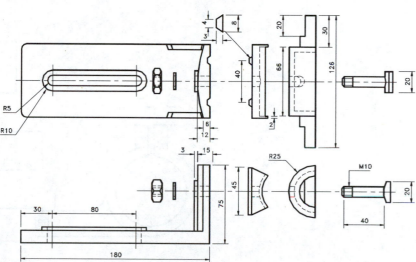

Fig. 14.43 Dimensioned views of the parts of Exercise 1

2. Figure 14.44 is an exploded and profiled 3D solid model drawing of part of a tool rest support from a lathe. Figures 14.45 and 14.46 show dimensioned orthographic views of the parts of the tool rest.

Working to the given dimensions, construct 3D solid model drawings of either the whole tool rest in an exploded view, or in an assembled view. Or take parts and construct 3D solid model drawing(s) of the parts you have selected.

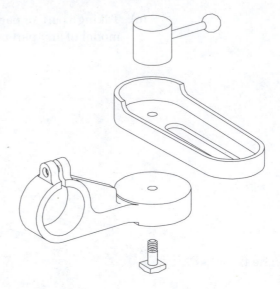

Fig. 14.44 Exercise 2

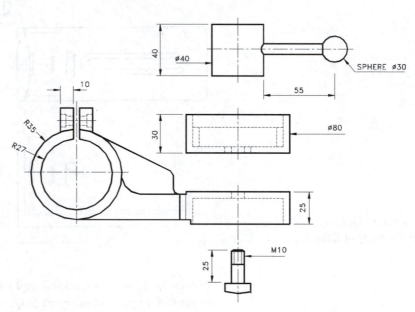

Fig. 14.45 Dimensioned views
of parts for Exercise 2

3. Figure 14.47 is an exploded, profiled 3D solid model drawing of a part from a marking device. Figure 14.48 gives dimensions of its various parts. Either:
   (a) Construct a 3D solid model drawing of the exploded device, or:
   (b) Construct a 3D solid model drawing of the assembled device, or:
   (c) Construct 3D solid model drawings of a selected part or selected parts of the device.

In each of your drawings include the marking scriber.

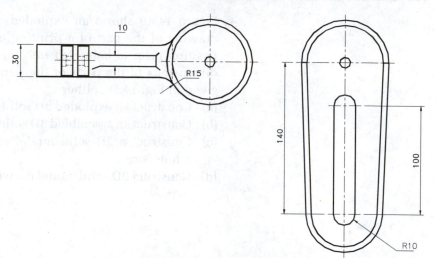

Fig. 14.46 Details of further
dimensions for Exercise 2

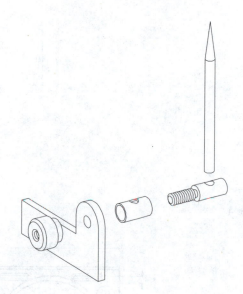

Fig. 14.47 Exercise 3

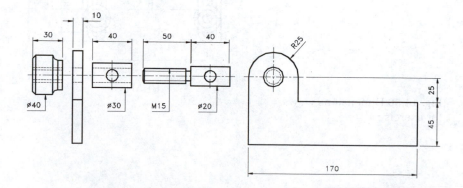

Fig. 14.48 Dimensions views
for Exercise 3

4. Figure 14.49 shows an exploded and profiled 3D solid model drawing of the part of a printing machine for holding paper in position prior to being fed into the machine. Figure 14.50 gives dimensions of the parts of the part. Working to the dimensions given in Fig. 14.50, either:

(a) Construct an exploded 3D solid model drawing of the part, or:

(b) Construct an assembled 3D solid model drawing of the part, or:

(c) Construct a 3D solid model of any selected item from the whole, or:

(d) Construct 3D solid model drawings of selected items from the part.

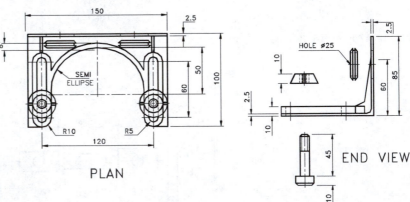

Fig. 14.49 Exercise 4

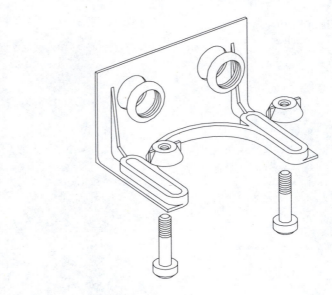

Fig. 14.50 Dimensions views for exercise 4

CHAPTER 15

The Rendering tools

Rendering

Fig. 15.1 The **Render** toolbar

Rendering is a system which produces photo-realistic coloured images from 3D solid drawings. Rendering in R14 usually follows a sequence such as:

1. A 3D solid model drawing is constructed.
2. The model is placed in a suitable UCS plane to allow lights to be included for illuminating the model.
3. Either colours or 'materials' are added to the model to give the rendering an appearance of having been made from the added materials.
4. The model is placed in a suitable viewing position.
5. The model is rendered. Backgrounds can be included in the rendering if required.

The Render toolbar

Right-click in any toolbar on screen and the **Toolbars** dialogue box appears. *Left-click* in the check box against **Render** and the **Render** toolbar appears on screen (Fig. 15.1).

Figure 15.2 shows the names of the tools in the toolbar.

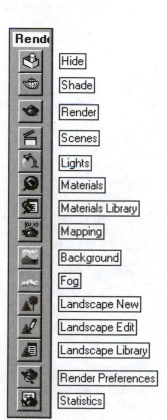

Fig. 15.2 The tools in the **Render** toolbar

Examples of rendering 3D models

Example 1

1. Construct a simple 3D solid model such as that shown in Fig. 15.3.

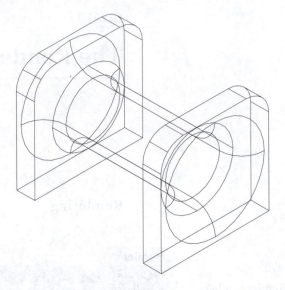

Fig. 15.3 The 3D model for
Example 1

2. Select the **Hide** tool, followed by a *left-click* on the model. The result is shown in Fig. 15.4. This is the same as calling **Hide** as described earlier.

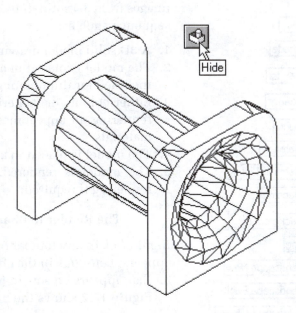

Fig. 15.4 The result of using
Hide

3. Select the **Shade** tool, followed by a *left-click* on the model. The model becomes shaded (Fig. 15.5). The method of shading depends upon the set variable **SHADEDGE**. See the **HELP** for the variable.

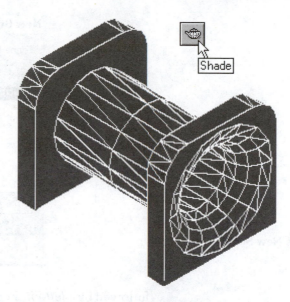

Fig. 15.5 The result of using
Shade

4. Select the **Render** tool. The **Render** dialogue box appears. Select
   current in the **Scene to Render:** list, followed by a *left-click* on the
   OK button. The model renders to the default lighting and colour
   (Fig. 15.6).

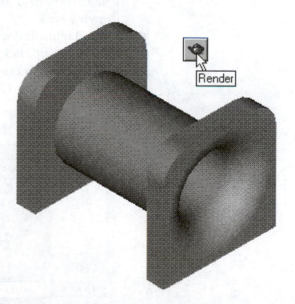

Fig. 15.6 The result of using
the **Render** tool

5. Select the **Scenes** tool. The **Scenes** dialogue box appears. *Left-click*
   on the **New...** button. The dialogue box is replaced with the **New
   Scene** box (Fig. 15.7). *Enter* a scene name in the **Scene Name:** box,

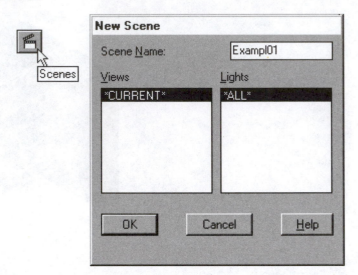

Fig. 15.7 The **New Scene**
dialogue box

followed by a *left-click* on the **OK** button. The scene name is added
to those already in the **Scene** dialogue box.

6. Select the **Lights** tool. The **Lights** dialogue box appears (Fig. 15.8).
   Lights for this example were added as follows:

   (a) Place the model in the **World UCS** and if necessary **Zoom** 0.5.
       If necessary also **Move** the model nearer the top of the R14
       drawing area.

   (b) In the **Lights** dialogue box select **Point Light** from the popup
       list. Then *left-click* on the **New...** button and the **New Point
       Light** dialogue box appears (Fig. 15.9). *Left-click* on the **Modify<**
       button and at the Command line:

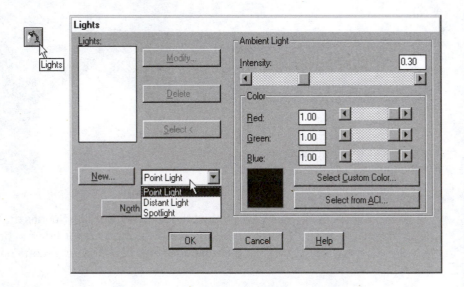

Fig. 15.8 The **Lights** dialogue
box

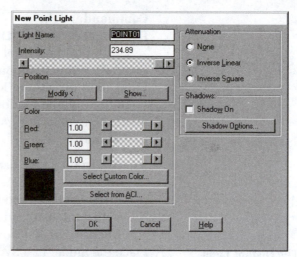

Fig. 15.9 The **New Point Light**
dialogue box

Command: _light
Enter light location <current<: *enter* .xy **of** *pick* a point immediately
    above the model
(need Z): *enter* 400 *right-click*
Command:

Fig. 15.10 The **Point light** icon

(c)   A light icon appears in position on the model. The icon is
      shown in Fig. 15.10 – in fact the icon appears in the drawing
      at such a small scale, that Fig. 15.10 is a large zoom of the icon.
(d)   The **Lights** dialogue box reappears. Select **Distant Light** from
      the popup list, followed by a *left-click* on the **New...** button.
      The **New Distant Light** dialogue box appears (Fig. 15.11). *Left-
      click* on the **Modify<** button and at the Command line:

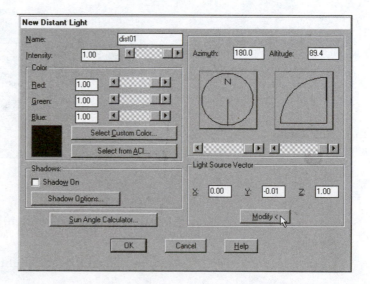

Fig. 15.11 The **New Distant
Light** dialogue box

Command: _light
Enter light direction TO <current>: *enter* .xy **of** *pick* a point about
    central to the model
(need Z): *enter* 50 (about half of the model height) *right-click*
Enter light direction FROM <current>: *enter* .xy **of** *pick* a point
    to the right and below the model
(need Z): *enter* 150 *right-click*
Command:

(e) A **Distant Light** icon appears at the selected position (Fig.
    15.12).
(f) Place another **Distant Light** to the left and below the model
    with it **Intensity** reduced to 70 – use the slider to the right of the
    Intensity figures box. Place its **direction from** height at 300.
7. Place the model in a **SW Isometric** viewing position.
8. **Zoom** the model to occupy most of the R14 drawing area.
9. *Left-click* on the **Render** tool icon. The **Render** dialogue box
   appears (Fig. 15.13). In the **Render** dialogue box, *left-click* on
   current, followed by another on the **OK** button. The result is shown
   in Fig. 15.14. Note the difference between this rendering and that
   of Fig. 15.6, in which default lighting was accepted.

Fig. 15.12 The **Distant Light**
icon

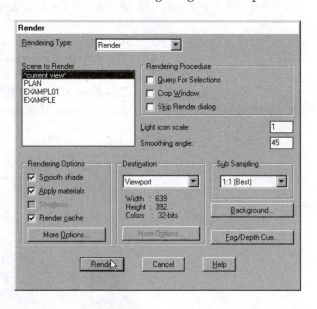

Fig. 15.13 The **Render**
dialogue box

Notes on lighting

1. R14 allows four types of lighting to be included with a rendering
   file:

Ambient: General overall lighting as if from all possible directions.

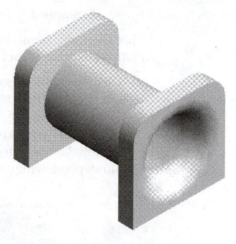

Fig. 15.14 Example 1

An ambient light value of 0.3 is generally accepted as the most suitable, but it can be increased or decreased if thought necessary. See Fig. 15.8. An area of the **Lights** dialogue box is devoted to **Ambient Light**.

Point: Light in all directions from the selected source. Point light diminishes with distance from its source

Distant: Light in parallel rays from a selected source. There is no diminution of the light no matter how far from the source at which the light is placed.

Spotlight: Light as if from a spotlight. The light is directional and in the form of a cone with a 'hotspot' cone forming a bright spot onto the model being illuminated.

2. It can be seen from all the light dialogue boxes that the intensity of the light can be varied, no matter which type is chosen.

3. It will also be seen from an examination of the light dialogue boxes that the colour of the light can be changed as required, either by altering the **Red:**, **Green:** and **Blue:** sliders or from a colour dialogue box.

4. In general at least four lights are advisable:

   Ambient at 0.3 intensity.
   Point light above the model to give a general illumination.
   A **Distant** light either front left or front right of a greater intensity than another **Distant** light on the alternate front left or front right.

5. Extra lights can be added as wished. In particular a light from behind the model, can be effective, either from directly behind, or from behind and below the model.

Example 2

This example, involving the model from Example 1, is shown in Plate VI because it includes the use of colour.

1. Select the **Materials Library** tool. The **Materials Library** dialogue box appears (Fig. 15.15). From the **Library List:** select **BRASS GIFMAP**. Then *left-click* on the **Preview** button. A preview of the selected material appears either on a sphere or a cube in the Preview box. A *left-click* in the box below the **Preview** button allows previewing on a sphere or on a cube from a small popup list.

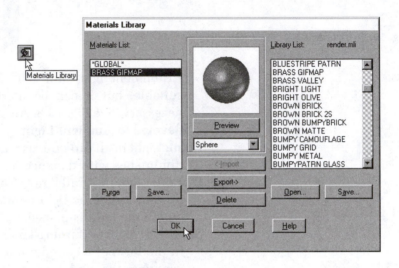

Fig. 15.15 The **Materials Library** dialogue box

2. *Left-click* on the **OK** button of the dialogue box.
3. Select the **Materials** tool. The **Materials** dialogue box appears (Fig. 15.16). Select **BRASS GIFMAP** and *left-click* on the **Attach<** button. Then *pick* the model.

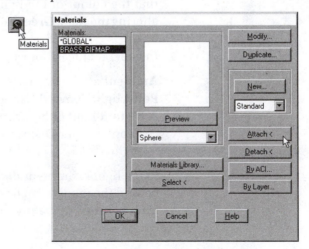

Fig. 15.16 The **Materials** dialogue box

4. Render the model which has now had the material **BRASS GIFMAP** attached.

Example 3

Figure 15.17 shows two profiled views of the 3D solid model for this example and Fig. 15.18 a rendering using the default lighting and materials.

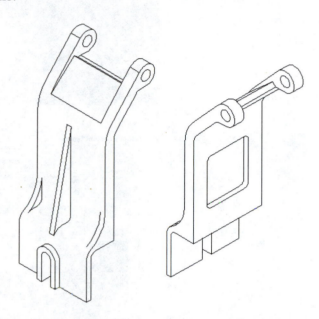

Fig. 15.17 Example 3. Profiled views of the 3D model

The final rendering is shown in Fig. 15.19. This rendering includes a background (**Whiteash.tga**) and lights are set to produce shadows. These two effects are obtained as follows:

Shadows

After setting the parameters for the lights, *left-click* on any of the light names in the **Lights** dialogue box, followed by another on the **Modify** button. The **Modify** light dialogue box for the chosen light will appear (Fig. 15.20). A *left-click* in the **Shadow On** check box of the dialogue box will cause the selected light to cast shadows in the rendering.

Background

Left-click on the **Background** tool icon in the **Render** toolbar. The **Background** dialogue box appears. In the dialogue box, backgrounds can be set in colour:

1. *Left-click* in the **Solid** check circle at the top of the dialogue box, followed by another in **AutoCAD Background** check circle.

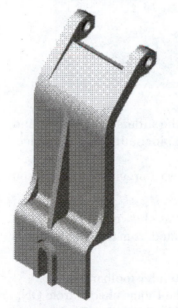

Fig. 15.18 Example 3. Default rendering

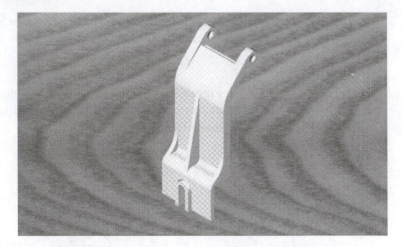

Fig. 15.19 Example 3

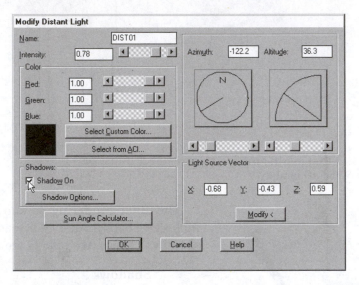

Fig. 15.20 Setting **Shadows ON** in the **Modify Distant Light** dialogue box

2. Either make up your own colour using the sliders **Red:**, **Green:** and **Blue:** or *left-click* on the **Select Custom Color** button and then select from the **Color** dialogue box.
3. A *left-click* on the **Preview** button allows a preview of the chosen background colour.

Or an **Image** can be set for a background as shown in Fig. 15.21 in which the file **Whiteash.tga** has been selected from the R14 **Textures** directory:

1. Select the **Background** tool from the **Render** toolbar.
2. In the **Background** dialogue box, set the **Image** check circle ON.
3. *Left-click* on the **Find File...** button (Fig. 15.21). The **Background Image** dialogue box (Fig. 15.22) appears. From the **Textures**

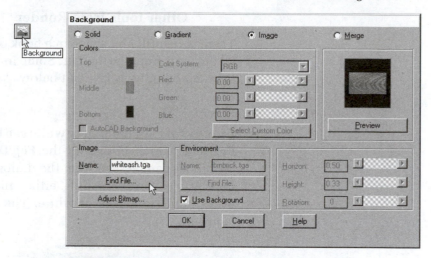

Fig. 15.21 The **Background**
dialogue box

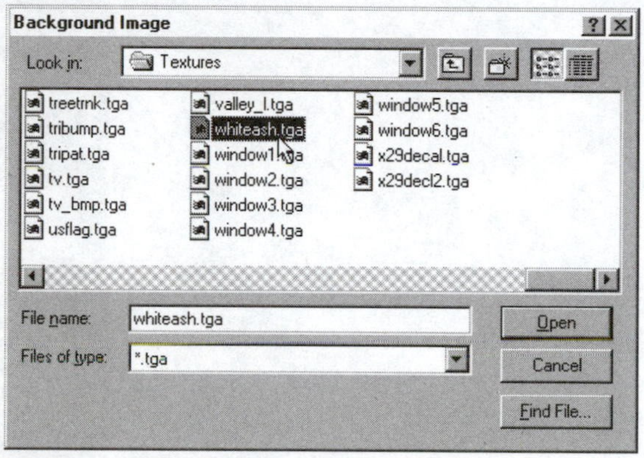

Fig. 15.22 The **Background**
Image dialogue box

directory, select the file **whiteash.tga**. *Left-click* on the dialogue
box **Open** button. The **Background** dialogue box reappears.

4. The selected background can be previewed by *clicking* on the
   Preview button as shown in Fig. 15.21.

Notes on renderings

1. Rendering inevitably takes time, no matter how fast the operating
   system of the computer being used. If shadows, materials and
   background are included with a 3D model, then rendering will take
   longer than rendering without these additions.
2. As a rendering is being applied, a series of comments will appear
   at the Command line indicating progress of the time being taken as
   the rendering proceeds.
3. A number of renderings of examples and exercises from previous
   chapters are included in the colour plates section.

Other tools from Render

There is insufficient space in a book of this nature to fully describe all the tools from the toolbar. Some indication of the effects of using the remaining tools is given below.

Fog

An effect of fog, coloured or white can be gained by first selecting the **Fog** tool, which brings up the **Fog/Depth Cue** dialogue box (Fig. 15.23). As can be seen from the dialogue box, a variety of different fog settings can be made – either included in the scene, or as a background, coloured or white. The depth of the fog can also be adjusted.

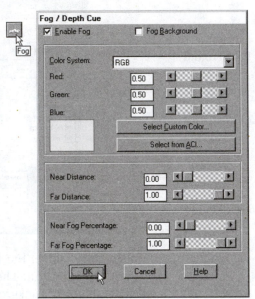

Fig. 15.23 The **Fog/Depth Cue** dialogue box

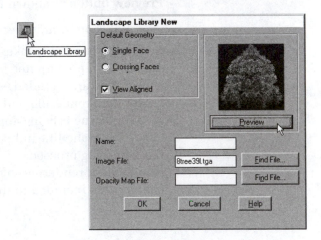

Fig. 15.24 The **Landcape Library New** dialogue box

Landscapes

A variety of landscape effects can be included in a scene with the aid of the **Landscape New**, **Landscape Edit** and **Landscape Library** tools. Figure 15.24 shows the secondary dialogue box when **Landscape Library** is called. A *left-click* on **New...** in the **Landscape Library** dialogue box (not shown) and the **Landscape Library New** dialogue box appears. In Fig. 15.24, the file **8tree391.tga** has been selected from the R14 **Textures** directory and a *left-click* on the **Preview** button shows the graphics in the Preview box.

Rendering Preferences

Finally, select the **Rendering Preferences** tool and the appropriate dialogue box comes to screen (Fig. 15.25). As can be seen from Fig. 15.25 settings can be made as wished to the methods by which renderings can be achieved.

Note: The reader is advised to experiment with the tools from the **Render** toolbar on some simple 3D models in order to understand the possibilities of rendering more fully.

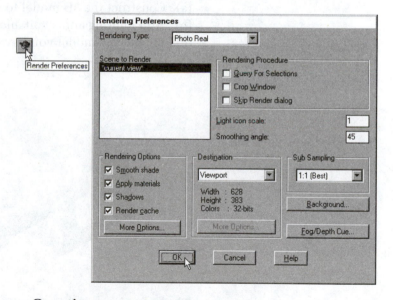

Fig. 15.25 The **Rendering Preferences** dialogue box

Questions

1. What is meant by the term 'rendering'?
2. What is the usual sequence by which a 3D solid model drawing is rendered?
3. What are the differences resulting from using the **Shade** tool and using the **Render** tool?

4. The results obtained by using the **Shade** tool are controlled by a set variable. What is its name?
5. Can you name the types of lights used in rendering?
6. What is meant by 'default lighting' when referring to the rendering of a 3D model?
7. Can you suggest the positions of lights for good general lighting of a 3D model prior to rendering?
8. What is the three-letter extension given to the file containing a library of materials?
9. How is a background scene applied to a rendering of a 3D model?
10. Can a profiled 3D model be rendered?

Exercises

If you have saved 3D model drawings resulting from answering exercises from previous chapters, now is the time to practise rendering them.

1. Figure 15.26 is a rendering of the 3D model, the dimensions for which are shown in the orthographic projection given in Fig. 15.27.
   (a) Construct the 3D model to the given dimensions.
   (b) Add lighting and a suitable material.
   (c) Render the model you have constructed.

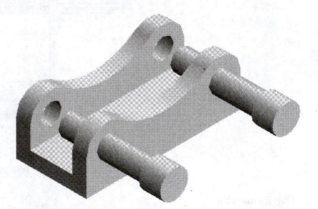

Fig. 15.26 Exercise 1

2. The dimensioned plan given in Fig. 15.28 shows a washer from a watering device. Construct a joined polyline of the plan, extrude the outline you have drawn to a height of 10; subtract from the extrusion a cylinder for the central hole. Add suitable lighting and a plastic type material. Place the 3D model you have constructed in a good viewing position and then render.

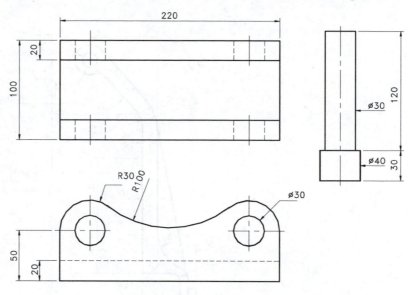

Fig. 15.27 Dimensions for
Exercise 1

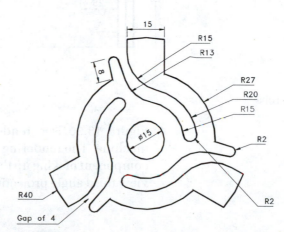

Fig. 15.28 Exercise 3

3. Figure 15.29 gives the dimensions for the rendered 3D model
   shown in Example 3 in this chapter. The model is part of a
   draughting machine used when construing technical drawings by
   hand.

   This is a fairly difficult exercise in the construction of a 3D
   model.

   (a) Working to the dimensions given in Fig. 15.29 construct a 3D
       model of the part.
   (b) Add suitable lighting and a metal material.
   (c) Place the 3D model in a suitable viewing position and render.

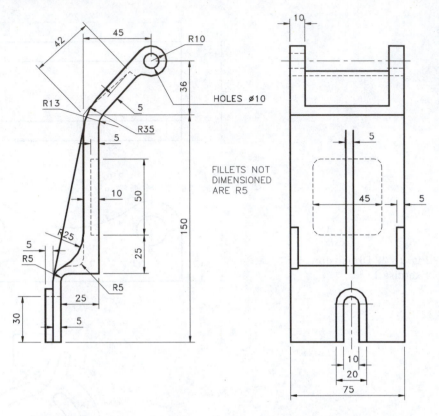

Fig. 15.29 Exercise 3

4. Figure 15.30 is a rendering of a part from a tool sharpening machine. The rendering has a different metallic material for each component making up the part. Figure 15.31 is a dimensioned two-view third angle projection of the components making up the part.

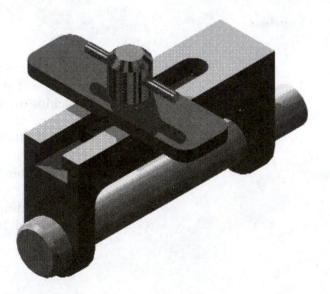

Fig. 15.30 Exercise 4

(a) Working to the dimensions given in Fig. 15.31 construct 3D models of each of the components making up the part.

(b) Move the components into positions as if they were correctly assembled.

(c) Add lighting and materials.

(d) Place the model in a suitable viewing position and render.

Another fairly difficult 3D model to construct.

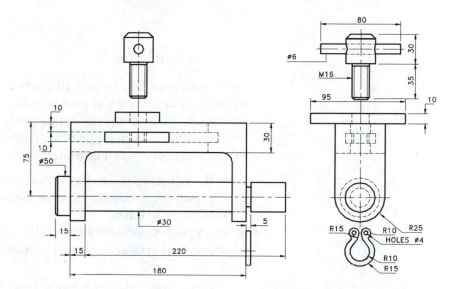

Fig. 15.31 Exercise 4. Dimensioned two-view third angle projection

Appendix A

Printing and plotting

Introduction

Most readers of this book will probably be working at computers already set up to print or plot to default, previously set printers or plotters. In many cases the printer will be the default Windows 95 printer which is used for printing from applications other than R14. Printers or plotters can be added to the computer in use by:

1. In the Windows 95 start-up window, *left-click* on the **Start** button.
2. Then *left-click* on **Settings** in the menu which appears, followed by another on **Printers**.
3. The **Printers** window appears, showing some icons. *Double-click* on the **Add Printer** icon and the **Add Printer Wizard** appears (Fig. A.1).
4. Select a manufacturer's name from the **Manufacturer's** list and then a printer or plotter from the **Printers:** list.
5. Insert the disk containing the driver for the chosen printer or plotter and add the device to those already loaded into Windows 95. The loaded driver can now be used by R14 users.

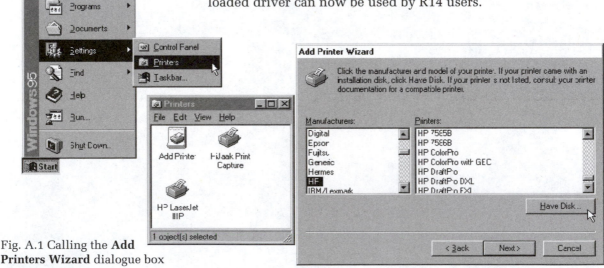

Fig. A.1 Calling the **Add Printers Wizard** dialogue box

Printing or plotting

When a drawing is to be printed or plotted, call the **Plot** tool.

1. As shown in Fig. A.2 the tool can be called either from the **File** pull-down menu, from the **Plot** tool in the **Standard** toolbar, or by *entering* plot at the Command line.

Fig. A.2 Calling the **Plot** tool

2. The **Print/Plot Configuration** dialogue box appears (Fig. A.3). As can be seen a variety of settings can be made in the dialogue box. To take a typical example:

    (a) *Left-click* in the **Hide** check box. The drawing is a 3D model drawing and it is wished to hide hidden lines in the printout.

    (b) *Left-click* on the **Window...** button. The **Window Selection** box appears (Fig. A.4).

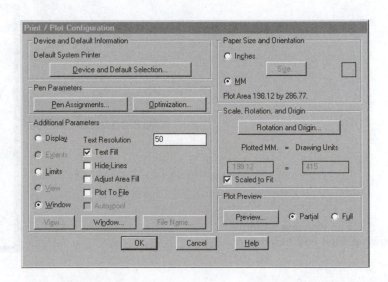

Fig. A.3 The **Print/Plot Configuration** dialogue box

(c) *Left-click* on the **Pick<** button. The box disappears allowing the operator to window the area of the drawing required in the print.

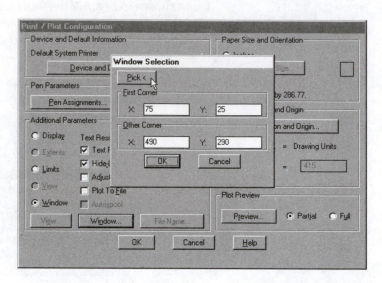

Fig. A.4 The **Window Selection** box

3. The **Window Selection** box reappears. *Left-click* on its **OK** button and the **Print/Plot Configuration** dialogue box reappears. *Left-click* in the **Full** check circle in the **Preview** area of the dialogue box followed by another on the **Preview** button. A preview of the drawing as it will appears when printed or plotted appears on screen (Fig. A.5).

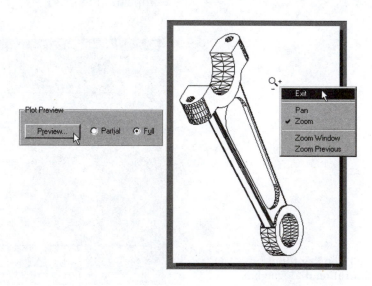

Fig. A.5 The **Preview** window showing what will be printed

4. *Right-click* near the icon in the preview window and again on **Exit**. The **Print/Plot Configuration** box reappears. *Left-click* on the **OK** button of the dialogue box and drawing is printed (or plotted).

5. If there is any detail in connection with the printer or plotter in use which is not correct a warning box such as that shown in Fig. A.6 will appear.

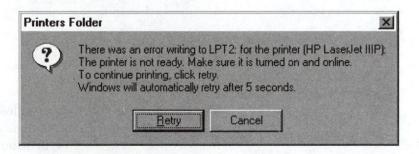

Fig. A.6 The **Printers Folder** warning box appearing if anything is incorrect

Note: The above is not the only method of printing or plotting, but is one that is widely used. Other set-ups can be configured.

Glossary of tools (Commands)

Introduction

Many of the tools shown in this glossary have not been described in the pages of this book. This book is intended for those learning how to use AutoCAD Release 14. In order to keep the book to a reasonable size on the grounds of cost to the reader, it has been necessary to restrict descriptions of tool usage to those considered to be essential to the beginner. It is hoped this glossary will encourage readers to experiment with those tools (commands) not described earlier.

Note: The letters in brackets after the tool (command) name show the abbreviation or key shortcuts for the tool.

3DARRAY – Creates an array of 3D models in 3D space.

3DFACE (3F) – Creates a three or four sided 3D mesh behind which other features can be hidden.

3DMESH – Creates a 3D mesh in 3D space.

3DSIN – Brings the **3D Studio File Import** dialogue box on screen.

3DSOUT – Brings the **3D Studio Output File** dialogue box on screen.

ABOUT – Brings the **About AutoCAD** bitmap on screen.

ACSIN – Imports an **ACIS** file into R14.

ACSOUT – Exports 3D solid models to **ACIS** file format.

ALIGN – Allows selected entities to be aligned to selected points in 3D space.

AMECONVERT – Converts AME solid models (from Release 12) into R14 solid models.

APPLOAD – Brings the **Load AutoLISP, ADS, and ARX files** dialogue box to screen.

ARC (A) – Creates an arc.

AREA – States in square units of the area selected from a number of points.

ARRAY (AR) – Creates **Perpendicular** or **Polar** arrays in 2D.

ASE – Provides links between AutoCAD and databases.

ASEADMIN – Allows access to databases.

ASEEXPORT – Exports data to databases.

ASELINKS – Manipulates links between AutoCAD and databases.

ASEROWS – Edits links between AutoCAD and databases.

ASESELECT – Creates links in rows between objects and databases.

ASEQLED – Executes SQL (Structured Query Links).

ATTDEF – Allows editing of attributes from the Command line.

ATTEDIT – Allows editing of attributes from the Command line.

AUDIT – Checks and fixes any errors in a drawing.

BHATCH (H) – Brings the **Boundary Hatch** dialogue box on screen.

BLIPMODE – Sets blips on or off (1 or 0).

BLOCK – Saves a drawing to a block within the drawing in which it was saved.

BMAKE (B) – Brings the **Block Definition** dialogue box on screen.

BMPOUT – Brings the **Create BMP File** dialogue box.

BOX – Creates a 3D solid box.

BOUNDARY (BO) – Brings the **Boundary Creation** dialogue box on screen.

BREAK – Breaks an object into parts.

CAL – For the calculation of mathematical expressions.

CALC – Brings the Windows 95 **Calculator** to screen.

CHAMFER (CHA) – Creates a chamfer between two entities.

CHPROP (CH) – Change properties of an entity through the **Change Properties** dialogue box.

CIRCLE (C) – Creates a circle.

CONE – Creates a 3D model of a cone.

COPY (CO) – Creates a single or multiple copies of selected entities.

COPYCLIP (Ctrl+C) – Copies part of a drawing to the Windows 95 **Clipboard.**

COPYLINK – Forms a link between an AutoCAD drawing and its appearance in another application such as a word processing package.

CYLINDER – Creates a 3D cylinder.

DBLIST – Creates a database list in a Text window for every entity in a drawing.

DDATTDEF (AT) – Brings the **Attribute Definition** dialogue box to screen.

DDATTE (ATE) – Edits individual attribute values.

DDATTEXT – Brings the **Attribute Extraction** dialogue box on screen.

DDCHPROP – Brings the **Change Properties** dialogue box on screen.

DDCOLOR (COL) – Brings the **Select Color** dialogue box on screen.

DDEDIT (ED) – Select text and the **Edit Text** dialogue box appears.

DDGRIPS (GR) – Brings the **Grips** dialogue box on screen.

DDIM (D) – Brings the **Dimensions Styles** dialogue box on screen.

DDINSERT (I) – Brings the **Insert** dialogue box on screen.

DDMODIFY (M) – Brings the **Modify** dialogue box for the selected entity on screen.

DDOSNAP (OS) – Brings the **Osnap Settings** dialogue box on screen.

DDPTYPE – Brings the **Point Style** dialogue box on screen.

DDRENAME – Brings the **Rename** dialogue box on screen.

DDRMODES (RM) – Brings the **Drawing Aids** dialogue box on screen.

DDESELECT (SE) – Brings the **Object Selection Settings** dialogue box on screen.

DDUCS (UC) – Brings the **UCS Control** dialogue box on screen.

DDUCSP (UCP) – Brings the **UCS Orientation** dialogue box on screen.

DDUNITS (UN) – Brings the **Units Control** dialogue box on screen.

DDVIEW (V) – Brings the **View Control** dialogue box on screen.

DDVPOINT (VP) – Brings the **Viewpoint Presets** dialogue box on screen.

DEL – Allows a file (any file) to be deleted.

DIM – Starts a session of dimensioning.

DIM1 – Allows the addition of a single addition of a dimension to a drawing.

Note: There are a large number of set variables controlling methods of dimensioning. These are not included here.

DIST (DI) – Measures the distance between two points in coordinate units.

DIVIDE (DIV) – Divides and entity into equal parts.

DONUT (DO) – Creates a donut.

DSVIEWER – Brings the **Aerial View** window on screen.

DTEXT (T) – Creates dynamic text. Text appears in drawing area as it is entered.

DVIEW (DV) – Instigates the dynamic view prompts sequence.

DXBIN – Brings the **Select DXF File** dialogue box on screen.

DXFOUT – Brings the **Create DXF File** dialogue box on screen.

DXFIN – Brings the Select DXF File dialogue box on screen.

EDGESURF – Creates a 3D mesh surface from four adjoining edges.

ELLIPSE (EL) – Creates an ellipse.

END – Finishes a drawing session and closes AutoCAD down.

ERASE – Erases selected entities from a drawing.

EXIT – Ends a drawing session and closes AutoCAD down.

EXPLODE (X) – Explodes a block or group into its various entities.

EXPLORER – Brings the Windows 95 Explorer on screen.

EXPORT (EXP) – Brings the **Export Data** dialogue box on screen.

EXTEND (EX) – To extend an entity to another.

EXTRUDE (EXT) – Extrudes a closed polyline.

FILLET (F) – Creates a fillet between two entities.

FILTER – Brings the **Object Selection Filters** dialogue box on screen.

GROUP (G) – Brings the **Object Grouping** dialogue box on screen.

HATCH – Allows hatching by the *entry* responses to prompts.

HATCHEDIT (HE) – Brings the **Hatchedit** dialogue box on screen.

HELP – Brings the **Help Topics** dialogue box on screen.

HIDE (HI) – To hide hidden lines in 3D models.

ID – Identifies a point on screen in coordinate units.

IMAGEADJUST (IAD) – Brings the **Image Adjust** dialogue box on screen.

IMAGEATTACH (IAT) – Brings the **Image Attach File** dialogue box on screen.

IMAGECLIP (IIM) – Brings the **Image** dialogue box on screen.

IMPORT (IM) – Brings the **Import File** dialogue box on screen.

INSERT – Allows the insertion of a block by response to prompts at the Command line.

INSERTOBJ (INS) – Brings the **Insert Object** dialogue box.

INTERFERE (IN) – Creates an interference solid from selection of several solids.

INTERSECT (INT) – Creates an interference solid from a group of two or more solids.

ISOPLANE – Sets the isoplane when constructing an isometric drawing.

LAYER (LA) – Brings the **Layer and Linetype** dialogue box on screen.

LENGTHEN (LEN) – Lengthen an entity on screen.

LIGHT – Brings the **Lights** dialogue box on screen.

LIMITS – Sets the drawing limits in coordinate units.

LINE (L) – Creates a line.

LINETYPE (LT) – Brings the **Layer and Linetype** dialogue box on screen.

LIST (LI) – Lists in an text window details of any entity or group of entities selected.

LOAD – Brings the **Select Drawing File** dialogue box on screen.

LOGFILEOFF – The Text window contents are no longer recorded.

LOGFILEON – The Text window contents are recorded.

LTSCALE (LTS) – Allows the linetype scale to be adjusted.

MATCHPROP (MA) – Brings the **Property Settings** dialogue box on screen.

MATLIB – Brings the **Materials Library** dialogue box on screen.

MEASURE (ME) – Allows measured intervals to be placed along entities.

MENU – Brings the **Select Menu File** dialogue box on screen.

MENULOAD – Brings the **Menu Customization** dialogue box on screen.

MIRROR (MI) – Creates an identical mirror image to selected entities.

MIRROR3D – Mirrors 3D models in 3D space in selected directions.

MLEDIT – Brings the **Multiline Edit Tools** dialogue box on screen.

MLINE (ML) – Creates mlines.

MLSTYLE – Brings the **Multiline Styles** dialogue box on screen.

MOVE (M) – Allows selected entities to be moved.

MSLIDE – Brings the **Create Slide File** dialogue box on screen.

MSPACE (MS) – Changes from Paperspace to Modelspace.

MTEXT (MT) – Brings the **Multiline Text Editor** on screen.

MVIEW (MV) – When in PSpace brings in MSpace objects.

MVSETUP – Allows drawing specifications to be set up.

NEW (Ctrl+N) – Brings the **Create New Drawing** dialogue box on screen.

NOTEPAD – Brings the Windows 95 **Notepad** on screen.

OFFSET (O) – Offsets selected entity by a stated distance.

OOPS – Cancels the effect of using **Erase** and brings back a drawing after **WBlock.**

OPEN – Brings the **Select File** dialogue box on screen.

ORTHO – Allows ortho to be set ON/OFF.

PAN (P) – Pans the R14 drawing editor in any direction.

PASTECLIP (Ctrl+V) – Pastes a bitmap from the **Clipboard** into the drawing area.

PASTESPEC (PA) – Brings the **Paste Special** dialogue box on screen.

PBRUSH – Brings Windows 95 **Paint** on screen.

PEDIT (PE) – Allows editing of polylines.

PFACE – Allows the construction of a 3D mesh through a number of selected vertices.

PLAN – Allows a drawing in 3D space to be seen in plan (UCS World).

PLINE (PL) – Creates a polyline.

PLOT (Ctrl+P) – Brings the **Plot/Print Configuration** dialogue box to screen.

POINT (PO) – Allows a point to be placed on screen.

POLYGON (POL) – Creates a polygon.

POLYLINE (PL) – Creates a polyline.

PREFERENCES (PR) – Brings the **Preferences** dialogue box on screen.

PREVIEW (PRE) – Brings the print/plot preview box on screen.

PSFILL – Allows polylines to be filled with patterns.

PSIN – Brings the **Select Postscript File** dialogue box on screen.

PSOUT – Brings the **Create Postscript File** dialogue box on screen.

PSPACE (PS) – Changes Modelspace to Paperspace.

PURGE (PU) – Purges unwanted data from a drawing before saving to file.

QSAVE – Quicksave. Saves the drawing file to its current name.

QUIT (Q) – Ends a drawing session and closes down AutoCAD.

RAY – A construction line from a point and (Usually) at an angle.

RECONFIG – Reconfigures the set up for rendering.

RECOVER – Brings the **Select File** dialogue box on screen to allow recovery of selected drawings as necessary.

RECTANG – Creates a pline rectangle.

REDEFINE – If an AutoCAD Command name has been turned off by **Undefine** turns the command name back on.

REDO – Cancels the last **Undo**.

REDRAW (R) – Redraws the contents of the R14 drawing area.

REDRAWALL (RA) – Redraws the whole of a drawing.

REGEN (RE) – Regenerates the contents of the R14 drawing area.

REGENALL (REA) – Regenerates the whole of a drawing.

REGION (REG) – Creates a region from an area within a boundary.

RENAME (REN) – Brings the **Rename** dialogue box on screen.

RENDER (RRE) – Brings the **Render** dialogue box on screen.

REPLAY – Brings the **Replay** dialogue box on screen from which bitmap image files can be selected.

REVOLVE (REV) – Forms a solid of revolution from outlines.

REVSURF – Creates a solid of revolution from a pline.

RMAT – Brings the **Materials** dialogue box on screen.

ROTATE (RO) – Rotates selected entities around a selected point.

ROTATE3D – Rotates a 3D model in 3D space in all directions.

RPREF (RPR) – Brings the **Rendering Preferences** dialogue box on screen.

RULESURF – Creates a 3D mesh between two entities.

SAVE (Ctrl+S) – Brings the **Save Drawing As** dialogue box on screen.

SAVEAS – Brings the **Save Drawing As** dialogue box on screen.

SAVEASR12 – Allows a drawing to be saved in Release 12 drawing file format.

SAVEIMG – Brings the **Save Image** dialogue box on screen.

SCALE (SC) – Allows selected entities to be scaled in size – smaller or larger.

SCENE – Brings the **Scene** dialogue box on screen.

SCRIPT (SCR) – Brings the **Select Script File** dialogue box on screen.

SECTION (SEC) – Creates a section plane in a 3D model.

SETVAR (SET) – Can be used to bring a list of the settings of set variables into an AutoCAD Text window.

SHADE (SHA) – Shades a selected 3D model.

SHAPE – Inserts an already loaded shape into a drawing.

SHELL – Allows MS-DOS commands to be entered.

SKETCH – Allows freehand sketching.

SLICE (SL) – Allows a 3D model to be cut into two parts.

SOLID (SO) – Creates a filled outline in triangular parts.

SOLPROF – Creates a profile from a 3D solid model drawing.

SPELL (SP) – Brings the **Check Spelling** dialogue box on screen.

SPHERE – Creates a 3D solid model sphere.

SPLINE (SPL) – Creates a spline curve through selected points.

SPLINEDIT (SPE) – Allows the editing of a spline curve.

STATS – Brings the **Statistics** dialogue box on screen.

STATUS – Shows the status (particularly memory use) in a Text window.

STLOUT – Saves a 3D model drawing in ASCII or binary format.

STRETCH (S) – Allows selected entities to be stretched.

STYLE (ST) – Brings the **Text Styles** dialogue box on screen.

SUBTRACT (SU) – Subtracts one 3D solid from another.

TABLET (TA) – Allows a tablet to be used with a pointing device.

TABSURF – Creates a 3D solid from an outline and a direction vector.

TBCONFIG – Brings the **Toolbars** dialogue box ion screen to allow configuration of a toolbar.

TEXT – Allows text from the Command line to be entered into a drawing.

TEXTQULTY – Sets the resolution for printing True Type text for plotting.

THICKNESS (TH) – Sets the thickness for the Elevation command.

TOLERANCE (TO) – Brings the **Symbol** dialogue box on screen from which geometric tolerance symbols can be selected.

TOOLBAR (TO) – Brings the **Toolbars** dialogue box on screen.

TORUS (TOR) – Allows a 3D torus to be created.

TRIM (TR) – Allows entities to be trimmed up to other entities.

TYPE – Types the contents of a named file to screen.

UNDEFINE – Suppresses an AutoCAD command name.

UNDO (U) (Ctrl+Z) – Undoes the last action of a tool.

UNION (UNI) – Unites 3D solids into a single solid.

VIEW – Allows a view to be controlled – deleted restored or saved.

VPLAYER – Controls the visibility of layers in paperspace.

VPOINT – Allows viewing positions to be set by x,y,z entries.

VPORTS – Allows viewport settings to be made.

VSLIDE – Brings the **Select Slide File** dialogue box on screen.

WBLOCK (W) – Brings the **Create Drawing File** dialogue box on screen.

WEDGE (WE) – Creates a 3D solid in the shape of a wedge.

WMFIN – Brings the **Import WMF File** dialogue box on screen.

WMFOPTS – Brings the **Import Options** dialogue box on screen.

WMFOUT – Brings the **Create WMF** dialogue box on screen.

XATTACH (XA) – Brings the **Select file to attach** dialogue box on screen.

XLINE – Creates a construction line.

XREF (XR) – Brings the **External Reference** dialogue box on screen.

ZOOM (Z) – Brings the zoom tool into action.

Set variables

Introduction

AutoCAD R14 is controlled by over 270 set variables, many of which are automatically set when making entries in dialogue boxes. Many are also automatically set or read only variables depending upon the configuration of R14.

Below is a list of those set variables which are of interest in that they often require to be set by *entering* figures or letters at the Command line. To set a variable, enter its name at the Command line and respond to the prompts which are seen.

To see all the set variables, *enter* set (or setvar) at the Command line:

Command: *enter* set *right-click*
SETVAR Variable name or ?: *enter* ? *right-click*
Variables(s) to list <*>: *right-click*

and a Text window opens showing a list of the first of the variables. To follow on the list press the **Return** key when prompted.

ANGDIR – Sets angle direction. **0** counterclockwise; **1** clockwise.
APERTURE – Sets size of pick box in pixels.
ATTDIA – Set to **1** INSERT uses a dialogue box; set to **0** no dialogue box for INSERT.
BLIPMODE – Set to **1** marker blips show; set to **0** no blips.
CMDIA – Set to **1** enables **Plot** dialogue boxes: set to **0** disables **Plot** dialogue box.

Note: DIM variables – There are between 50 and 60 variables for setting dimensioning, but most are in any case set in the **Dimension Styles** dialogue box or as dimensioning proceeds. However, one series of the **DIM** variables may be of interest:

DIMBLK – Sets a name for the block drawn for an operator's own arrowheads. These are drawn in unit sizes and saved as required.
DIMBLK1 – Operator's arrowhead for first end of line.

DIMBLK2 – Operator's arrowhead for other end of line.

DRAGMODE – Set to **0** no dragging; set to **1** dragging on; set to **2** automatic dragging.

DRAGP1 – Sets regeneration drag sampling. Initial value is 10.

DRAGP2 – Sets fast dragging regeneration rate. Initial value is 25.

EDGEMODE – Controls the use of **Trim** and **Extend**. Set to **0** does not use extension mode; set to **1** uses extension mode.

FILEDIA – Set to **0** disables dialogue boxes; set to **1** enables dialogue boxes.

FILLMODE – Set to **0** entities created with **Solid** are not filled; set to **1** they are filled.

MIRRTEXT – Set to **0** text direction is retained; set to **1** text is mirrored.

PELLIPSE – Set to **0** creates true ellipses; set to **1** polyline ellipses.

PICKBOX – Sets selection pick box height in pixels.

PICKDRAG – Set to **0** selection windows picked by two corners; set to **1** selection windows are dragged from corner to corner.

QTEXTMODE – Set to **0** turns off Quick Text; set to **1** enables Quick Text.

SAVETIME – Sets Automatic Save time. Initially 120. Set to **0** disables Automatic Save time.

SHADEDGE – Set to **0** faces are shade, edges are not highlighted; set to **1** faces are shaded, edges in colour of entity; set to **2** faces are not shaded, edges in entity colour; set to **3** faces in entity colour, edges in background colour.

SKETCHINC – Sets the **Sketch** record increment. Initial value is **0.1**.

SKPOLY – Set to **0** and **Sketch** makes line; set to **1 and** Sketch makes polylines.

SURFTAB1 – Sets mesh density in the M direction for surfaces generated by the **Surfaces** tools.

SURFTAB2 – Sets mesh density in the N direction for surfaces generated by the **Surfaces** tools.

TEXTFILL – Set to **0** True Type text shows as outlines only; set to **1** True Type text is filled.

TILEMODE – Set to **0** Paperspace enabled; set to **1** tiled viewports in Modelspace.

TOOLTIPS – Set to **0** no tool tips; set to **1** tool tips enabled.

TRIMMODE – Set to **0** edges not trimmed when **Chamfer** and **Fillet** are used; set to **1** edges are trimmed.

UCSFOLLOW – Set to **0** new UCS settings do not take effect; set to **1** UCS settings follow requested settings.

UCSICON – Set **OFF** and the UCS icon does not show; set to **ON** and it shows.

Glossary of computer terms

This glossary contain some of the more common computing terms.

Application – The name given to software packages that perform the tasks such as word processing, Desktop Publishing, CAD etc.

ASCII – American national standard code for information interchange. A code which assigns bits to characters used in computing.

AT – Advanced technology. Applied to PCs which have an 80286 processor (or better).

Attribute – Text appearing in a drawing, often linked to a block.

Autodesk – The American company which produces AutoCAD and other CAD software packages.

BASIC – Beginners all-purpose symbolic instruction code. A programming language.

Baud rate – A measure of the rate at which a computer system can send and receive information (measured in bits per second).

BIOS – Basic input/output system. The chip in a PC that controls the operations performed by the hardware (e.g. disks, screen, keyboard etc.).

Bit – Short for binary digit. Binary is a form of mathematics that uses only two numbers: 0 and 1. Computers operate completely on binary mathematics.

Block – A group of objects or entities on screen that have been linked together to act as one unit.

Booting up – Starting up a computer to an operating level.

Bus – An electronic channel that allows the movement of data around a computer.

Byte – A sequence of 8 bits.

C – A computer programming language.

Cache – A section of memory (can be ROM or RAM) which holds data that is being frequently used. Speeds up the action of disks and applications.

CAD – Computer-aided design. Should not be used to mean computer-aided drawing.

CAD/CAM – Computer-aided design and manufacturing.

CD-ROM – Computer disc read only memory. A disk system capable of storing several hundred Mb of data – commonly 640 Mb. Data can only be read from a CD-ROM, not written to it.

CGA – Colour graphic adaptor. A screen display with a resolution of 320 × 200 in four colours. Not used much with modern CAD systems.

Chips – Pieces of silicon (usually) that have the electronic circuits that drive computers formed on their surface.

Clock speed – Usually given in megaherz (MHz) – this is the measure of the speed at which a computer processor works.

Clone – Refers to a PC that functions in a way identical to the original IBM PC.

CMOS – Complimentary metal oxide semiconductor. Often found as battery powered chips which control features such as the PC's clock-speed.

Command Line – In AutoCAD the Command Line is a window in which typed commands are entered, and which display the prompts for, and responses to, these commands.

Communications – Describes the software and hardware that allow computers to communicate.

Compatible – Generally used as a term for software able to run on any computer that is an IBM clone.

Co-processor – A processor chip in a computer that runs in tandem with the main processor chip, and can deal with arithmetic involving many significant figures ('floating-point' arithmetic). Often used in CAD systems to speed up drawing operations.

CPU – Central processing unit. The chip that drives a PC.

Data – Information that is created, used or stored on a computer in digital form.

Database – A piece of software that can store, handle and organise large amounts of information.

Dialogue box – A window that appears on screen in which options may be presented to the user, or which requires the user to input information requested by the current application.

Directories – The system in MS-DOS for organising files on disk. Could be compared with a folder (the directory) containing documents (the files).

Disks – Storage hardware for holding data (files, applications etc.). There are many types: the most common are hard disks (for mass storage) and floppy disks (less storage) and CD-ROMs (mass storage).

Display – The screen allowing an operator to see the results of their work at a computer.

DOS – Disk operating system. The software that allows the computer to access and organise stored data. MS-DOS (produced by the Microsoft Corporation) is the DOS most widely used in PCs.

DTP – Desktop publishing. DTP software allows for the combination of text and graphics into page layouts which may then be printed.

EGA – Enhanced graphics adaptor – A screen display with a resolution of 640 × 350 pixels in 16 colours.

EMS – Expanded memory specification. RAM over and above the original limit of 640 Kb in the original IBM PC. PCs are now being built to take up to 128 Mb RAM (or even more).

Entity – A single feature or graphic being drawn on screen, e.g. a line, a circle, a point, etc. Sometimes linked together to form a block, where the block then acts as a single entity.

File – A collection of data held as an entity on a disk.

Fixed disk – A hard disk that cannot usually be easily removed from the computer; as distinct from floppy disks which are designed to be easily removable.

Floppy disk – A removable disk that stores data in magnetic form. The actual disk is a thin circular sheet of plastic with a magnetic surface, hence the term 'floppy'. It usually has a firm plastic case.

Flyout – A number of tool icons which appear when a tool icon which appear when a main tool icon (which shows a small arrow) is selected.

Formatting – The process of preparing the magnetic surface of a disk to enable it to hold digital data.

Gigabyte (Gb) – In computing terms 1 Gb is 1,073,741,824 bytes (not 1,000,000,000).

GUI – Graphical user interface. Describes software (such as Windows) which allows the user to control the computer by representing functions with icons and other graphical images.

Hardcopy – The result of printing (or plotting) text or graphics on to paper or card.

Hard disk – A disk, usually fixed in a computer, which rotates at high speed and will hold large amounts of data (often several gigabytes).

Hardware – The equipment used in computing: the computer itself, disks, printers, monitor etc.

Hertz (Hz) – The measure of 1 cycle per second. In computing terms, often used in millions of herz – (megaherz or MHz) as a measure of the clock speed.

IBM – International Business Machines. An American computer manufacturing company – the largest in the world.

Intel – An American company which manufactures the processing chips used in the majority of PCs.

Joystick – A small control unit used mainly in computer games. Some CAD systems use a joystick to control drawing on screen.

Kilobyte (K) – In computing terms 1 K is 1,024 bytes (not 1,000).

LAN – Local area network. Describes a network that might typically link PCs in an office by cable, where distances between the PCs is small.

LED – Light-emitting diode.

Library – A set of frequently used symbols, phrases or other data on disk, that can be easily accessed by the operator.

Light pen – Stylus used to point directly at a display screen sensitive to its use.

Megabyte (Mb) – In computing terms 1 Mb is 1,048,576 bytes (not 1,000,000).

Memory – Any medium (such as RAM or ROM chips) that allows the computer to store data internally that can be instantly recalled.

Message box – A window containing a message for the user which appears when certain tools or command are selected or executed.

MHz – Megahertz. 1,000,000 hertz (cycles per second).

Mouse – A device for controlling the position of an on-screen cursor within a GUI such as Windows.

Microcomputer – A PC is a microcomputer; a minicomputer is much larger and a mainframe computer is larger still. With the increasing capabilities of microcomputers, the term seems to be dropping out of use.

Microsoft – The American corporation which produces the Windows operating system and many other software packages.

MIPS – Millions of instructions per second. A measure of a computer's speed – it is not comparable with the clock speed as measured in MHz because a single instruction may take more than a single cycle to perform.

Monitor – A computer's display screen.

Mouse – A device for controlling the position of an on-screen pointer within a GUI such as Windows.

MS-DOS – Microsoft disk operating system.

Multitasking – A computer that can carry out more than one task at the same time is said to said to be multitasking. For example in AutoCAD Release 14, printing can be carried out 'in the background', while a new drawing is being constructed.

Multi-user – A computer that may be used by more than one operator simultaneously.

Networking – The joining together of a group of computers, allowing them to share the same data and software applications. LANs and WANs are examples of the types of networks available.

Object – A term used in CAD to describe an entity, or group of entities that have been linked together.

Operating System – Software and in some cases hardware, that allows the user to operate application software and organise and use data stored on a computer.

PC – Personal computer. Should strictly only be used to refer to an IBM machine, but is now in general use.

Pixels – The individual dots on a computer display.

Plotter – Produces hardcopy of, for instance, a drawing produced on computer by moving a pen over a piece of paper or card.

Printer – There are many types of printer: dot-matrix, bubble-jet and laser are the most common. Allows material produced on a computer (graphics and text) to be output as hardcopy.

Processor – The operating chip of a PC. Usually a single chip, such as Intel's 80386, 80486 or Pentium chip.

Programs – A set of instructions to the computer that has been designed to produce a given result.

RAM – Random access memory. Data stored in RAM is lost when the computer is switched off, unless previously saved to a disk.

RGB – Red, green blue.

ROM – Read only memory. Data and programs stored in a ROM chip are not lost when the computer is switched off.

Scanner – Hardware capable of being passed over a document or drawing and reading the image into a computer.

Software – Refers to any program or application that is used and run on a computer.

SQL – Structured query language. A computer programming language for translating and transferring data between an application such as AutoCAD and a database.

Tool – A tool represent a command which may be executed by selecting an on-screen icon.

Tool tip – A tool tip appears when the mouse cursor is moved over a tool icon – a small box appears carrying the name of the tool.

Toolbar – A toolbar contain a number icons, each representing a different tool.

UNIX – A multi-user, multitasking operating system (short for UNICS: uniplexed information and computing systems).

VDU – Visual display unit.

Vectors – Refers to entities in computer graphics which are defined by the end points of each part of the entity.

VGA – Video graphics array. Screen displays with resolution of up to 640 × 480 pixels in 256 colours. SVGA (super VGA) allows resolutions up to 1024 × 768 pixels.

Virtual memory – A system by which disk space is used to allow the computer to function as if more physical RAM were present. It is used by AutoCAD (and other software) but can slow down a computer's operation.

WAN – Wide area network. A network of computers that are a large distance apart – communication is often done down telephone lines.

Warning box – A window containing a warning or request which the user must respond to, which appears when certain circumstances are met or actions are made.

Weitek – Makers of math co-processor chips for 80386 and 80486 computers. Important for AutoCAD users, because the addition of a Weitek co-processor chip speeds up drawing construction processes considerably.

WIMP – Window, icon, menu and pointing device. A term that is used to describe some GUIs.

Winchesters – Hard disks. Refers to the company which made the first hard disks. An out-of-date term.

Window – An area of the computer screen within which applications such as word processors may be operated.

Workstation – Often used to refer to a multi-user PC, or other system used for the purposes of CAD (or other applications).

WORM – Write once, read many. An optical data storage system that allows blank optical disks to have data written onto them only once.

WYSIWYG – What you see is what you get. What is on the screen is what will be printed.

XMS – Extended memory specification. RAM above the 1 Mb limit.

XT – Extended Technology. Was used to refer to the original 8086 and 8088 based computers.

Index